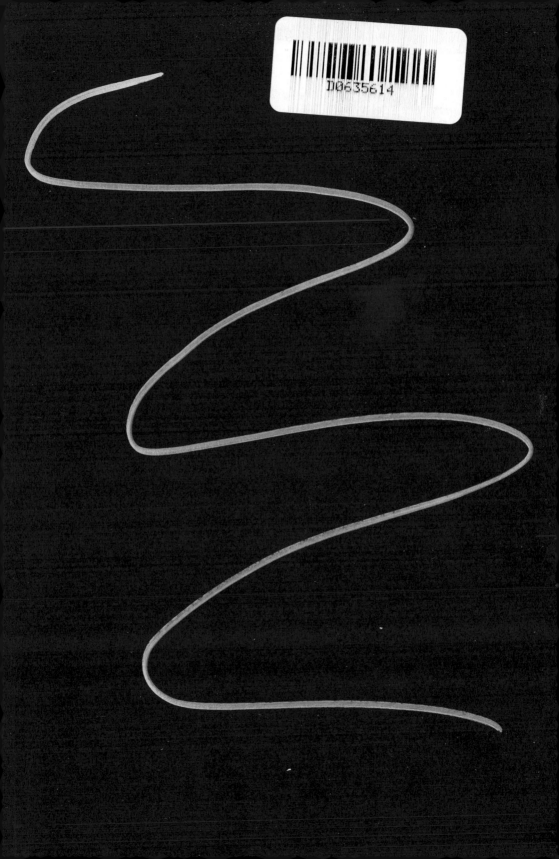

THE CIVIL WAR

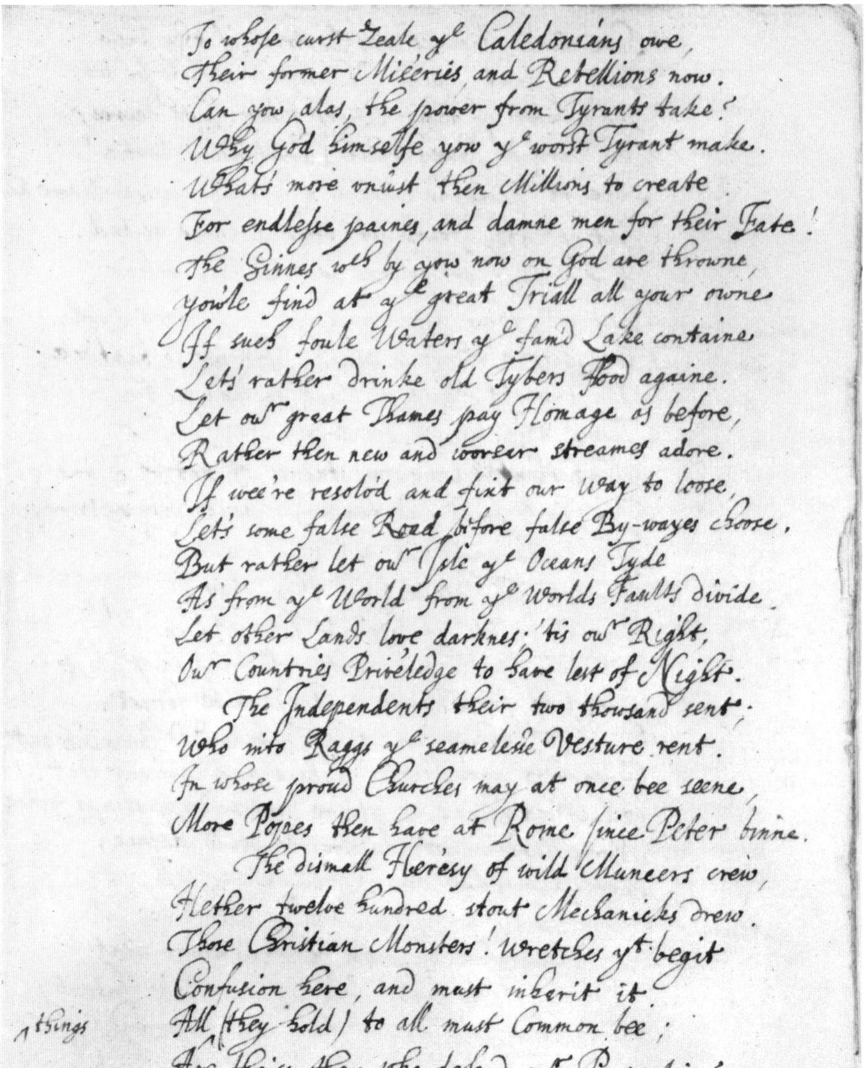

To whose curst Zeale ye Caledonians owe,
Their former Miseries, and Rebellions now.
Can yow, alas, the power from Tyrants take?
Why God himselfe yow ye worst Tyrant make.
What's more vniust then Millions to create
For endlesse paines, and damne men for their Fate!
The Sinnes wch by yow now on God are throwne,
yow'le find at ye great Triall all your owne
If such foule Waters ye fam'd Lake containe,
Let's rather drinke old Tybers flood againe.
Let our great Thames pay Homage as before,
Rather then new and worser streames adore.
If wee're resolv'd and fixt our Way to loose,
Let's some false Road, b'fore false By-wayes choose.
But rather let our Isle ye Oceans Tyde
As from ye World from ye Worlds Faults divide.
Let other Lands love darknes; 'tis our Right,
Our Countries Priviledge to have lest of Night.
The Independents their two thousand sent,
Who into Raggs ye seamelesse Vesture rent.
In whose proud Churches may at once bee seene,
More Popes then have at Rome since Peter binne.
The dismall Heresy of wild Muncers crew,
Hether twelve hundred stout Mechanicks drew.
Those Christian Monsters! Wretches yt begit
Confusion here, and must inherit it.
things All (they hold) to all must Common bee;
Are theise they who defend our Propertie!

Omen. –
God Saturne tooke to hide his pleasant rap[illegible]

The Civil War, III 65–92, in Panshanger MS D/EP/F.48

ABRAHAM COWLEY

The Civil War

EDITED BY ALLAN PRITCHARD

UNIVERSITY OF TORONTO PRESS

University of Toronto
Department of English Studies and Texts
20

printed in Canada by
University of Toronto Press, Toronto and Buffalo
ISBN 0-8020-5263-0
LC 75-185731

Acknowledgments

For permission to print *The Civil War* from the Panshanger MSS I am indebted to Lady Monica Salmond and to the Hertford County Record Office, respectively the owner and the custodian of the manuscripts. I am grateful to Mr Peter Walne, the Hertford County Archivist, and to his staff for their co-operation and helpfulness. I owe a similar debt to the Bodleian Library and the British Museum, which have allowed me to use manuscripts in their possession as well as their other resources. The National Register of Archives also provided indispensable assistance. Through the Register I learned that letters by Cowley were to be found among the Panshanger MSS, and my investigation of the letters led to my discovery of a copy of the long-lost complete text of *The Civil War*. My work on this edition of the poem has been aided by the University of Toronto, which allowed me a period of leave, and by the Canada Council, which granted me a fellowship. Publication of the book is made possible through subventions from the Humanities Research Council, using funds supplied by the Canada Council, and from the Publications Fund of University of Toronto Press. Colleagues at the University of Toronto, including J.A. Carscallen and D.I.B. Smith, have been generous in their help.

ALLAN PRITCHARD
University College
University of Toronto

Contents

THE CIVIL WAR

NOTES

APPENDIXES AND INDEX

References and Abbreviations

Except where special reason exists for using another text, references to Cowley's English works are to the two volumes of A.R. Waller's edition, as being the most nearly complete and most generally available. Since Waller does not number the lines of the poems or provide a very satisfactory index of titles, references to his edition have frequently been given by page number. For *The Puritan and the Papist* John Sparrow's edition has been used because it is much superior to Waller's. All references to the Bible are to the Authorized Version. References to classical texts are to the editions of the Loeb Classical Library. Copies of all Civil War newspapers and pamphlets cited will be found either in the British Museum Library (principally in the Thomason Collection) or in the Bodleian Library (principally in the Wood Collection). Since most of these publications can be located without undue difficulty through D. Wing's *Short-Title Catalogue* and through G.K. Fortescue's *Catalogue* of the Thomason Collection, the location of the copy used has been specified only in exceptional cases. Falconer Madan's *Oxford Books* should be consulted by those who seek fuller titles and more bibliographical details than have been provided here for the Oxford publications of the Civil War period. For works printed before the nineteenth century, the place of publication has been given only when it is not London. The brief forms of reference listed below have been used throughout for a number of works frequently cited. Certain generally accepted abbreviations have also been employed, including *OED* for *The Oxford English Dictionary*, and *RES* for *The Review of English Studies.*

THE TEXTS OF *The Civil War*: SIGLA

A British Museum, Additional MS 36913
D Bodleian, Douce MS 357
C1 Hertford County Record Office, Panshanger MS D/EP/F.48
C2 Hertford County Record Office, Panshanger MS D/EP/F.36
P *A Poem on the Late Civil War* (1679), the British Museum copy, 1077.h.4

EDITIONS OF COWLEY

Essays: Essays, Plays and Sundry Verses ed. A.R. Waller (Cambridge 1906)
Poems: Poems ed. A.R. Waller (Cambridge 1905). To avoid confusion, Cowley's *Poems* of 1656 are cited as: *Poems* (1656).
The Puritan and the Papist: in *The Mistress with other Select Poems of Abraham Cowley* ed. John Sparrow (London 1926), pp.19-28

OTHER WORKS

Butler, *Hudibras*: Samuel Butler, *Hudibras* ed. John Wilders (Oxford 1967)
Clarendon, *History*: Edward Hyde, Earl of Clarendon, *The History of the Rebellion and Civil Wars in England* ed. W.D. Macray (Oxford 1888). Reference is by book and paragraph.
Clarendon, *Life: The Life of Edward Earl of Clarendon ... Written by Himself* (Oxford 1827)
Gardiner: Samuel R. Gardiner, *History of the Great Civil War 1642-49* (London 1886)
Loiseau: Jean Loiseau, *Abraham Cowley, sa vie, son œuvre* (Paris 1931)
Nethercot: Arthur H. Nethercot, *Abraham Cowley, The Muse's Hannibal* (Oxford and London 1931; reissued, New York 1967)
Sprat, 'Life': Thomas Sprat, 'An Account of the Life and Writings of Mr Abraham Cowley,' prefaced to *The Works of Mr Abraham Cowley* (1668)
Wood, *Life and Times: The Life and Times of Anthony Wood* ed. A. Clark (Oxford 1891-5)

INTRODUCTION

1

The Survival of the Suppressed Poem

Although a part of Abraham Cowley's *The Civil War* was published almost three hundred years ago, most of the poem has remained unprinted and unknown until the present edition. Cowley mentioned the work in the preface to his *Poems* in 1656, stating that he had written a poem in three books on the Civil War, which he left unfinished when the tide turned against the Royalist cause after the first Battle of Newbury, but he gave the impression that he had destroyed all copies of it. In 1679, twelve years after his death, a somewhat truncated version of the first book was published, with the title *A Poem on the Late Civil War*; but it was assumed that the remainder of the poem was irrecoverably lost until the recent discovery of two manuscript copies of the whole poem among the Cowper family papers in the Panshanger MSS at the Hertford County Record Office.[1] The present edition is based primarily upon the more authoritative of these two copies. It provides a version of Book I that contains numerous minor variations from the version previously printed, as well as a hitherto unknown final passage; and it provides for the first time a text of Books II and III, more than two thirds of the poem. Thus it offers a substantial addition to the body of Cowley's poetry.

The reasons why Cowley did not complete or publish the poem appear in his statement in the preface to his *Poems* (1656): '... I have cast away all such pieces as I wrote during the time of the late troubles, with any relation

1 I mentioned my discovery of the existence of one of these manuscripts in 'Six Letters by Cowley,' *RES*, n.s. XVIII (1967) 256. The other manuscript has subsequently come to view as a result of the recent cataloguing of the Panshanger MSS by the staff of the Hertford County Record Office.

to the differences that caused them; as among others, *three Books of the Civil War it self*, reaching as far as the first *Battel* of *Newbury*, where the succeeding *misfortunes* of the *party* stopt the *work*; for it is so uncustomary, as to become almost *ridiculous*, to make *Lawrels* for the *Conquered.'* Continuing in a passage which brought him into some disfavour in Royalist circles and which was deleted in later editions of his works, he declared that the supporters of the defeated cause should lay down their pens as well as their swords, that they should do nothing to revive the memory of the conflict but rather seek reconciliation. He concluded: 'And I would have it accounted no less unlawful to *rip up old wounds*, then to *give new ones*; which has made me not onely abstain from printing any things of this kinde, but to burn the very copies, and inflict a severer punishment on them my self, then perhaps the most rigid Officer of *State* would have thought that they deserved.'[2]

As this statement suggests, *The Civil War* is a poem that was overtaken by history before it was completed. Cowley evidently began to write it early in the war, while he was still confident of a Royalist triumph. When his party suffered severe reverses after the Battle of Newbury in September 1643, he felt that it would be futile either to continue the poem or to publish what he had already written. The following years could not have brought any reason for him to change his mind or return to the project. Sometime between 1644 and 1646 he left England and abandoned his literary activities to serve as secretary to Lord Jermyn at the court of the exiled Queen Henrietta Maria in France.[3] He returned to England in 1654, but he was regarded with such suspicion by the Commonwealth government that he was imprisoned in the following year. During his confinement he prepared the collected edition of his verse published as the *Poems* in 1656.[4] For reasons which may or may not be stated candidly in his preface to this edition, he was clearly anxious to make his peace with the government of Oliver Cromwell. The preface was so conciliatory that it appears to have offended both Charles II and his chief minister, Sir Edward Hyde.[5] Nothing could have been more contrary to Cowley's purposes than to have included in the *Poems* such a fiercely Royalist work as *The Civil War*. It is unlikely,

2 Sigs. (a)4-(a)4^{v}. In accordance with Cowley's wishes, Sprat suppressed the offending passage of the preface in his edition, *The Works of Mr Abraham Cowley* (1668). See his 'Life,' prefaced to this edition, sigs. a1^{v}-a2. The suppressed passage is printed by A.R. Waller in the notes to his edition of Cowley, *Poems*, p.455.

3 On the date of Cowley's departure for France, see Nethercot, pp.91-2.

4 See Sprat, 'Life,' sig. a2, and Nethercot, pp.141-59.

5 See Nethercot, pp.160, 188-91, 198-9.

indeed, that the poem could have been openly or safely published in England at any time during the Commonwealth period.[6]

After the Restoration it would have been possible for Cowley to publish the poem, if one assumes that, contrary to the impression he gives in the 1656 preface, he still had a copy of it in his possession; but there is no evidence that he considered printing the work. Presumably he retained the view he expressed in 1656 that the poem had long since ceased to serve its intended purpose. It was outdated, so closely tied to historical happenings seventeen or more years in the past as to be scarcely intelligible to those of a new generation. Furthermore, publication of the poem would have made Cowley appear as one who had been over-optimistic and lacking in powers of political and military analysis, since the outcome of the war had been very different from that which he predicted. A special additional reason against publication lay in the fact that he had incorporated various lines and passages from the poem in the *Davideis* and other works published in 1656.[7]

Cowley may have been dissatisfied, too, with the literary qualities of the work, and have felt that its publication could not help and might well harm his currently very high reputation as a poet. He was not unwilling to print uncompleted works, as the publication of the *Davideis* in 1656 demonstrates, but he may have regarded *The Civil War* as the draft of a poem which had never been brought to a state of sufficient perfection to deserve publication. He more than once made it clear that he wished only the best and most finished of his work to be published, and he expressed the view that even Shakespeare's reputation had been damaged because the dramatist or his editors allowed inferior work to be published.[8]

At the time of Cowley's death in 1667, his statement eleven years earlier that he had written a poem about the Civil War was still remembered, but the assumption seems to have been generally made that the work had been lost or destroyed. In his account of Cowley in his *Memoires* (1668) David Lloyd wrote: '... and its [sic] pity his three Books of the Civil Wars, reaching as far as the first Battel of *Newbury*, are lost.'[9] Cowley's literary executor, Thomas Sprat, did nothing to dispel the belief that the poem no longer

6 Even after the Restoration some aspects of the poem seem to have been regarded as possibly sensitive or dangerous, for when the first book was published in 1679 as *A Poem on the Late Civil War* a number of proper names were replaced by dashes or initials. See p.63, below.

7 See pp.52-4, below.

8 See 'The Preface,' *Poems* (1656), sigs. (a)1^{v}-(a)2.

9 *Memoires of the Lives ... of those Noble, Reverend, and Excellent Personages, That Suffered ... in our late Intestine Wars*, p.620

existed. When he published his folio edition, *The Works of Mr Abraham Cowley* (1668), he included no part of the poem, and he made no mention of the work in his prefatory 'Account of the Life and Writings,' although he stated that he had added to the previously published works of the poet, 'all that I could find in his Closet, which he had brought to any manner of perfection.'[10] If Sprat had access to a copy of *The Civil War* he must have felt bound by the direction Cowley had given in his will that he should not publish any work unworthy of his name,[11] and he probably considered that *The Civil War*, which the poet had not chosen to publish in his lifetime, was to be placed in this prohibited category. Sprat clearly took Cowley's direction seriously, since he omitted other writings by the poet from his edition, notably the youthful *Poetical Blossoms*, which Cowley had earlier excluded from his *Poems* in 1656, and the letters, which Sprat regarded as too intimate for publication.

Printers and publishers, however, were not all bound by such scruples as Sprat's, and some of them stood ready to print any unpublished work by so popular a poet as Cowley. In 1679 an anonymous publisher, who can be identified from the *Term Catalogues* as Langly Curtis,[12] seized upon the opportunity to print a manuscript of the first book of *The Civil War* which had somehow come into his hands. The title-page of this quarto volume of 32 pages reads: 'A Poem on the Late Civil War. By Mr. Abraham Cowley. London, Printed 1679.' An unsigned preface, 'The Publisher to the Reader,' opens with the following statement: '*Meeting accidentally with this* Poem *in Manuscript, and being informed that it was a Piece of the incomparable Mr.* A C'*s, I though it unjust to hide such a* Treasure *from the World. I remember'd that our Author in his Preface to his* Works, *makes mention of some* Poems *written by him on the* late Civil War, *of which the following Copy is questionably*[13] *a part.*' Curtis did not state clearly, and may not have realized, that the work which he published was the opening of the poem in

10 Sig. A1^{v}
11 Cowley's will is printed by Nethercot, pp.296-7.
12 See *The Term Catalogues, 1668-1709* ed. E. Arber (London 1903-6), I 359. Information about Curtis appears at scattered places in George Kitchin's *Sir Roger L'Estrange* (London 1913). He was a non-conformist and defender of Titus Oates, frequently in trouble with the authorities for his publications. Cowley's political and religious views must have been uncongenial to him, but in 1679 he may have been prompted to publish the poem not only by Cowley's high literary reputation but also by the general interest in works relating to civil wars that was caused by the agitation surrounding the Popish Plot.
13 The word 'questionably' remained unchanged when this preface was first reprinted with the poem by Tonson in *Miscellany Poems* in 1706, but in Tonson's next edition in 1716 it was altered to 'unquestionably'.

three books Cowley had mentioned in 1656. At the conclusion of his text he printed the statement: '*The Author went no further.*'

A Poem on the Late Civil War was reprinted in Jacob Tonson's *Miscellany Poems* in 1706, 1716, and 1727,[14] and in the first volume of *The Works of the English Poets* (1779), the publication for which Samuel Johnson provided his life of Cowley. It was included in the two most complete modern editions of Cowley's work by Alexander Grosart (1881) and A.R. Waller (1905-6). Although the attribution of the poem to Cowley has not passed entirely without question, those who have studied his work closely have not doubted that the poem is his.[15] While the existence of the Cowper manuscript copies was unknown, however, the editors and students of Cowley could only conjecture what can now be demonstrated, that *A Poem on the Late Civil War* is part of the poem described by Cowley in 1656; and they could do little to disprove the statement of the publisher in 1679: '*The Author went no further.*'

The two Cowper manuscripts of the poem have remained unknown until the present time because they have been, ever since the seventeenth century, part of the private archive of the Cowper family, housed first at Hertford Castle and later at Panshanger House. Those who have studied Cowley have not examined the Cowper papers because they had little reason to suppose that any connection existed between the poet and the Cowpers. The manuscripts of *The Civil War* have finally come to light following the deposit of the great collection of papers from Panshanger House at the Hertford County Record Office.

These two manuscripts evidently came into the possession of the Cowper

14 In *The Dial of Virtue: A Study of Poems on Affairs of State in the Seventeenth Century* (Princeton 1963), pp.38*n*, 245, Ruth Nevo states that the poem was printed in 1693 in *Examen Poeticum* (the first edition of the third part of *Miscellany Poems*), but it is not in copies of the 1693 edition that I have examined. It appears in the second edition, *Examen Poeticum: Being the Third Part of Miscellany Poems* (1706), pp.383-413. On its title-page this volume is dated MDCCVI. A separate title-page for Cowley's poem has the date 1709, but this is probably a misprint for 1706, since signatures are continuous.

15 In *The Works of the English Poets*, I (1779), the poem was described as 'possibly genuine' (p.323*n*). Grosart termed the attribution 'somewhat doubtful' in the 'Memorial-Introduction' to his *The Complete Works in Verse and Prose of Abraham Cowley* (Edinburgh: Chertsey Worthies' Library, 1881), I cxxxiii. A.R. Waller appears to have had no doubt that the work was Cowley's when he printed it in his edition, *Essays, Plays and Sundry Verses* (Cambridge 1906), pp.465-81. The attribution has been accepted and confirmed by Nethercot, Loiseau, and other modern students of Cowley. In his *Abraham Cowley*, pp.81, 403, Loiseau pointed out that the poem has a number of verbal parallels with the *Davideis*.

family as part of the literary collection made in the later seventeenth century by Sarah, Lady Cowper (*c*1644-1720). One of them is a fair scribal copy of the poem in a commonplace book owned by her. The other, consisting of three little leaflets, is clearly the original from which the scribal copy was made. It is written seemingly in three different hands, the first two of which are small and not always very legible. Presumably Sarah Cowper somehow acquired this manuscript and then employed an experienced scribe to make the more legible copy in her commonplace book.

Sarah was the wife of Sir William Cowper, the second baronet, a landed gentleman, active in politics, who had Hertford Castle as his principal residence. Her main claim to distinction has been that she was the mother of the first Earl Cowper, the Lord Chancellor, and the great-grandmother of William Cowper, the poet, but she deserves to be remembered also for the interest she took in the poetry of her time. Her diaries for the years 1700-16, which survive among the Panshanger MSS, show that in her old age she became austerely religious, but as a younger woman she clearly possessed wide literary interests. Two of her commonplace books have been preserved in which, beginning about 1670, she copied, or sometimes had others copy, poetry not only by Cowley but also by Buckingham, Rochester, Sedley, and others. She appears to have attached special importance to *The Civil War* since she not only preserved her original manuscript but also went to the trouble of having a scribal copy made in one of these commonplace books. In addition, she copied in her own hand a series of short extracts from the poem into her other commonplace book.[16]

Sarah Cowper did not record the source from which she obtained the original manuscript, but it seems almost certain that she acquired it from Cowley's friend, Martin Clifford. There is no evidence that she ever knew Cowley himself, but her reminiscences of her earlier life in the diary she kept in her old age show that she knew Clifford well.[17] She mentions one occasion, at least, on which she received a manuscript from him, his own

16 A fuller description of the manuscripts of *The Civil War* is given below. The second commonplace book is a leather-bound volume, labelled on its spine, 'Paper Booke' (Panshanger MS D/EP/F.37). On its first page it has the title, 'The Medley', and the inscription, evidently added by Sarah Cowper in her old age: 'If in the Dayes of my Youth, I had not Diverted my Thoughts with such stuff as this Book Contains; the unhappy Accidents of my Life, had been more than Enough to ha' made me Madd'. The passages from *The Civil War* are copied on pp.258-9; most of them are from Book I, but Book II (ll.131-2) and Book III (ll.313-14, 561-2, 595-601) are represented.

17 With the permission of the Clarendon Press, I use again here a little material from my 'Six Letters by Cowley,' but the article contains some more detailed information about Sarah Cowper, Martin Clifford, and their friendship.

translation of Minucius Felix. Their friendship presumably developed in the years 1671-7, when Clifford, in the final period of his life, was Master of the Charterhouse. Sir William and Lady Cowper were at this time his neighbours, for their London house was in Charterhouse Yard. Probably Lady Cowper prevailed upon Clifford to give her a copy of the unpublished poem by Cowley, and to give her other literary manuscripts in his possession also. Among her papers and those of her husband are to be found six holograph letters by Cowley. These letters do not bear the name of the persons addressed in them, but one was almost certainly written to the Duke of Buckingham, with whom Clifford was closely connected, and the others were probably written to Clifford himself. Sarah Cowper's commonplace books include verse by Buckingham which has been published only in relatively recent times from the Duke's own commonplace book. That Clifford was the person from whom she obtained some of these manuscripts is confirmed by the fact that the initials 'M C' appear in the margin of one of her commonplace books beside a copy of Cowley's 'To the Duke of Buckingham' and beside verse by Buckingham.[18]

Sarah Cowper could have found no person more likely than Martin Clifford to have possessed manuscripts of unpublished work by both Cowley and Buckingham; his only possible rival would be Thomas Sprat. Clifford's close friendship with Cowley appears to have continued unbroken from the time when they were students together at Trinity College, Cambridge, to the end of the poet's life. In testimony of this friendship, Sprat dedicated his life of Cowley to Clifford. During the years following the Restoration, Clifford was secretary to the Duke of Buckingham, who was patron both of Cowley and Sprat. The latter served at the same period as Buckingham's chaplain. Although Cowley evidently allowed very little circulation of the manuscript of *The Civil War* and even created the impression that he had destroyed his own copy, we may reasonably conjecture that at some time he gave a copy to Clifford. An alternative possibility is that Sprat, serving as Cowley's literary executor, found the poem among Cowley's papers and presented it to Clifford. In either case, it seems evident that we owe the unexpected survival of *The Civil War* to Sarah Cowper's youthful interest in Cowley's poetry, to the friendship she formed with the elderly Martin Clifford, and to the care her descendants showed in preserving her papers.

The Civil War is a poem Cowley left unfinished and did not wish to be published, but the reasons he gave against publication in 1656 were political and historical circumstances that have long since lost their force; indeed, the

18 The 'Paper Booke' (or 'The Medley'), pp.221, 354, 360, etc. On Cowley's 'Buckingham' see Appendix B, below.

very considerations that caused Cowley to avoid publication in 1656 make the poem in some respects the more interesting now. *The Civil War* should perhaps be judged as the draft of a poem that may not have satisfied Cowley's own standards, rather than as a perfected final version, but it provides a significant addition not only to the body of his poetry but also to the genre of the seventeenth-century political poem. It is the most extended and ambitious of Cowley's political poems, and it is unique as the attempt by a poet of stature to give epic treatment to the great events of the Civil War. It is interesting, too, for the close and sometimes surprising connections it has with several of Cowley's other works.

2
Circumstances of Composition

The Civil War clearly belongs to Cowley's period of residence in Oxford, the Royalist headquarters, to which he had migrated from Cambridge upon the outbreak of the conflict. The poet does not explicitly tell us that he writes in an Oxford setting, but early in the poem he praises the university for its loyalty and extols its happiness in harbouring the King and in escaping the Puritan vandalism from which his own university had suffered (I 345-64). In the last book he informs us that he was engaged in celebrating 'My Kings great acts in Verses not unfit' (III 546) when the news of the Battle of Newbury and the death of Falkland reached Oxford, late in September 1643. These verses may well have been part of *The Civil War* itself, for there is no other surviving poem of this date to which the description could be applied.

The circumstances that brought Cowley to Oxford and into the service of the royal cause have been described by Sprat and the poet's other biographers.[1] They appear clearly enough in Cowley's own writings. Although the poet tells us in his *Libri Plantarum* (1668) that he had in his youth a prophetic vision of the Civil War, when he saw armies fighting in the sky,[2] there is little other evidence that he was any quicker than most of his contemporaries to perceive the approach of the catastrophe. His early verse leaves no doubt, however, that he was ready to defend the King and the Church of England against any attack that might come. From his days at Westminster School onwards, he missed few opportunities of eulogizing the King and satirizing the Puritans. During his Cambridge years, as the great religious

1 See specially Sprat's 'Life,' sigs. A2-a1; Nethercot, pp.67-89; and Loiseau, pp.43-86.
2 *Poemata Latina* (1668), pp.316-17

and political crisis developed, he reaffirmed his loyalty to the King in a series of occasional and complimentary poems which combine apprehension with optimism or the profession of optimism. These poems contain some close anticipations of passages in *The Civil War*.[3]

When the young Prince of Wales visited Cambridge in March 1642, Cowley must have been a natural choice for the honour of providing a play for his entertainment, by reason of his strong royalism as well as his literary reputation. Alluding to the fact that the royal family had already abandoned London as being hostile, Cowley declared in the Prologue to this play, *The Guardian*: 'We perish, if the *Round-heads* be about.'[4] Since Cambridge was in a strongly Puritan area, it was inevitable that he should leave it soon after the outbreak of the Civil War, six months later. In his essay, 'Of My self,' he writes of his departure from the university and the quiet life of learning and letters he had known there, stating that he was 'torn from thence by that violent Publick storm which would suffer nothing to stand where it did, but rooted up every Plant, even from the Princely Cedars to Me, the Hyssop.'[5] The exact date of his migration is not known, but Sprat states that the poet's 'affection to the Kings Cause drew him to *Oxford*, as soon as it began to be the chief seat of the Royal Party.'[6] This suggests that Cowley made his move by the end of 1642,[7] since the King first established himself in Oxford late in October and returned to make the city his more permanent headquarters a month later.

Little is known of the details of Cowley's life in Oxford, but Wood states that he resided in St John's College.[8] Sprat tells us that he continued with the same studies he had pursued at Cambridge, and that 'he speedily grew familiar to the chief men of the Court and the Gown, whom the Fortune of the War had drawn together.'[9] The friendship that he developed during this period with Lucius Cary, Viscount Falkland, is particularly interesting in relation to *The Civil War*, since the poem concludes with an extended elegy for that much lamented figure. We know from another source that Cowley

3 A few of these parallels have been indicated in the notes in the present edition (I 11-12, 74, 79, 97-102, 112-13).
4 *Poems*, p.31
5 *Essays*, p.458
6 'Life,' sig. A2v
7 Anthony Wood gives a slightly later date, stating that Cowley's migration occurred at the beginning of 1643 (*Fasti Oxonienses*, Part II, col. 210, in *Athenae Oxonienses* ed. P. Bliss, IV [London 1820]).
8 Loc. cit.
9 'Life,' sig. A2v

while at Cambridge had attracted Falkland's attention as early as 1638.[10] In 1639 he paid tribute to Falkland's character and learning in his poem, 'To the Lord Falkland. For his safe Return from the Northern Expedition against the Scots,' declaring:

> He is too good for *War*, and ought to be
> As far from *Danger*, as from *Fear* he's free.[11]

By the time Cowley came to Oxford, Falkland must have been heavily occupied by his duties as Secretary of State, but Sprat testifies that the poet's friendship with him ripened during the much troubled final period of his life. Addressing himself to Cowley's old friend, Martin Clifford, Sprat writes:

> And particularly, though he was then very young, he had the entire friendship of my Lord *Falkland* one of the Principal Secretaries of State. That affection was contracted by the agreement of their Learning and Manners. For you may remember, Sir, we have often heard Mr. *Cowley* admire him, not only for the profoundness of his knowledge, which was applauded by all the world, but more especially for those qualities which he himself more regarded, for his generosity of mind, and his neglect of the vain pomp of humane greatness.[12]

Sprat's statement is amply corroborated by *The Civil War*, which in its final lines provides the fullest evidence of Cowley's affection and admiration for Falkland.

Sometime presumably during his period in Oxford, Cowley developed an acquaintance with Henry Jermyn, later Lord Jermyn and Earl of St Albans, that had a greater effect upon his career than his friendship with Falkland. This acquaintance led to his entering the service of Jermyn and of Queen Henrietta Maria, whose secretary and favourite Jermyn was. In this service Cowley remained for many years, following the Queen into exile in France. It seems unlikely, however, that this acquaintance with Jermyn had yet developed very far when he wrote *The Civil War*. Sprat states that Cowley was introduced to Jermyn after the death of the poet's close Cambridge friend, William Hervey, by Hervey's brother who was Jermyn's cousin, but Sprat shows here his usual vagueness about dates.[13] William Hervey, whom

10 See Robert Cresswell's letter to Falkland, 12 May 1638, printed by Kurt Weber in his *Lucius Cary, Second Viscount Falkland* (New York 1940), p.126.

11 *Poems*, p.20

12 'Life,' sigs. A2^{v}-a1

13 'Life,' sig. A2^{v}. On the vagueness and inconsistency of Sprat's dating of the events of Cowley's period in Oxford, in the Latin and English versions of his life, see

Cowley commemorated in a moving elegy,[14] died on 16 May 1642. Jermyn, however, had been obliged to leave England in March 1641, because of his implication in the Army Plot against Parliament, and he did not join the Royalist circle in Oxford until the middle of July 1643, when he accompanied the Queen on her return from her journeys to the Continent and in the north of England.[15] Cowley's employment by Jermyn and the Queen can scarcely have begun until sometime after that date. In *The Civil War* Cowley expresses his devotion to the Queen, and he praises Jermyn for his military skill and courage, but he gives no indication that at the time he writes he is specifically in their service.

During the earlier part of his period in Oxford, before his opportunity to enter the employment of Jermyn occurred, Cowley no doubt looked about for various ways of serving the Royalist cause. According to Sprat, 'he was present and in service in several of the Kings Journeys and Expeditions.'[16] If he took part in military service before he wrote *The Civil War*, however, it was probably not very extensive, for it has left no obvious mark on the poem. At the time of his arrest in 1655 he was described in a Commonwealth newspaper as 'more famous by his pen then by his sword,'[17] and this description is indisputably accurate, even if it was made maliciously. Cowley may have seen some military action, but he must have numbered himself among those to whom Learning and the Arts gave the different task that he describes in *The Civil War* (I 231–2):

unapt themselves to fight,
They promised noble pens the Acts to write.

Cowley no doubt felt a special obligation to use his pen in support of the cause to which he was dedicated, for at the beginning of the Civil War his reputation stood higher than that of almost any other Royalist poet. His statements in his 1656 preface suggest that he may have written or begun

Nethercot, pp.90-2. Wood (loc. cit.) states that Cowley was introduced to Jermyn at a later time by Stephen Goffe in Paris, but his account has usually been regarded as less reliable than Sprat's.

14 'On the Death of Mr. William Hervey'

15 Cowley's modern biographers have sometimes mistakenly assumed that Jermyn was present in Oxford when Cowley arrived there (for example, Loiseau, p.83). Jermyn's movements and activities during the relevant period can be discovered from the frequent allusions to him in the Queen's letters. See *Letters of Queen Henrietta Maria* ed. M.E.A. Green (London 1857), pp.120, 181, 222, *et passim.*

16 'Life,' sig. A2^v

17 *The Weekly Intelligencer of the Commonwealth*, 17-24 April 1655, cited by Nethercot, p.141

to write a number of works defending the Royalist cause. One such poem, *The Puritan and the Papist*, was published in 1643. It appeared anonymously, but it is attributed to him in early manuscript copies, and his authorship seems to be established beyond dispute.[18] This poem has close affinities with some passages in *The Civil War* (especially in the first book), but it is a much shorter work and relatively restricted in its scope. Cowley probably wrote it in the early months of 1643,[19] before he turned to the more ambitious project of *The Civil War*.

Internal evidence suggests that Cowley began *The Civil War* in the summer or early autumn of 1643, and it seems to confirm his statement in the 1656 preface that he gave up work on the poem in the unfortunate period for the Royalist cause which followed the first Battle of Newbury. He may have begun Book I in the spring, but, to judge by surviving versions, his work cannot have been very far advanced by the beginning of the summer, for in line 372 he refers to the death of John Hampden, which occurred on 24 June. The latest events described in Book I are the Battle of Roundway Down and the reunion of the King and Queen at Kineton, both of which took place on 13 July, but an apparent allusion to Nathaniel Fiennes as a '*Barbarous Coward*' (l.561) indicates that the book was not completed until sometime after 26 July, the date of Fiennes' surrender of Bristol.[20] It may possibly have been finished in August or early September, before some of the events described in Books II and III had taken place. Cowley may have allowed this book some circulation in Royalist circles in Oxford while the events it dealt with were still relatively fresh. In contrast to Books II and III, which survive only in the Cowper MSS, Book I (lacking its final lines) survives in two other seventeenth-century manuscript copies, and still another

18 See John Sparrow's discussion in his edition, *The Mistress with other Select Poems of Abraham Cowley*, pp.198-9.

19 This poem has sometimes been assigned to the autumn of 1643, but internal evidence suggests the early part of the year. For example, Cowley appears to allude to Lord Brooke, who was killed in March, as still alive (ll.91-6). John Sparrow states that a manuscript of the poem in his possession has the date, 20 May 1643 ('The Text of Cowley's Satire *The Puritan and the Papist*,' *Anglia*, LVIII [1934] 102). Some of the parallels with *The Civil War* are indicated in the notes in the present edition.

20 Fiennes' trial by court martial for the surrender of Bristol was delayed until December 1643, but the accusation of cowardice was first brought against him both by members of his own party and by Royalists immediately after the fall of the city. An anonymous Royalist commentator describes him as 'that bloudie Coward' in *The Earle of Essex His Letter to Master Speaker. July 9. 1643. With some briefe Animadversions on the said Letter* (Oxford 1643, received by Thomason 4 August), p.6.

manuscript evidently provided the text for the 1679 publication, *A Poem on the Late Civil War*.[21]

Books II and III carry the action little more than two months beyond the date of the last events recorded in Book I. Book II includes military actions in the Midlands during the spring and early summer that were excluded from Book I by the structural scheme Cowley adopted; but the narrative moves beyond the events of 13 July only to 4 September, the date of the Royalist capture of Exeter. An allusion is made, however, to the forthcoming Battle of Newbury, fought on 20 September (I.356).[22] Book III moves only sixteen days further ahead to that battle. Nothing in these two books suggests that when Cowley wrote he had knowledge of events much later than Newbury and its immediate aftermath. John Pym, who died on 8 December, is mentioned as if still alive (II 545). Oliver Cromwell, who became increasingly prominent in the months after Newbury, is nowhere mentioned in the poem, although he had a leading part in some of the military actions described by Cowley.[23] This suggests that Cowley completed *The Civil War* (so far as the poem ever was completed) before Cromwell emerged as one of the unmistakably dominant figures in the Parliamentary party and army. Probably he wrote of the events of the summer and autumn of 1643 very close to the time of their occurrence.

Cowley could have chosen no period more apparently favourable than the summer of 1643 in which to embark on a poem intended to celebrate the Royalist triumph over the rebels. The later part of June and the beginning of July was, as Anthony Wood records, a period of great rejoicing in Oxford, during which the Royalists celebrated with bonfires, bell-ringing, and proclamations of thanksgiving the news of victories that arrived almost daily.[24] The Royalists were generally optimistic because of their military successes, and they had good reason to expect that they would shortly achieve a complete triumph. By the beginning of July the King's forces had won a notable series of victories in the west, including Stratton (16 May),

21 See pp.63-4, below.

22 Cowley's statement that he shortly expects the fall of Plymouth (II 354-5) may suggest a date in or about the later part of November, since the Royalists made a strong effort during this period to capture the city. See the note on these lines.

23 Cromwell had a particularly prominent part in the action at Gainsborough in which Charles Cavendish was killed (II 143). See his own account of the battle, in *The Writings and Speeches of Oliver Cromwell* ed. W.C. Abbott (Cambridge, Mass. 1937-47), I 243-6. It is possible, of course, that Cowley was reserving some subjects to which he gives unexpectedly little attention, such as Parliament's negotiations with the Scots, and the Solemn League and Covenant, for treatment in later books of the poem.

24 *Life and Times*, I 101-3

and they appeared to be well on the way to clearing the Parliamentary forces entirely from the western counties. In the north the Royalist commander, the Earl of Newcastle, had signally defeated the forces of the Fairfaxes at Adwalton Moor (30 June), leaving Parliament with only one northern stronghold, Hull. The way seemed to be opening for a double Royalist advance on London from the west and the north, and it appeared likely that the Parliamentary forces would prove to be too weak and divided to meet such an attack successfully. During the month of June the Earl of Essex's army was much reduced and weakened by disease which afflicted it while it was camped near Thame in Oxfordshire. Disputes had broken out between Essex and the commander of the Parliamentary army in the west, Sir William Waller. The death of Hampden on 24 June removed from the Parliamentary councils the man who had done more than any other to reconcile the conflicting elements in his party.

Cowley's expectation of a quick and complete Royalist victory can only have been strengthened by many of the later events of the summer, and it need not have been seriously undermined until the Battle of Newbury. Throughout the summer the Royalist armies continued to be brilliantly successful in the west. They defeated Waller at Lansdown on 5 July, and annihilated his army at Roundway Down on 13 July; they captured Bristol, the second city of England, on 26 July, and Exeter on 4 September; they carried out siege operations against Plymouth, the only important remaining Parliamentary stronghold in the south-west, and they moved against Gloucester. By the end of July, as Thomas May states, the Parliamentary cause seemed 'to be quite suncke beyond any hope of recovery, and was so believed by many men.'[25]

In August the Parliamentary forces began to rally, although Royalists did not immediately perceive that the tide was turning against their cause. The citizens of London fitted out an expedition under the Earl of Essex, which succeeded on 5 September in raising the Royalist siege of Gloucester. During the next two weeks Essex managed to lead his army back toward London, until he reached the neighbourhood of Newbury. Here he was finally intercepted by the King's army, but he was able to preserve most of his force intact in this battle and subsequently to bring his army to London. Thus the Royalists failed in their attempt to destroy the principal Parliamentary army; and after Newbury the King did not dare to advance on London but returned to Oxford.

Cowley, as *The Civil War* shows, did not immediately recognize or admit the disastrous consequences for his party of Essex's success in relieving

25 *The History of the Parliament of England* (1647), III 90

Gloucester and leading his army back to London. Like other Royalist writers in the period following the battle,[26] he did his best to maintain that Newbury was a victory for his cause. But, if the writers were unwilling to admit failure, realization of the ill consequences of the battle nonetheless grew quickly in Royalist circles, as Clarendon testifies: 'upon the King's return to Oxford, there appeared nothing but dejection of mind, discontent, and secret mutiny.'[27] There is evidence enough in the last book of *The Civil War* that Cowley, although he puts the best face he can upon events, shared in the dejection Clarendon describes. The fact that the poem, which begins in a heroic and celebratory mode, concludes in satire and elegy suggests the degree to which the poet's cause and his literary design were defeated even before he gave up work on the poem. If he retained any intention of continuing with the poem after the consequences of Newbury had become clear, the events of the later part of the winter probably caused him to abandon the design. In January 1644 the Scots entered the war, driving back the Earl of Newcastle, whose earlier victories Cowley had celebrated, and in the following months the Royalists suffered numerous reverses, culminating in their decisive defeat at Marston Moor in July. Cowley remained in the Royalist service, but the optimism that inspired *The Civil War* and was necessary for its continuation could not long survive the Battle of Newbury.

26 See, for example, *Mercurius Aulicus*, 20-1 September 1643, pp.527-30; and *A True and Impartiall Relation of the Battaile ... neare Newbery* (Oxford 1643).
27 *History*, VII 238

3
History and Propaganda

As Cowley implies in his description of *The Civil War* in his 1656 preface, '*three Books of the Civil War it self,*' military action is central in the poem, although the scope of the poem is much wider than military history, and his treatment of events is that of a poet and propagandist, rather than that of a chronicler or historian. Cowley is concerned with the religious and political issues and the personalities of the war as well as with military action, but no one could complain of him as Ben Jonson complained of Samuel Daniel: 'Daniel wrott Civill Warres, and yett hath not one batle in all his Book.'[1] Cowley describes the important campaigns and battles of the first year of the war, to the time of Newbury, especially those which were, or could be claimed as, Royalist victories; and the structure of his poem is determined to a large degree by the military events of this period, although it is influenced also by literary, especially epic, tradition.

In organizing his account of events Cowley was confronted by the problem that the action of the war did not follow any simple or orderly pattern. In the period he deals with, there took place the two major battles of Edgehill and Newbury in central England, but important campaigns were fought also in the west and the north, and fighting occurred simultaneously and sporadically over much of the country. The solution that Cowley devised to this problem is the one that has generally been adopted by later historians of the Civil War: he makes a compromise between the chronological and

1 *Ben Jonson's Conversations with William Drummond of Hawthornden* ed. R.F. Patterson (London 1923), p.20. Jonson's criticism may, of course, be taken to refer to the style rather than the actual amount of military description.

regional treatment of events. His scheme is basically chronological, but he departs at times from strict chronology in order to give a coherent account of events in a particular region or theatre of war.

The opening part of Book I, which serves as a general introduction to the poem, includes a contrast between the divided England of the present and the united England of the past, and a review of the antecedents of the Civil War (ll.1-168). Cowley then describes the gathering together of the King's army, which followed the raising of the royal standard at Nottingham on 22 August 1642; and he goes on to give an account of events in central England during the first three months of the war, including the first skirmish at Powick Bridge near Worcester, on 23 September, the first major battle, Edgehill, on 23 October, the subsequent royal advance to Brentford in the environs of London, and the King's return to Oxford on 29 November, when the design to attack London was abandoned (ll.169-364). Cowley next gives a brief description of events in central England during the later winter and the spring of 1643, including the deaths of the Parliamentary leaders, Lord Brooke and John Hampden (ll.365-92); but, since little fighting took place in the area during this period, he soon moves on to celebrate the successful Royalist western campaign led by Sir Ralph Hopton, Prince Maurice, and the Marquis of Hertford, which culminated in the crushing defeat of the Parliamentary army of Sir William Waller at Roundway Down on 13 July (ll.393-490). In the later part of the book he describes the victories won in the north by the Earl of Newcastle against the Parliamentary armies of Sir Thomas and Lord Fairfax, the most notable of which was Adwalton Moor on 30 June (ll.509-46).

Books II and III, which cover a shorter period of time than Book I, are not so fully taken up as it is by the narrative of events, but military action remains the dominant subject of the first half of Book II and the middle part of Book III. Book II opens with an account of the war in the central and northern Midlands during March and April, including the Battle of Hopton Heath and Prince Rupert's capture of Birmingham and Lichfield (ll.1-136). Cowley next turns his attention to events in Lincolnshire, particularly the death on 28 July of the Royalist hero, Charles Cavendish (ll.137-56), and to those in the southern Midlands, including the sickness which devastated Essex's army at Thame in Oxfordshire during the month of June (ll.157-96). He then resumes his history of the western campaign from the point at which he had left it in Book I, describing the Royalist capture of Bristol on 26 July (ll.197-276) and of Exeter on 4 September (ll.277-352), and the commencement of the Royalist siege of Gloucester on 10 August (ll.357-64). In the remaining section of Book II history is partly displaced by epic fiction as Cowley describes a council in Hell, in which Satan declares his support and aid for the rebels (ll.365-617). The opening of Book III is given largely to a satirical description of the zeal of the Puritans of London in raising a force for the relief of Gloucester, and to satire of the sects which compose this force (ll.1-198). The story of military events is resumed with an account of the King's abandonment of the siege of Gloucester on 5 September, and the skirmish between Royalist and Parliamentary armies at Aldbourne Chase on 18 September (ll.199-250). There follows a description of the Battle of Newbury, on 20 September (ll.251-380), a satirical catalogue of the rebels who fell in the engagement (ll.381-454), and finally a series of elegies for the Royalist fallen, concluding with that for Falkland (ll.455-648).

Since Cowley wrote *The Civil War* before any ordered or comprehensive history of the period he was dealing with had been published, he had to piece together the history of events for himself. No doubt he relied partly upon his own observation, partly upon such informal sources of information as his acquaintance in the Royalist circles in Oxford provided, and partly upon the newspapers and pamphlets that were being printed in large numbers. His opportunity for observation of important events was probably quite limited. The attendance in the King's expeditions to which Sprat refers may have taken place at a later date than the poem, since Cowley's descriptions of battle provide no definite evidence of first-hand knowledge,[2] but he must have witnessed the setting out and return of royal armies and other events of the kind that Anthony Wood describes in his account of life in Oxford during the war.[3] It is impossible to estimate how much information came to him in informal ways, but his friendship with Falkland and the acquaintance Sprat states he held with 'the chief men of the Court and the Gown' should have provided him with opportunities of acquiring knowledge of events. The evidence suggests, however, that Cowley remained consistent to his bookish habits of study and work, and that he acquired most of his information from the newspapers and pamphlets, relying heavily upon the official and semi-official Royalist accounts of events printed in Oxford. *The Civil War* contains very little information that Cowley could not have found in the Royalist newspapers, newsbooks, and pamphlets printed in 1642 and 1643, and the poem frequently seems to be specifically indebted to these publications.

2 Cowley's description of the sights and sounds of combat at Newbury (III 339-50) may suggest that he witnessed this battle, but a later passage (III 529-46) seems to indicate that he received news of the battle elsewhere, presumably in Oxford, which he mentions in l.530.

3 See Wood's *Life and Times*, I 69-105.

Cowley's most important single source for the history of events in 1643 was probably *Mercurius Aulicus*, the newspaper skilfully edited by John Berkenhead, which was published weekly in Oxford beginning in January of that year, and which was in effect the official Royalist journal of news and propaganda.[4] The poet frequently appears to follow the version of events it provides, to reflect its emphases, and to establish the same links between events as it does. For example, the details of his description of the Battle of Adwalton Moor and the Earl of Newcastle's heroism (I 529-40) are almost certainly drawn from the account in *Mercurius Aulicus*.[5] His statement that Henry Hastings had twice vanquished Sir John Gell and Sir William Brereton in encounters earlier than the Battle of Hopton Heath (II 22-5) probably rests upon a careful reading of *Mercurius Aulicus*, for the journal had reported two such occasions, in January and February. His linking of the deaths of Hampden and Brooke as exemplifying the workings of providence in the Royalist cause (I 372-80) may also have been suggested by *Mercurius Aulicus*. In many instances *Mercurius Aulicus* should be regarded as representing the view of events that was general in Royalist circles, rather than as a direct source for *The Civil War*, but there can be little doubt that Cowley read the newspaper with close attention, and it seems likely that he sometimes had issues of it in front of him when he wrote.

In addition to *Mercurius Aulicus*, Cowley made extensive use of various Royalist accounts of particular military actions which were published in separate pamphlets, usually in Oxford. These reports were often written by officers who had played a part in the engagement they described, and *Mercurius Aulicus* sometimes referred its readers to them for a fuller description of actions than it had space to provide. There can be little doubt, for example, that Cowley drew the details of his account of the Battle of Stratton (I 433-56) from such a pamphlet, *The Round-Heads Remembrancer* (Oxford 1643). For his account of the Battle of Roundway Down (I 471-82), he probably made some use of *Mercurius Aulicus* but went for other details to *Sir John Byrons Relation* (York 1643). His description of the Battle of Hopton Heath and the heroic death of the Earl of Northampton (II 22-81) seems to derive from *The Battaile on Hopton-Heath* ([Oxford] 1643), and his account of the battles of Aldbourne Chase and Newbury (III 199-380) derives, in part at least, from *A True and Impartiall Relation* (Oxford 1643), attributed to Lord Digby.

4 The first editor of *Mercurius Aulicus* was Peter Heylin, but Berkenhead appears to have become the effective editor long before he officially succeeded Heylin in September 1643. See P.W. Thomas, *Sir John Berkenhead 1617-79, A Royalist Career in Politics and Polemics* (Oxford 1969), pp.30-5.

5 When details concerning Cowley's use of printed sources are not given here they will be found in the notes on the relevant passages of *The Civil War*.

Cowley no doubt made similar use of the proclamations, declarations, and speeches that were issued in the King's name (although often penned by Falkland, Clarendon, and others), and of Royalist sermons and pamphlets on the political and religious issues of the conflict. In addition to numerous pamphlets on special subjects, some comprehensive surveys and indictments of the crimes of the rebels had appeared in time to be of service to him, including two intelligent and effectively written works published in Oxford in 1643: *A Letter from Mercurius Civicus to Mercurius Rusticus*, attributed to John Berkenhead, and *The True Informer, Who in the following Discourse, or Colloquy, Discovereth unto the World the chiefe Causes of the sad Distempers in Great Brittany, and Ireland*, the authorship of which is unknown.[6] The poet must have read also Parliamentary newspapers and pamphlets, which, as Clarendon states, 'were everyday printed at London, and as constantly sent to Oxford,'[7] but he read these to refute rather than to borrow.

The Civil War belongs in many respects to the stream of Royalist propaganda that issued forth from Oxford in 1642-3. Cowley's treatment of events is to be understood in the context of the propaganda warfare of this period waged between *Mercurius Aulicus* and its chief Parliamentary opponent, *Mercurius Britanicus*, and their cohorts of followers. For example, his statement that de la Vieuville was cold-heartedly slain by the rebels after his capture at Aldbourne Chase (III 235-44), and his insistence that the Parliamentary forces had the advantage of the ground at Newbury (III 253, 307, 321, 363, 481-4) reflect the emphasis of the Royalist journals and pamphlets. Both points were vigorously denied by the Parliamentary writers. The very words and phrases he employs are often loaded with special meanings they had acquired in the verbal warfare of the period. Much in *The Civil War* that now appears flat or pointless had heated significance in the propaganda battle at the time Cowley wrote.

The Civil War is polemical to the degree that Cowley implies when he describes in the 1656 preface his decision to destroy it and similar writings: he declares that the members of the defeated party should dismantle 'all the

6 The *Letter* is concerned particularly with London, but it has a wide scope. On the attribution to Berkenhead, see Thomas, *Berkenhead*, pp.107-14. *The True Informer* appeared in several editions and issues in 1643, with both genuine and forged Oxford imprints (the forgeries being London printings); one has the title *The Historical Passages of England*. Thomason received a copy on 12 April. (See Madan's *Oxford Books*, nos. 1304, 1305, 1306, 1422.) The Royalist writings of the period are so homogeneous that it is perilous to argue direct influence, but this work provides some close verbal parallels with *The Civil War*, and one may suspect that Cowley was familiar with it.

7 *Life*, I 161

Works and *Fortifications* of *Wit* and *Reason*'[8] by which they had defended their cause. He writes in the poem with the constant purpose of rallying opinion on the Royalist side, of raising the morale of his party, and of crushing the Parliamentarians. He appears to have learned rapidly those arts of political propaganda that were developed during his period in Oxford under the leadership of Berkenhead and others. His desire to defend the Royalist cause did not make him entirely unscrupulous in his handling of facts. His poem contains many elements of fiction, but the fiction is not often presented in a way that would lead the reader to confuse it with fact. He made the most of his poetic license in introducing a fictitious speech of King Charles before the Battle of Newbury (III 277-328), and a fictitious or largely fictitious catalogue of the rebel dead following that battle (III 385-456), but in the first of these two instances he may have considered his practice to be sanctioned not only by epic precedent but also by the historiographical tradition stemming from Thucydides.[9] In some other cases where fact and fiction are confused Cowley was probably misled by his sources, as in the absurd allegation that Papists served in the Parliamentary army (III 183-6), and in the inflation of a trivial incident on the river near Brentford into an important engagement (I 325-32). However, if he rarely presents fiction as fact, he invariably interprets the facts in the way most favourable to the Royalist cause, and where facts are disputed he always prefers a Royalist version.

Cowley's natural bias in the treatment of events appears in the fact that he claims both of the two principal battles fought during the period covered by his poem, Edgehill and Newbury, as Royalist victories, although they were indecisive enough to be claimed as victories also by the Parliamentarians.[10] His bias appears too in the emphasis he gives to certain events or aspects of events, and in his omission or near-omission of others. Thus, while he celebrates the victories of Edgehill and Brentford, he passes silently over the fact that the campaign of which these battles were part ended in

8 *Poems* (1656), sig. (a)4

9 In the dedicatory epistle of his *The Civile Wares* (1609) Samuel Daniel states that he departs from historical truth only in 'framing speaches to the persons of men according to their occasions; as C. Salustius, and T. Liuius (though Writers in Prose, yet in that kinde Poets) haue, with diuers other antient and modern Writers, done before me' (sig. A2v).

10 This is not to say that Cowley entirely hides the truth about the outcome of the two battles. He makes the most of the limited Royalist success at Edgehill in I 207-320, but he later refers to '*Edghills* almost-*Victory*' (II 42). In III 377-8, he admits openly that the result of Newbury was disappointing, and in subsequent passages he deplores the terrible cost of that battle.

failure, when the King, faced by strong Parliamentary forces, decided not to risk another battle and abandoned his attempt to advance on London. He makes only the briefest allusion, by way of a pun, to the Parliamentary capture of Reading (II 157-8), which was really a major blow to the Royalists.[11] He describes very elaborately the disease that ravaged Essex's army in June 1643, interpreting it as divine punishment upon the rebels (II 159-92), while he makes no direct reference to the fact that Royalist Oxford was severely afflicted by a similar disease during the same period. He makes no allusion whatever to the fiasco of Edmund Waller's plot in London, in May 1643, an episode that brought only discredit upon the Royalist cause, as well as disgrace upon a fellow poet.

The extent to which Cowley's treatment of history is polemical can be assessed by comparing his version of events with Clarendon's in *The History of the Rebellion.* By the time he wrote *The Civil War* Cowley had probably become acquainted with Sir Edward Hyde, the future Lord Clarendon, who admired his poetry and shared his friendship with Falkland.[12] Cowley's biases are generally the same as Clarendon's and his treatment of events is often strikingly similar. *The Civil War* can be elucidated more frequently by reference to Clarendon's *History* than to any other single work, with the possible exception of *Mercurius Aulicus.* But Clarendon is distinctly more moderate, detached, and objective than Cowley, and the nature of *The Civil War* as propaganda frequently emerges from the comparison with the *History*.

While Clarendon is by no means totally uncritical of the King, is strongly critical of some of the royal advisers and military leaders, and comments candidly on various failures in the management of the royal cause, Cowley, in contrast, is completely uncritical of the King and his advisers, and he does his best to conceal all Royalist political and military blunders. In *The Civil War* he develops a eulogy of the happy years preceding the war (I 79ff) which has affinities with a famous passage in Clarendon's *History*, but he avoids the criticism of Charles' attempt at personal government that is stated or implied in Clarendon's account. Cowley half-conceals beneath a witty conceit the humiliation of the terms of the Treaty of Ripon made by the King with the Scots in 1640 (I 104); Clarendon emphasizes the ill manage-

11 See C.V. Wedgwood, *The King's War* (London 1958), p.194. Royalist leaders regarded the surrender of Reading as so discreditable that they made the commander responsible, Richard Feilding, face a court martial.

12 Clarendon praises Cowley's poetry in his *Life* (I 34). He appears to have been offended by Cowley's attempt to make peace with Cromwell's government in 1656, as has been noted above. It must have seemed to him then that the poet had moved from one false extreme to another.

ment and disastrous consequences of the negotiation. Cowley makes no mention of the facts that the Royalists violated a truce in their attack on Brentford in November 1642, and failed to observe properly the articles of agreement through which they obtained the surrender of Bristol in July 1643. Clarendon recognizes the need to offer explanation and justification in both instances, and in the second he expresses some real regret for a Royalist fault. Cowley does not admit the skill and heroism of Essex's relief of Gloucester, or the blunder of the Royalist commanders in subsequently allowing Essex to take his forces from Gloucester to Newbury before intercepting them; Clarendon has high praise for the first and strong criticism for the second. Similar differences appear between Cowley's and Clarendon's accounts of the Battle of Newbury, and even in their accounts of the death of Falkland. Cowley, although he shows some sign of being moved by Falkland's own spirit of charity, blames his death primarily on the rebels; Clarendon, strong though his Royalist bias is, blames it primarily upon the war.[13]

The difference between Cowley's and Clarendon's treatment of events arises partly no doubt from intrinsic differences between the characters of the two men, and from differences in experience and principle. Cowley lacked any of Clarendon's practical experience of politics when he wrote *The Civil War*, and he had developed little of Clarendon's breadth of view. It is significant that during the period prior to the conflict, while Hyde was actively opposing some of the King's policies in Parliament, Cowley was writing panegyrics of the monarch which stand out as extreme even in an age of extravagant panegyrics. Nor can it be entirely accidental that, even though Cowley made the friendship of the eminently moderate Falkland at Oxford, he found his later place in the service of Jermyn and Henrietta Maria, leaders of a circle which Clarendon regarded as dangerously extreme and which he worked against. But the difference between Clarendon's treatment of history and Cowley's is to be accounted for partly also by the differences in purpose and in the circumstances of composition of the two works. In *The History of the Rebellion* Clarendon wrote of the events of 1642-3 several years after they occurred, and he had the advantage of perspective and detachment impossible for Cowley.[14] Furthermore, Clarendon could allow himself considerable freedom and candour, because he did not write for

13 See Clarendon, *History*, I 159; II 107-30; VI 136; VII 130, 204-14, 217.

14 Clarendon wrote the original version of the earlier part of his *History*, which embraces the period covered by Cowley's poem, in 1645-8. He later incorporated in his first and second books extensive passages written in 1668-9. See C.H. Firth, 'Clarendon's "History of the Rebellion",' *English Historical Review*, XIX (1904) 26-54, 246-62, 464-83.

immediate publication: the *History* was not published until 1702-4, long after his death, and it appeared then in an expurgated version. Cowley, on the other hand, wrote very close in time to the events he described, and, until unforeseen reverses occurred, he no doubt intended his work to be quickly published as a contribution to the Royalist propaganda campaign.

If Cowley had any reservations concerning the character and policies of Charles and his advisers, it would have been quite contrary to his purposes to have admitted even a hint of doubt or criticism in *The Civil War*, for to do so would have been to give aid to the King's enemies. Thus Charles stands in the poem not merely as a paragon of virtue, which in private life he may have been, but also as the ideal monarch and as a great general. Happily for Cowley, the Royalist generals included men like Prince Rupert, Sir Bevil Grenville, and Sir Ralph Hopton, whose military exploits better qualified them for heroic treatment, but even Rupert possessed faults and made mistakes that Cowley had to conceal.[15] In such battles as Stratton, a great Royalist victory won in the face of overwhelming odds, Cowley had a fit subject for celebration, and his hyperbole needed scarcely to move beyond the truth,[16] but in other instances he had to exercise all his ingenuity to conceal defeat or to represent a doubtful action in the light most favourable to his cause.

As Cowley can admit no fault in the Royalists, so he can scarcely admit any merit in the rebels. He credits some of the Parliamentary leaders with Machiavellian skill but none with virtue. Thus Hampden is represented (just as Cromwell was later to be represented by Royalists) as a man of great intelligence and subtlety who uses his abilities to evil ends (I 377-92). In the poet's eyes all rebels are absolutely evil, and he makes no distinction between such relatively moderate figures as Hampden and Pym and such extremists as Harry Marten. He is reluctant even to allow courage to the Parliamentary soldiers, although he makes an exception in the case of their defence of Lichfield (II 135-6), prompted perhaps by the fact that Rupert

15 Rupert has often been held responsible for the failure of the Royalists to achieve a complete victory at Edgehill, because he allowed his cavalry to pursue the enemy too far from the field, an action which Cowley treats circumspectly (I 271-2). The poet makes no direct allusion to the fact that Rupert quickly became notorious for ruthlessness and plunder, being nicknamed by his opponents 'Prince Robber', but he does not see reason, as other Royalist writers did, to excuse the Prince's burning of Birmingham as an accident. See II 69-94 and note.

16 Little discrepancy appears between Cowley's view of this action (I 433-56) and that of such a scrupulous modern historian as Mary Coate in her *Cornwall in the Great Civil War and Interregnum 1642-60* (Oxford 1933): 'Stratton fight is nothing less than the triumph of forces spiritual and psychological over brute superiority of numbers and the tactical advantages of position ...' (p.70).

had paid public tribute to the bravery of his opponents in this action. During the end of the period covered by the poem the rebels in truth provided a better subject for heroic treatment than the Royalists. There was a genuinely epic quality in the energy and spirit of the Londoners in raising troops for Essex, in Essex's remarkable achievement in relieving Gloucester,[17] and in the courage of the London trained bands at Newbury; but Cowley could respond only with satire, and with the poetic fiction of the council in Hell, which evades unpalatable historical reality.

Cowley's treatment of the political issues that lie behind the conflict rests upon the conservative assumptions common to the Royalist writers of the period. His purpose is, in the words he gives to King Charles in the poem, 'things well establisht to defend' (III 291). The poet possessed an exceptionally strong personal commitment to order, as his writings show from the beginning to the end of his career,[18] and like many members of his party he viewed the outbreak of rebellion as the coming of chaos. He expresses again and again in *The Civil War* his belief in a traditional conception of order and degree. His view of the proper political and social order is frequently conveyed by images of divinely established cosmic order such as appear in the official sixteenth-century homily on obedience, in Hooker, or in the speech of Shakespeare's Ulysses in *Troilus and Cressida*:[19] the obedience of the stars to law in their movements through the heavens, or the allegiance rivers show in rendering tribute to the sea. Rebellion is described in images that suggest the violation or disruption of the natural order: earthquake, tempest, deluge, disease, and madness. Imagery of order and light is consistently associated with the Royalists, and imagery of disorder and darkness with the rebels.

The Civil War is a political poem rather than a political treatise. Cowley does not set forth his position regarding the political and constitutional issues of the war in any systematic way, and he implies his views as often as he states them. It is clear, however, that he adheres to the principles and arguments expounded in such official Royalist statements as *His Majesties Answer to ... The Declaration, or Remonstrance of the Lords and Commons,*

17 J.A.R. Marriott describes Essex's relief of Gloucester as 'the finest military achievement in the Civil War' (*The Life and Times of Lucius Cary, Viscount Falkland* [London 1907], p.312).

18 See Robert Hinman's comprehensive treatment of this subject in his *Abraham Cowley's World of Order* (Cambridge, Mass. 1960).

19 See 'An Exhortation Concerning good Order, and obedience to Rulers, and Majestrates' (first published in 1547), *Certaine Sermons or Homilies Appoynted to be Read in Churches* (1635), I 69; the first book of Hooker's *Of the Laws of Ecclesiastical Polity*; and *Troilus and Cressida*, I iii 74-137.

of the 19th of May, 1642 (1642), and in such popular and influential discourses as the younger Dudley Digges' *The Unlawfulnesse of Subjects Taking Up Armes Against their Soveraigne, in what case soever* ([Oxford] 1643). Like the authors of these works, and like Royalist writers generally in the period following Parliament's issuing of the Militia Ordinance in March 1642,[20] he regards himself as a supporter of the traditional constitution. He holds that the constitution has been violated, not by the King, but by the pretended or self-styled Parliament, the two houses sitting at Westminster, which have taken to themselves the right to make law without the royal assent and in violation of the royal prerogative. Professing to champion the subject's liberty and property, Parliament has in actuality illegally imprisoned the King's subjects and illegally taxed and confiscated their property. In Cowley's view the Royalist party is the true defender of liberty as well as of order.

Many of the political statements and implications of the poem are to be understood in the light of the great debate taking place during the period when Cowley wrote, on the questions of the duty of obedience and the right of resistance. In the arguments and examples he uses the poet follows the pattern established by such Royalist writers as Dudley Digges, Henry Ferne, and Thomas Morton in their controversy with Parliamentary writers like Henry Parker and William Prynne, who attempted to justify the resort of their party to armed revolt.[21] Thus Cowley places the barons who forced King John to sign Magna Carta, and Simon de Montfort, leader of the baronial opposition to Henry III, in the company of the most evil and notorious rebels of English history (II 457-68), with the purpose of refuting Parliamentary writers such as Prynne, who made heroes of these men and appealed to their example as precedent for their own rebellion in the name of liberty.[22] Cowley's unfavourable allusion to the rebels against Henry III

20 On the political debate of this period see J.W. Allen, *English Political Thought 1603-1660* (London 1938), I 415-521; and Ernest Sirluck, Introduction, *Complete Prose Works of John Milton,* II (New Haven 1959), 1-52.

21 The most heated phase of the debate began with Parker's *Observations upon some of his Majesties Late Answers and Expresses* [July 1642], which drew a series of Royalist replies, including Ferne's *The Resolving of Conscience* (Cambridge 1642), and Morton's *The Necessity of Christian Subjection* ([Oxford] 1643).

22 See Prynne's *The Soveraigne Power of Parliaments* (1643), Part I, p.38, etc. On the importance attached to Magna Carta by lawyers and parliamentarians in the Tudor and early Stuart periods see Faith Thompson, *Magna Carta, Its Role in the Making of the English Constitution 1300-1629* (Minneapolis 1948), pp.167-374. Cowley had precedent, however, for his unfavourable view of the rebels against John in the anonymous Elizabethan play, *The Troublesome Raigne of King John* (1591), and in 'An Homily Against Disobedience, and wilfull Rebellion,' *Certaine*

has special point in view of the fact that Sir Robert Cotton's life of that king was republished in 1642 as Parliamentary propaganda, with a title suggesting a parallel between Henry and Charles.[23]

Cowley's allusions to biblical history have the same kind of polemical significance as his allusions to medieval British history. Like Clarendon,[24] he protests against the application of 'Texts of wicked Princes' to King Charles by Parliamentary preachers and pamphleteers (II 597). The comparison of Charles to a wicked or erring monarch of the Old Testament was implied in Stephen Marshall's famous sermon, *Meroz Cursed* (1641), and it became increasingly open in Parliamentary literature after the outbreak of the war.[25] In opposition, Royalist writers tried to show that no good biblical precedent could be found for resistance to Charles or rebellion against him. Parliamentary writers argued, for example, that divinely sanctioned precedent for resistance to royal authority existed in Jeroboam's rebellion against King Rehoboam: Rehoboam took the advice of evil counsellors and acted tyrannically, and God forbade him to fight against the rebellion led by Jeroboam (1 Kings 12). *Mercurius Aulicus* and the Royalist pamphleteers rejected this argument and protested against the comparison of Charles to Rehoboam.[26] Cowley's allusion to Rehoboam and Jeroboam gains its point from this debate: he describes the followers of the latter, those who 'cut old Jacobs Stemme,' as suffering the torments of Hell, and maintains that even though Rehoboam was a tyrant, and even though God and fate decreed the success of the rebels, divine punishment was the inevitable consequence of the heinous sin of rebellion (II 443-8). The apparent implication is that rebellion is in no circumstances justifiable.

The political views Cowley expresses in *The Civil War* differ markedly from those he expresses in some later works. In parts of the *Davideis* that

Sermons (1635), II 315-16. This homily, first published *c*1571, was reissued in 1642 as Royalist propaganda, by an editor who used the initials 'G.I.', with the title: *The Doctrine of the Church of England, Established by Parliament against Disobedience and wilfull Rebellion.*

23 *The Troublesome Life and Raigne of King Henry the Third. Wherein five Distempers and Maladies are set forth ... Sutable to these unhappie times of ours*; *and continued with them till the King tied his Actions to the rules of his great and good Councell, and not to passionate and single advice*

24 Clarendon condemns this type of Puritan 'wresting and perverting of Scripture' (*History*, VI 40).

25 See, for example, John Goodwin, *Anti-Cavalierisme, Or, Truth Pleading as well the Necessity, as the Lawfulness of this present War* [1642]; and Hezekiah Woodward, *The Kings Chronicle*: *In two Sections*; *Wherein We have the Acts of the wicked and good Kings of Iudah fully declared, with the Ordering of their Militia, and grave Observations thereupon* (1643).

26 See *Mercurius Aulicus*, 24 May 1643, p.276.

were evidently written during the 1650s he appears much more critical of monarchical government than in *The Civil War*.[27] In the ode 'Brutus' (1656) he approves by implication violent resistance to an established ruler in the defence of liberty. In *A Discourse by Way of Vision, Concerning the Government of Oliver Cromwell* (1661) he expresses a more favourable view of Magna Carta than the earlier work seems to imply.[28] The contrast between his views in *The Civil War* and in these later works provides some measure of the extreme position into which he was driven in that poem by the pressures of debate. Yet his political views in *The Civil War* are no more extreme than those of most other Royalist writers during the period to which the poem belongs. In upholding the doctrine of non-resistance Cowley was doing no more than reasserting an ancient commonplace, which was set forth in the sixteenth-century homilies on rebellion and which was revived and given renewed emphasis by such Royalists as Digges and Morton. Like these writers, Cowley is concerned to show that armed resistance to the King would be unjustified even if Charles were – as he is not – a tyrannical and ungodly monarch. There is no need to assume that Cowley or other Royalists like Digges and Morton were attempting to justify absolutism, but they had a lively fear of anarchy, and at a time of active revolt against the King they could admit no sanction for rebellion.[29]

Cowley values degree no less than order, and his treatment of social issues rests upon the same conservative assumptions as his treatment of politics. Although he was, according to John Aubrey,[30] the son of a grocer, his aristocratic class bias is as intense as that of most Royalist writers. He shares the view, common among Royalists, that the rebellion is to a large extent an uprising of 'base mechanicks' and tradesmen discontented with their traditionally established place in the social order, and he condemns the rebels at every opportunity as socially inferior to their opponents. Thus he draws a contrast similar to that made by Clarendon and other Royalists between the high social rank of the King's officers slain at Newbury and the low rank of the rebels who fell. In one respect, indeed, his class prejudice appears more intense than Clarendon's. Clarendon concedes that the London

27 See the speech of Samuel in Book IV of the *Davideis* (*Poems*, p.371). As Nethercot has pointed out (pp.153-5), this section of the *Davideis* and the 'Brutus' ode may be read as part of Cowley's attempt to conciliate Cromwell's government.

28 In the *Discourse* Cowley refers to 'the most sacred of our *English* Laws, the Petition of Right, and *Magna Charta*' (*Essays*, p.371).

29 J.W. Allen has emphasized that Royalist writers generally in 1643 were not arguing for royal absolution (*English Political Thought*, I 512, etc).

30 *Brief Lives* ed. A. Clark (Oxford 1898), I 189. Aubrey's statement has been questioned because the poet's father described himself in his will as a stationer, but he may have been both a grocer and a stationer. See Nethercot, pp.1-3.

trained bands, consisting of middle-class and humbler men, fought splendidly at Newbury and forced the abandonment of the old contempt in which the Royalists had held them. Cowley, however, remains blinded to the reality of their achievement, and he continues to satirize the citizen militia just as he had done in his earlier writings, following the tradition established by Jonson and Beaumont, as if nothing had changed.[31]

Like other seventeenth-century Anglicans, Cowley views the church as an integral part of the established social and political order. Writing in the context of the raging controversy of the early 1640s concerning church government, he defends the traditional ecclesiastical system against all attacks and deplores the damage it had recently suffered at the hands of the Puritans. He laments the fragmentation of the church caused by the development of numerous Puritan sects and by the sudden emergence of anarchy and excesses of all kinds in religion; and he represents the new sects as old heresies in revived form. His emphasis upon the great number and the heretical nature of the Puritan sects may be read as an attempt to refute claims such as that made by John Milton in *The Reason of Church-Government* (1642) when he argued that an episcopal system was not necessary to prevent schism. Milton asked what heresies would appear if the episcopacy were abolished: 'What sects? What are their opinions? Give us the Inventory.'[32] Cowley provides a very long inventory or catalogue of the sects (III 59-186). He does not display much concern for strict accuracy but engages in the kind of attempt to 'confute by scandalous misnaming' that Milton charges against the defenders of the episcopacy.[33] He endeavours to associate with the contemporary Puritans not only the notorious excesses of the Anabaptists of Münster in the previous century but also a whole series of ancient heresies, many of which could scarcely be demonstrated to have any modern counterpart, for example, the 'Angelicalls' or Angelici, which Epiphanius had mentioned in the fourth century as an extinct sect whose doctrines he had been unable to discover.[34] In an apparent allusion to *The Doctrine and Discipline of Divorce*, Cowley seems to include Milton himself among the new heretics (III 95-6). But accuracy in detail is secondary to Cowley's purpose. By drawing up a lengthy catalogue of heresies he makes his point concerning the fragmentation of the church and the revival of heresy. In

31 See III, 303 and note. Cf. Jonson's *Underwood*, XLIV, and *Everyman in his Humour*, III v 149-52; Beaumont's *The Knight of the Burning Pestle*, V i and ii; and Cowley's *The Guardian*, I v.

32 *Complete Prose Works of John Milton*, I (New Haven 1953), 787

33 Ibid., p.788

34 *Adversus Octoginta Hæreses* (Migne, *Patrologiæ Cursus Completus, Series Græca*, XLI, cols. 1038-9)

this he follows a pattern established in numerous Anglican pamphlets of the period, for example, John Taylor's *A Swarme of Sectaries* (1641), Richard Carter's *The Schismatick Stigmatized* (1641), and the anonymous *The Division of the Church of England* (1642);[35] and he anticipates by a few years two more exhaustive and better-known treatises of the same kind, Ephraim Pagitt's *Heresiography* (1645) and the Presbyterian Thomas Edwards' *Gangræna* (1646).

Although Cowley follows some of the common patterns of Anglican polemical writing, he displays tendencies that link him with the Laudian rather than the moderate party in the Church of England. As his earlier writings show, he was strongly hostile toward the Puritans from the beginning of his career, attacking them as socially low, as irrational, as hypocritical, and as the enemies of learning and the arts.[36] At Cambridge he may, like his friend Crashaw, have come under the influence of the Laudian party, and there may be significance in the fact that at Oxford he is said to have resided at St John's, Laud's college.[37] There is no evidence that he was subsequently inclined to follow Crashaw in joining the Church of Rome, even though he was attached for many years to the Catholic circle of Henrietta Maria and Jermyn. Sprat's praise of his loyal devotion to the Church of England appears to be quite justified.[38] He developed, however, a greater sympathy for Roman Catholicism than many of his Anglican contemporaries, as his elegy for Crawshaw suggests.[39] In *The Puritan and the Papist* he defends the Church of England as the *via media* between the false extremes of Puritanism and Roman Catholicism, but in his reaction against Puritanism in *The Civil War* he aligns himself with those right-wing Anglicans who were much closer to the Roman Catholic than to the Puritan extreme. He introduces unfavourable allusions to Papists and makes it clear that his real allegiance is to the Church of England, but he goes so far as to state that he prefers Roman Catholicism to the excesses of Puritanism:

> If such foule Waters the fam'd Lake containe
> Let's rather drinke old Tybers Flood againe.

35 See Don M. Wolfe's discussion of pamphlets of this type, Introduction, *Complete Prose Works of John Milton*, I 135-7.

36 See, for example, 'A Vote,' and *The Guardian*, Prologue, and IV vii.

37 The President of St John's during the period of Cowley's presumed residence was Richard Baylie, Laud's disciple and kinsman by marriage. See W.C. Costin, *The History of St. John's College, Oxford, 1598-1860* (Oxford 1958), pp.30, 34.

38 'Life', sig. e1v. There is a story that Cowley died a Catholic, but it appears to be quite false. See Nethercot, pp.131, 135.

39 'On the Death of Mr. Crashaw'

Let our great Thames pay Homage as before,
Rather then new and worser streames adore.
If wee're resolv'd and fixt our Way to loose,
Let's some false Road before false By-wayes choose. (III 73-8)

He includes in his catalogue of notorious heretics 'Wicleffians, Hussites, and the Zwinglian crew' (III 179), although Wyclif, Hus, and Zwingli were generally admired by English Protestants as pioneers of the Reformation.[40] His reasons for placing them (or their followers) with the heretics is no doubt the fact that they were heroes especially of the Puritan party,[41] but he runs the risk of providing ammunition for the Puritan propagandists. Cowley protests against the Puritan habit of attaching the label 'Papist' to Royalists and Anglicans, but he is sometimes injudicious enough to make statements that could have been used by Puritans in support of their thesis that Royalist circles were thick with Roman Catholics and Roman Catholic sympathisers.

The Civil War frequently suffers from the narrowness and limitations of party propaganda, and it sometimes displays a bitterness, vindictiveness, and bloodthirstiness quite out of keeping with the conventional image of the poet as a gentle and moderate spirit, which is derived principally from his essays and other late writings. Cowley's decision to suppress the work testifies, in part at least, to his own recognition of these faults. It was clearly not in the character of the relatively young and fiercely committed poet who wrote *The Civil War* to achieve the exceptional detachment that appears in Marvell's 'Horatian Ode' or the striking moderation that sometimes appeared among the active military leaders, as in the famous and moving instance of the letter Sir William Waller addressed to Hopton in the spring of 1643.[42] But, in any case, such liberty was scarcely possible for the polemical writer in the heat of the propaganda warfare. In its treatment of history and politics *The Civil War* is not justly to be compared with Marvell's 'Horatian

40 See, for example, John Foxe's enormously influential Book of Martyrs, *Actes and Monumentes* (1570), pp.523-52, 701-48, 995-1005. Peter Heylin appears to have stirred controversy by maintaining in an Oxford disputation in 1627 that Wyclif and Hus were heretics from the Anglican as well as the Roman viewpoint, but his argument won Laud's approval. See George Vernon, *The Life of the Learned and Reverend Dr Peter Heylin* (1682), pp.26-30.

41 See, for example, John Milton's *Of Reformation* and *The Reason of Church-Government, Complete Prose Works*, I 525-6, 788. In the latter Milton writes that Christ's 'best Disciples in the reformation ... were call'd Lollards and Hussites' by their enemies of the bishops' tribe, just as they are now termed Brownists or Puritans.

42 The best text of the letter is the one given by Mary Coate in her *Cornwall in the Great Civil War* (p.77).

Ode' or even with Clarendon's *History*. The juster comparison is with *Mercurius Aulicus*, with the political verse of Cleveland, and with the other explicitly polemical writings of the period of the Civil War. There may be some instances where Cowley appears unusually biased and extreme even when judged by the criteria generally accepted by the participants in the propaganda battle, but on the whole he emerges from the comparison with contemporary polemical writers not as one who is exceptionally immoderate, although certainly as one who possesses many of the common limitations.

While *The Civil War* is strongly partisan, designed as a contribution to a hoped-for Royalist victory, Cowley sometimes views the war in a wider perspective, as a tragedy for England in which there can be no victory. This sense of tragedy sounds strongly in the final words of the poem, in the conclusion of the elegy for Falkland. Cowley is bitter against the rebels for having killed this paragon of men, and he hopes that his dead friend's spirit will inspire the Royalists to victory. But finally, as if in meditating on Falkland's character he has absorbed something of that man's charitable spirit and hatred of bloodshed, and as if his death has shocked him into an increasing sense of the horror of the war, he asks not for victory but for peace, and he seems to admit the possibility of forgiveness and reconciliation.

4
Literary Tradition

If *The Civil War* is shaped by current history and polemics, it is shaped also by literary tradition. Cowley views the events of his time with a vision formed partly by his reading of the literature of the past, and he turns not only to the newspapers and pamphlets but also to Virgil and Lucan. On its most ambitious level the poem is an attempt to give epic treatment to current history, to celebrate the great men and the great deeds of the Royalists in the manner traditional in heroic poetry. Cowley was too much at the mercy of unfolding forces of history and too much committed to the needs of propaganda to allow *The Civil War* to be in any full sense an epic, but he succeeds in giving the poem enough of the epic scope and quality to raise it to a higher literary level and to make it more permanently interesting than the ordinary work of propaganda.

The epic scope of the poem appears partly in Cowley's setting the current conflict in a broad perspective of human history, his relating of events in the present to events in the past, English, classical, and biblical. He uses allusion to earlier English history sometimes to intensify the sense of the tragedy of the current condition of the nation. Thus the poem opens with a contrast between the England of the past, united in heroic endeavour and victorious over her foreign enemies, and the England of the present, torn by internecine strife. On the other hand, he frequently draws parallels between the present war and the conflicts of the past. He establishes the heroism and virtue of the Royalists and the villany of their opponents by associating them with appropriate figures from legend or history. Sir Bevil Grenville is compared with Decius, and Charles Cavendish with Hector, and the Royalist Cornish forces are linked with King Arthur. Conversely, the Parliamentarians are associated with the most overweening and evil rebels and regicides in classical myth and history and in biblical and English history: with the giants who warred with the gods in Greek myth, with Marius, Sulla, and Catiline, with Korah and Ahitophel, and with the murderers of Edward II, just as the new Puritan sects are linked with the notorious heresies of the past. This use of history not only serves Cowley's polemical purposes as a technique of favourable and invidious comparison, but it serves also to create the sense that the Civil War is an episode in the age-old conflict between the forces of order and disorder, of good and evil, of God and Satan.

The sense that the conflict has a universal and timeless dimension is reinforced further by the introduction of a supernatural level, which is in keeping both with epic tradition and with the providential reading of history general in the seventeenth century. Cowley incorporates in his poem a characteristically Renaissance mixture of classical and Christian elements, including Cupids, angels, Furies, Alecto, Satan, and the Christian God. Infernal or satanic elements are associated with the Parliamentarians most notably in the elaborate description at the end of Book II of a council or parliament in Hell, where Satan plots his assistance to the rebels, but this passage is part of a larger pattern in the poem. Alecto appears at the opening of Book II, sowing discord and declaring her pleasure at the activities of the rebels. In Book III the Furies aid the rebels in raising forces for the relief of Gloucester, and they reappear as allies of the rebels on the battlefield at Newbury. Similarly, divine forces are constantly associated with the Royalists. Sometimes these belong to the world of fiction and convention. Cupids appear at Kineton, to prepare for the reception of the King and Queen, as if they had strayed from a court masque.[1] On a more serious level, angels and God himself are seen as supporting the Royalist cause. Occasionally, indeed, Cowley views the war as a divine judgment upon the whole nation for its sins, but, like many of his contemporaries, he seems to feel no difficulty in reconciling this view with a belief that God supports his own party. Books I and III both conclude in prayer for victory and peace.

Although the structure of the poem is determined in great part by historical events, it is moulded also by epic tradition. Cowley appears to have in mind a common epic pattern, found for example in Tasso and later followed by Milton. In this pattern the forces of good secure an initial success; there is then an upsurge of the forces of evil, but in the conclusion good achieves an overwhelming triumph. The first two parts of this three-part

1 I 497-500. C.V. Wedgwood comments on the masque-like spirit of this passage in her discussion of *A Poem on the Late Civil War* in her *Poetry and Politics under the Stuarts* (Cambridge 1960), p.76.

structure appear in *The Civil War*, and it is evident particularly in his handling of the second part that Cowley is thinking in epic terms, as he describes the council in Hell with Satan's determination to aid the rebels, the subsequent flight of the Furies unleashing evil passions among the inhabitants of London, and the frantic efforts of the Londoners to prepare an army to resist the King. The third part of the structure, of course, could not be completed, because history did not allow the conclusion intended and desired by Cowley.

The character of *The Civil War* as a heroic poem appears also in Cowley's use of a series of the traditional epic conventions. He follows epic precedent, for example, in employing the convention of the formal speeches delivered by the leaders of opposing armies before battle, giving such speeches to Charles and Essex before Newbury. In the epic manner he provides catalogues of military leaders and the fallen in battle, adapting this convention also to give a satiric catalogue of the Puritan sects whose members compose the Parliamentary army. His attempt to achieve an epic elevation of style is frequently apparent, and he makes some use of one special mark of epic style, the epic or Homeric simile.

It is evident that when Cowley wrote *The Civil War* he possessed already much of that comprehensive knowledge of epic tradition which was subsequently revealed by the *Davideis* and the notes he provided for that poem. Many of his notes to the *Davideis* shed light on his practice in *The Civil War*, for example a discussion of the convention of the epic catalogue in which he criticizes the manner in which it had been handled by a number of classical poets.[2] Cowley wrote *The Civil War* in circumstances that cannot have allowed him time for long premeditation or leisurely composition, but he came to the poem almost immediately from his years of study at Cambridge, and he possessed a mind extraordinarily well stored with literary knowledge. If he had already begun his work on the *Davideis* at Cambridge, as Sprat states,[3] the studies of epic poetry he had made for that poem must have been relatively fresh in his mind. According to Sprat, he continued his studies for a time at Oxford. Probably during the period when he wrote

2 Book III, note 8

3 Sprat states that he often heard Martin Clifford declare that Cowley 'finish'd the greatest part' of the *Davideis* while he was a young student at Cambridge ('Life,' sig. c1). Nethercot (pp.153-5) has shown that part of the poem was written or extensively revised during the 1650s, and Frank Kermode has suggested that the whole poem was written between 1650 and 1654 ('The Date of Cowley's *Davideis*,' *RES*, xxv [1949] 154-8). Clifford's statement as reported by Sprat may, however, be taken as evidence that Cowley had at least begun his studies for the poem during his Cambridge years.

The Civil War he had access to college libraries and to the Bodleian, '*Bodleys* noble worke,' as he terms it in the poem (I 351).[4]

Cowley was no slavish imitator of classical literary models, and there is no need to question Denham's praise of his combination of originality with learning:

> To him no Author was unknown,
> Yet what he wrote was all his own.[5]

It is understandable, however, that one student of his literary sources has been driven to write that a passage in the *Davideis* contains details 'taken from almost all Latin and Greek poets.'[6] Cowley not only possessed a vast knowledge of literature but he often worked by an assimilative method and drew in a single passage simultaneously upon a whole series of sources,[7] ranging from classical poetry to the English poetry that was appearing even at the time he was writing. It is scarcely possible to identify all the influences that went into the making of *The Civil War*, and it is often difficult to separate one strand of influence from another with any confidence. One may, however, point to some of the literary models which were in Cowley's mind as wrote, and which he must have hoped would be in the minds of his readers, since many elements in the poem gain added significance when they are seen in relation to literary tradition or understood as allusion to a particular work.

None of the classical poets left more easily discernible marks of influence upon *The Civil War* than Virgil. This is as one would expect, since Cowley declared his admiration for Virgil in many passages of his writings,[8] and it has always been recognized that the Roman poet is a major influence upon his work. As the author of the *Davideis* he has been described as the most Virgilian of English epic poets before Milton.[9] Among the Virgilian elements common to the *Davideis* and *The Civil War* is Cowley's occasional use of

4 Cf. Cowley's later praise of the Bodleian in his 'Ode. Mr. Cowley's Book presenting it self to the University Library of Oxford'.

5 'On Mr Abraham Cowley *His Death and Burial amongst the Ancient Poets*' (*The Poetical Works of Sir John Denham* ed. T.H. Banks [New Haven 1928]), ll.29-30

6 John M. McBryde, 'A Study of Cowley's Davideis,' *Journal of Germanic Philology*, II (1899) 525

7 This point has been well made by E.M.W. Tillyard in his discussion of the relation of the *Davideis* to its possible models and sources, in his *The English Epic and its Background* (Oxford 1966), p.424.

8 See, for example, 'The Motto,' and numerous notes to the *Davideis*.

9 Elizabeth Nitchie, *Vergil and the English Poets* (New York 1919), p.133

the half-line or hemistich; in a note to the *Davideis* he claims to be the first English poet to follow Virgil in employing it.[10] The classical supernatural machinery of *The Civil War* unmistakably derives in part from the *Aeneid*, for example the description of Alecto blowing her trumpet to cause discord and war (II 5-12).[11] Similarly, Cowley's commemoration of the deeds and laments for the deaths of Royalist heroes sometimes echo Virgil's celebration of the heroes of the *Aeneid*. Some lines in his elegy for Charles Cavendish (II 150-4) are virtually a translation of Virgil's lines on the death of Pallas. So also, his descriptions of battle show the influence of the *Aeneid*, for example his picture of the behaviour of the horses at the opening of the Battle of Newbury (III 342). In a description of the King's horse (III 267-74), he draws not upon the *Aeneid* but upon two passages in the *Georgics*. Minor verbal echoings of Virgil appear frequently in the poem. Thus the opening lines of the first book,

> What rage does *England* from it selfe divide
> More then Seas doe from all the world beside,

and other lines in the third book (79-80) obviously recall Virgil's well-known allusion to the Britons in the *Eclogues* (I 66): 'et penitus toto divisos orbe Britannos.'

The usefulness of Virgil to Cowley was, of course, limited by the fact that Virgil's subject and purposes in the *Aeneid* were very different from his own. For a poem that was concerned with national history rather than national legend, and that took civil war as its subject, he found his principal classical model in Lucan's *Pharsalia*. English interest in Lucan, which had been stimulated by the translations of Marlowe and Thomas May, was strong at the time Cowley wrote. During the Civil War English poets turned naturally to Lucan, as studies of Marvell's 'Horatian Ode' have suggested.[12] That Cowley fully shared the contemporary interest in Lucan is shown by the fact that he frequently refers to the poet in his notes to the *Davideis* and *Pindarique Odes*,[13] as well as by the evidence of influence which appears in *The Civil War*.

10 See *The Civil War*, I 430, and II 521; and the *Davideis*, Book I, note 14.
11 When detailed or exact references to Cowley's literary sources are not given here they will be found in the notes on the passages of *The Civil War* which are cited.
12 See, for example, R.H. Syfret, 'Marvell's "Horatian Ode",' *RES*, n.s. XII (1961) 160-72.
13 See, for example, *Davideis*, Book I, notes 1 and 57, Book III, notes 8, 38, and 46; *Pindarique Odes*, 'The 34. Chapter of the Prophet Isaiah,' stanza 3, note 4; 'The Plagues of Egypt,' stanza 4, note 2, and stanza 5, note 2.

Cowley's affinity with Lucan is suggested by the very title of his poem, *The Civil War*, for Lucan's epic, although commonly known as the *Pharsalia*, is properly titled *De Bello Civili*. To Lucan more than any other poet Cowley probably owes his conception not merely of an epic on civil war but of an epic that gives a highly polemical treatment of the conflict, a poem that deplores the evil of civil war and at the same time expresses a fiercely partisan viewpoint. Cowley declares his horror of civil war in the opening lines of his first two books in much the manner of Lucan at the opening of the first two books of the *Pharsalia*: both poets emphasize the unnatural and self-destructive nature of the conflict, viewing it as disease and madness and as the coming of chaos, as a war in which there can be no true victory. At the beginning of both poems the contrast is developed between the past when a united nation was victorious against foreign enemies, and the present (or, in the case of Lucan, the relatively recent past) when the nation destroys itself by internal conflict. In the eyes of both poets, moreover, the fault lies with one party in the conflict, principally with that of Caesar for Lucan and entirely with the rebels for Cowley. Lucan's Pompey and Cowley's Charles represent the traditional values of their nations, opposing tyrannical innovation. Charles stands for liberty in Cowley's view, just as Pompey does in Lucan's, since Cowley regards the Puritans and Parliamentarians as the real enemies of liberty.

Cowley sometimes appears to fuse contemporary history with Lucan's accounts of events. For example, his description of the Royalist siege of Lichfield and the vigorous rebel defence of the city (II 107-12) is no doubt based primarily upon current news sources, but the action seems to be associated in his mind with Scaeva's defence of the siege line at Dyrrachium against Pompey's attack in the *Pharsalia* (VI 169-79): in both cases the defenders hurl stones at their assailants and cut off the hands of the attackers as they clutch the battlements; and Lucan's comment on the defenders (VI 262): 'Infelix, quanta dominum virtute parasti,' seems to be echoed in Cowley's lines (II 135-6):

> Unhappy men! who can your curses tell?
> Damn'd, and infam'ed for fighting *ill soe well*!

Similarities appear also beween Lucan's description of the Battle of Pharsalia and Cowley's account of Newbury, although Newbury is not for Cowley so crushing a defeat of the cause he supports as Pharsalia is for Lucan. Cowley not only follows Lucan's precedent in giving the opposing leaders, Charles and Essex, formal speeches before the battle, but he may also have drawn some of the arguments in the speech he invents for Charles from the similar arguments and exhortations in the speeches of Lucan's Caesar and Pompey. Like Lucan, too, he laments that on the side he supports the nobility perished, while on the other side only plebeians fell. This coincidence arises from historical circumstances, but there can be little doubt that Cowley writes with some sense of the parallel between Newbury and Pharsalia as seen by Lucan.

The Civil War does not appear to embody so many substantial verbal echoings of Lucan as of Virgil, but the influence of Lucan's methods and style is pervasive, and Cowley could have justified his own practices more often by the precedent of Lucan than by that of Virgil. The relative structural looseness of his poem and the apparent lack of a sense of proportion that he displays in his treatment of various events arise partly from the fact that he wrote in haste, close in time to the actions which he described, but he may have considered himself to be taking advantage of a freedom allowed by Lucan's precedent. The epigrammatic qualities and conceits of his style are developed partly from the Donne tradition but partly no doubt also from Lucan; and Lucan provided the fullest precedent for the use of such a style in a heroic poem. In particular, Cowley seems to follow Lucan in developing at every opportunity elements of the grotesque, horrific, and macabre. His closeness in taste and style to Lucan appears if one compares his description of an action on the Thames near Brentford in which ships are set afire and in which those who try to escape death by fire find death by drowning (I 325-32) with Lucan's description of a similar situation in a sea battle (III 680-90). Cowley's elaborately gruesome and grotesque description of Essex's army racked by disease (II 159-91) is a counterpart of Lucan's descriptions of the suffering of Pompey's army from thirst and disease (IV 292-336, VI 80-105).

As his notes to the *Davideis* and the *Pindarique Odes* show,[14] Cowley was strongly interested not only in Lucan but in Lucan's contemporary, Statius, and in the later Roman poet, Claudian. In *The Civil War* (I 535) he makes an allusion to Capaneus, a heroic figure of Statius' *Thebaid*, and some details in his description of Hell (II 365-86) may also derive from the *Thebaid*.[15] His contrivance of a parliament in Hell, in the later part of Book II, probably has its closest classical counterpart in Claudian's *In Rufinum Liber Primus* (ll.25-139). In Claudian's poem, Alecto, angry because of the

14 For example, Cowley alludes to Statius in no fewer than six of the notes to Book III of the *Davideis* (21, 33, 37, 46, 48, 53). In note 46 he defends his own use of hyperbole by reference to the precedent of Statius and Claudian. His verse includes the translation, 'Claudian's Old Man of Verona.'

15 McBryde (pp.518, 525) discusses the influence of Statius on this passage in the form in which it appears in the *Davideis*.

peace that prevails among men, summons an infernal council, where such figures as Discord, Hunger, and Age take their places on iron seats, and hear a speech which has a general similarity with that of Cowley's Beelzebub, and which brings a similar result, the unleashing of a force of discord and destruction among men. In writing *The Civil War* Cowley may also have been influenced by the alternation of extreme panegyric and extreme invective that is characteristic of Claudian, and by the conceited qualities of his style. He adapted at least one of Claudian's conceits, that of the adjacency of fire and snow on Aetna in the *De Raptu Proserpinae*, for his own poem (II 333-6).

If classical literary tradition provides one frame of reference for *The Civil War*, the Bible provides another. The ease and frequency of Cowley's scriptural allusion may have been developed partly in biblical studies that he had made for the *Davideis*. In his fusion of biblical and Christian elements with classical myth Cowley may occasionally have in mind the distant precedent of Dante, whose inferno provides a prototype for that which he constructs in the later part of Book II; but probably a stronger influence is Tasso's *Gerusalemme Liberata*.[16] Tasso had already brought together many of the diverse elements that are joined in Cowley's poem. He had described an infernal council presided over by Satan, he had introduced the Virgilian figure of Alecto, spreading destruction and strife, and he had given both devils and angels an influence on events.[17] Tasso's poem had relevance for Cowley not only because it was widely regarded as the outstanding example of the Christian neo-classical epic but also because the Civil War was in Cowley's eyes almost as much a holy war as the Crusade was for Tasso, even though in one passage (I 21-30) he develops a contrast between the Crusades and the current war. The spirits of his rebels, like those of Tasso's infidels, plunge into Hell upon death, while the souls of the Royalist dead rise to be welcomed into Heaven as martyrs.

Apart from the classics, however, the strongest literary influences upon *The Civil War* were probably provided by English poets, ranging from Spenser to those contemporary with Cowley. In a well-known passage in his essay 'Of my Self,'[18] Cowley tells us that he decided to become a poet because of the joy he found as a child in reading Spenser. When he wrote

16 The extent of Cowley's knowledge of Italian is uncertain, as Nethercot points out (p.33), but Tasso's poem was no doubt known to him in Edward Fairfax's translation (1600), if not in the original. Tasso's work has frequently been regarded as one of the principal models for the *Davideis*. See Tillyard, *The English Epic*, pp.423-4, and Loiseau, pp.329-30.

17 See especially Books IV, VIII, and IX of the *Gerusalemme Liberata*.

18 *Essays*, pp.457-8

The Civil War the influence of Spenser was no longer so strong upon him as it had been in his earlier years, but it was not dead. There are in his poem not only little incidental echoes of Spenser, such as the phrase 'confused Noyse' in a rhyme with 'voice' (I 143-4), which derives from the *Epithalamion* (ll.138-9), but also indications of a deliberate attempt to associate his work with that of the greatest heroic poet whom England had yet produced. Spenser's influence appears in his occasional use of an allegorical method. Such figures as Religion and Schism, Loyalty and Sedition stand in opposed positions at the opening of the Battle of Edgehill (I 213-42), and the figure of Rebellion appears among the fiends in Hell (II 401-20). Cowley's description of Rebellion seems designed to bring similar figures in Spenser to the reader's mind; it is not modelled on a single person in *The Faerie Queene*, but it suggests a whole series of figures of sedition, doubleness, or false-seeming in the earlier poem. His lines (II 405-6),

> Faire seem'd her hew, and modest seemd her guise;
> Her Eyne cast up towards Heaven in holy wise,

have some suggestion of Spenser's description of Archimago, with his hypocritically ostentatious piety (I i 29).[19] Rebellion's doubleness of face and tongue and her destructive and seditious quality suggest Spenser's Ate, 'mother of debate,/ And all dissention,' the breaker of sceptres and defiler of churches, who appears beautiful upon first sight (IV i 19-31). Similarly Cowley's description of Rebellion's speech (II 413-14),

> Her wicked Mouth spoke proud and bitter things,
> Blasphem'ed Gods Church, and curst anoynted Kings,

seems to echo Spenser's description of the speech of the Blatant Beast (VI xii 28):

> And spake licentious words, and hateful things
> ...
> Ne Kesar spared he a whit, nor Kings.

That Cowley is deliberately establishing a link between *The Civil War* and *The Faerie Queene* is indicated also by his use of Spenserian archaisms such as 'Eyne' (II 406) and other favourite words of Spenser such as 'grisly' (II 411).

19 Spenser's description of Speranza (I x 14), a figure in a very different category, may also have been in Cowley's mind.

In writing *The Civil War* Cowley may have turned not only to Spenser but also to the two followers of Spenser who had anticipated him in giving heroic treatment to English civil wars, Daniel and Drayton. In *The Civil Wars* and *The Barons' Wars* Daniel and Drayton had already made the attempt to adapt the material of English history to the model of Lucan's *Pharsalia*; they had described in much detail the horrors of civil war; they had introduced into their poems figures of nemesis or mischief who spread discord among men; and they had contrasted times when England was united at home and victorious abroad with times when it was torn by internal strife.[20] Drayton was before Cowley in contrasting a period of civil war with the time when the English fought together to free the Saviour's tomb, and in contrasting the harmony of the stars with the disharmony of men.[21] Neither Daniel nor Drayton had for Cowley the prestige of Lucan or Spenser, and it is rarely possible to isolate their influence from that of their common classical and English models, but a comparison of his work with theirs is instructive as showing the extent to which Cowley adapts literary commonplaces that had already been developed or domesticated in English heroic and historical poetry.

For Daniel and Drayton the horror of civil war belonged to the past, and with the evil past they were able to contrast the peaceful present time of the reigns of Elizabeth and James. For Cowley the contrast between past and present is reversed, and he looks nostalgically to the peaceful period in which they wrote. There are some apparent echoings of Drayton's *Poly-Olbion* in *The Civil War* which suggest that Cowley turned to the earlier poet's descriptions of a still peaceful England in order to read his accounts of the areas that in his own time had become the scenes of bloodshed. Thus Cowley's description of the river Tamar as favouring its Cornish or Royalist bank and as turning away from its Devon side, held by the rebels (I 409-14), may well have been suggested by Drayton's description of the river's 'equall sides' in the *Poly-Olbion*, and his lines seem to gain special point if Drayton's words are recalled.

A number of the Elizabethan plays that had provided heroic treatment of earlier English history and civil wars were no doubt also in Cowley's mind

20 See, for example, Daniel, *The Civil Wars*, Book I, stanza 2, III 54, VI 30ff; and Drayton's *The Barons' Wars*, Canto I, stanzas 1-11, II 4-8, 67-8. Cf. Thomas May's *The Reigne of King Henry the Second* (1633), in which Satanic forces are represented as working to destroy the peace and power of England and as attempting to reduce the nation to civil war.

21 Compare Cowley, I 21-6, and I 299-304, with Drayton, *The Barons' Wars*, II 45, and IV 51. Other poets had, of course, also anticipated Cowley in developing these themes. On the contrast between civil strife and holy crusade, cf. Shakespeare, *Henry IV, Part I*, I i 1-29.

when he wrote *The Civil War*. His knowledge and interpretation of medieval English history probably derive from Shakespeare and Marlowe, as well as from such chroniclers and historians as Holinshed. His account of the heroic exploits of the English in the Hundred Years War (I 37-58) may well be influenced both by Shakespeare's *Henry V* and the anonymous Elizabethan play, *The Raigne of King Edward the Third*. The latter play may have led him into an inaccuracy, for he appears to follow the anonymous dramatist in conflating two historically separate events (I 47). His themes and his political views have much in common with those Shakespeare develops in *Richard II*, *Henry IV*, *Henry V*, *Henry VI*, and *Richard III*.

Seventeenth-century poets as diverse as Donne and Denham have left some mark of their influence on *The Civil War*. There is no need to reopen here the large and much discussed subject of Donne's stylistic influence on Cowley, but one may point to a probable example of Cowley's more specific indebtedness to Donne: it seems likely that he has in mind Donne's description of the flight of the soul to Heaven in *The Second Anniversary* when he describes the flight of Falkland's soul.[22] Denham's *Cooper's Hill*, which was immediately popular when published in its first version in 1642, very close to the time of composition of *The Civil War*, must have interested Cowley both for its political commentary and for its author's notable skill in handling the medium of the closed heroic couplet.[23] Cowley appears to echo Denham in his description of the Thames (I 333-44).

A particularly interesting case of contemporary literary influence is that of Crashaw's free version of Marino, 'Sospetto d'Herode.'[24] Crashaw's poem was not published until 1646, but a manuscript copy is dated 1637.[25] Cowley had presumably become familiar with the work at Cambridge through his friendship with Crashaw. His description of Hell, Lucifer, and the infernal

22 Cowley was undoubtedly familiar with other descriptions of the flight of the soul, including Lucan's in the *Pharsalia* (IX 1-18), and Chaucer's in *Troilus and Criseyde* (V 1807-27), but his contrast between this world's imperfect and the next world's perfect knowledge (III 571-84) suggests Donne's poem (ll.251-320).

23 On the basis of the version of Book I published in 1679, B. O Hehir suggests that *The Civil War* may be the earliest poem to show the influence of *Cooper's Hill*. See his *Expans'd Hieroglyphicks: A Critical Edition of Sir John Denham's Coopers Hill* (Berkeley and Los Angeles 1969), pp.294-5.

24 McBryde (pp.503-12) discussed this influence in relation to the *Davideis*, but he had no reason to suppose that Cowley knew Crashaw's poem before its publication, since it had appeared in *Steps to the Temple* (1646), ten years before the *Davideis* was printed.

25 See L.C. Martin's introduction to his *The Poems English Latin and Greek of Richard Crashaw* (second edition, Oxford 1957), p.lxxxviii. Quotations from the 'Sospetto d'Herode' are from this edition (pp.109-26).

council in the later part of Book II appears to be decidedly influenced by Crashaw. He follows Crashaw's sequence in moving from the general description of Hell to a description of Lucifer, and then to the flight of the Furies, who work on the sleeping inhabitants of London in Cowley's poem as they work on the sleeping Herod in Crashaw's.

Much in this pattern might, of course, have been derived by Cowley from other sources, but there are a remarkable number of similarities in detail between the works of the two poets. For example, Crashaw describes Satan as seated on 'a burnisht Throne of quenchlesse fire' (stanza 6), while Cowley describes Lucifer as rising 'from his direfull throne/Of burnisht Flames' (II 517-18). In speech Crashaw's Satan asks: 'what though it cost/Mee yet a second fall?' (stanza 32); Cowley's Lucifer declares: 'Had I another Heav'en I'de venture't here' (II 535). Crashaw's Satan has a glance like 'the fatall Light/Of staring Comets,' and 'His breath Hells lightning is' (stanza 7); Cowley writes of his figure of Rebellion: 'And from her stareing eyes feirce Lightning flew' (II 412), and 'her Breath was Flame' (II 416). Crashaw describes the torments of the damned: 'In .../ (His shop of flames) hee fryes himselfe' (stanza 8), and 'the black soules boile in their owne gore' (stanza 37); Cowley uses similar detail: 'In such feirce flames the Traytour now is fried' (II 451), and 'drown'd in boyling blood' (II 491). Crashaw writes of the flight of the Fury over the earth (stanza 48):

> The field's faire Eyes saw her, and saw no more,
> But shut their flowry lids for ever.

Cowley describes the effect of the similar flight in his poem thus: 'Th'affrighted Night shuts close her trembling eyes' (III 6). Such parallels as these between the two poems are numerous. Taken together they suggest that Crashaw's poem was known to Cowley long before its publication and that it made a strong impact upon him.

Cowley must have read with special interest the work of the Royalist poets of Oxford which was appearing even as he was engaged in writing *The Civil War*. Since he was not a member of the university, he could not contribute to *Musarum Oxoniensium* Επιβατηρια (Oxford 1643), a volume in which Oxford men celebrated the Queen's return from the Continent and the north. In *The Civil War* (I 491-508), however, he commemorates this event in much the same spirit as a number of the poets who contributed to that volume, and his lines have some close affinities with poems published there by William Cartwright, John Berkenhead, and John Fell. In a similar fashion, his lines on the death of Grenville (I 466-72) seem to embody some echoes of poems by Cartwright and others published in *Verses on the Death of the*

Right Valiant Sr Bevill Grenvill ([Oxford] 1643); and his lines on the death of Northampton (II 52–64) contain ideas and images which were probably suggested to him by the anonymous *An Elegy on the Death of the Right Honourable Spencer, Earle of Northampton* [Oxford 1643]. Such poems as these provide an important context for *The Civil War*,[26] but, if Cowley read and sometimes drew upon the scattered occasional verse of other Royalist poets, he must have done so with the consciousness that his own work was much more ambitious and comprehensive than any treatment of the war attempted by the other poets.[27]

The existence of close affinities between passages in *The Civil War* and various contemporary occasional poems suggests the degree to which Cowley amalgamates with epic tradition a series of the prevailing literary types of his period, including Renaissance courtly verse and panegyric, elegy, and satire. Even a form so remote from epic as the court masque exerts a persistent influence on *The Civil War*. Such allegorical figures as those which appear before the Battle of Edgehill (I 213-42) belong as much to the world of the masque as to that of Spenser. The pattern whereby figures of disorder, grotesque antimasque elements, intrude only to be swept away or reduced to order by figures of virtue and authority, which was strongly established in the Jacobean and Caroline masque, leaves its mark on *The Civil War* in a number of sudden transformation scenes. In Jonson's *Pleasure Reconciled to Virtue* the very presence of Hercules is sufficient to transform a landscape or banish disorder; in D'Avenant's *Salmacida Spolia* (1640), the last of the pre-war masques, the plots of Discord to disrupt the tranquility of England are instantaneously defeated by the divine wisdom of the King; so in Cowley's poem the presence of the King is enough to raise a great army, as if by magic or divine power, that of Newcastle is sufficient to create order from chaos, the very name of Rupert is capable of vanquishing the enemy, and the Queen can win a great victory by an influence she exercises even in her absence.[28] It is unfortunate for Cowley that the masque conventions ultimately proved inadequate in the face of the hard realities of the war.

When Cowley develops in *The Civil War* panegyrics of King Charles and Queen Henrietta Maria, princes Rupert and Maurice, the Earl of Newcastle, Lord Jermyn, Lord Digby, Sir Ralph Hopton, and others, he frequently

26 This context is well indicated by the Bodleian MS Douce 357, where the first book of *The Civil War* is transcribed with a large collection of the occasional Royalist verse of the 1640s, including poems by Denham and Cleveland.

27 Such extended verse histories of the Civil War as A. Cooper's Στρατολογια (1660) are much later in date than Cowley's poem, and they are negligible in their literary quality.

28 See *The Civil War*, I 169-78, 519-22, 202, 505-8. Cf. I 189-92.

draws not so much upon epic conventions for the celebration of heroes as upon the Renaissance conventions for the praise of kings and courtiers in which he was already well practised before he began to write the poem. For the inclusion of the funeral elegy in the heroic poem he had excellent precedent in epic practice, as we may be reminded by his paraphrase of Virgil's lines on the death of Pallas in his elegy for Charles Cavendish, but he gives both elegy and satire a larger place in *The Civil War*, especially in the final book, than they had in classical epic. He provides elegies, sometimes brief but sometimes lengthy and elaborate, for most of the notable Royalists who fell in the first year of the war, including the earls of Lindsey, Northampton, Sunderland, and Carnarvon, the Marquis de la Vieuville, Lord Falkland, and Sir Bevil Grenville, as well as Cavendish. To these heroic figures he opposes a gallery of satirical portraits of the rebel leaders and fallen: the Earl of Essex, Lord Wharton, Lord Brooke, John Hampden, Sir William Waller, and the apparently fictitious characters in his satirical catalogue of the rebel dead at Newbury.

In its satiric aspects *The Civil War* owes some obvious debt to the Jonsonian tradition in which Cowley had earlier worked, for example in his comedy, *The Guardian.* His satiric character sketches of the rebels in Book III and elsewhere, which provide some of the liveliest passages in the poem, derive in part from Jonson's portraits of Puritans in *The Alchemist* and *Bartholomew's Fair*, and they have some affinities with the polemical characters in prose or verse written in considerable numbers by Royalists in the 1640s to ridicule their enemies.[29] Cowley is, however, one of the pioneers of the Royalist satire of the Civil War period, and his work in *The Civil War* and *The Puritan and the Papist* precedes most of the surviving satire of John Cleveland, who emerged later in the decade as the most effective and popular of the Royalist satirical poets.

Charles Lamb suggested that as a comic dramatist Cowley provides the link between the earlier Stuart and the Restoration eras,[30] and a similar claim might be made for his non-dramatic satire. If his satiric characters recall Jonson, they also point the way to Butler and Dryden. Such a character sketch as Cowley's Simon Blore, the women's tailor turned preacher, visionary, and soldier (III 434-50) comes close to satiric characters in Butler's *Hudibras*, for example Cerdon, the cobbler, preacher, and warrior (I ii

29 The relevant literary traditions are discussed by William P. Holden, *Anti-Puritan Satire 1572-1642* (New Haven 1954); and Benjamin Boyce, *The Polemic Character 1640-61* (Lincoln, Neb. 1955).

30 *Specimens of English Dramatic Poets*, in *The Works of Charles and Mary Lamb* ed. E.V. Lucas (London 1903-5), IV 432

409-40). Cowley mixes satire of socially low characters with a rationalistic satire of fanaticism in much the manner of Butler, and, occasionally at least, he provides lines and touches of ridicule and wit that reach Butler's inspired level.

Cowley anticipates Butler so closely in his treatment of such subjects as the rebels' practice of celebrating defeats as victories (I 308-16) that one may be tempted to speculate concerning the possibility of Butler's having knowledge of *The Civil War*. Butler could well have known Book I of Cowley's poem before he began *Hudibras*, since it appears to have had some circulation in manuscript, presumably among Royalists; and he may possibly have seen the last two books while he was engaged upon the later part of *Hudibras*, since in the years 1670-3 he was in the service of the Duke of Buckingham, who was also the employer or patron of Sprat, Cowley's literary executor, and of Martin Clifford, the probable possessor of the original Cowper manuscript.[31] There is no need, however, to assume that Butler was directly influenced by Cowley. The conclusion which can most safely be drawn is that there exists a real continuity between the Royalist satire of the 1640s and the work of Butler. The two hitherto unknown books of *The Civil War* give Cowley a more important place in the development of that satire than he has previously been granted.

It has sometimes been supposed that Dryden was responsible for the republication in Tonson's *Miscellany Poems* of the version of Book I of *The Civil War* first printed in 1679.[32] Since the work did not appear in any edition of the *Miscellany Poems* until 1706, six years after his death, he is really most unlikely to have had any connection with the publication, but he may well have known this part of the poem. His own practice and the critical comments he made in his later years upon Cowley and certain other writers

31 On Butler's service of Buckingham, see Wilders' introduction to his edition of *Hudibras*, p.xx. In the summer of 1670 Butler travelled to Versailles with Buckingham and Sprat. Clifford probably remained in Buckingham's employment until his appointment, no doubt through the Duke's influence, as Master of the Charterhouse in 1671.

32 Grosart in his edition of Cowley's *Works* (I cxxxiii) and Ruth Nevo in *The Dial of Virtue* (pp.38n, 245) seem to assume that Dryden was the editor of the volume of *Miscellany Poems* in which Cowley's poem was printed. The phrase 'Publish'd by Mr. *DRYDEN*' appears on the title page of the *Third Part of Miscellany Poems* in 1716, but not on that of the edition of 1706, which seems to have been the first to include Cowley's poem. Hugh Macdonald points out that in reality Dryden probably had only a slight connection even with volumes of the *Miscellany Poems* published during his lifetime, although his name was regularly attached to them (*John Dryden, A Bibliography of Early Editions and of Drydeniana* [Oxford 1939], p.67).

suggest that *The Civil War* would have appeared faulty to his mature taste.[33] He might have criticised this poem as he criticised the *Pharsalia*, for its 'broken action, tied too severely to the laws of history,' and he might have considered that Cowley, like Lucan, 'crowded sentences together, was too full of points, and too often offered at somewhat which had more of the sting of an epigram, than of the dignity and state of an heroic poem.'[34] Yet *The Civil War* should have interested him, not only as the work of a poet whom he had idolized during his youth, but also for certain affinities with his own poetry.[35] In its heroic treatment of contemporary history Cowley's poem anticipates *Annus Mirabilis*, and as a work in closed couplets, combining the satiric with the epic, it foreshadows *Absalom and Achitophel*.[36] It exemplifies on a large scale the close relation between poetry and politics, the interplay between art, learning, and propaganda, which is at the centre of much of the work of Dryden and of a number of his contemporaries, including Andrew Marvell as well as Butler.

33 Dryden's comments on Cowley are conveniently gathered together by John Aden in his *The Critical Opinions of John Dryden: A Dictionary* (Nashville 1963), pp.37-8, 60.

34 'Preface,' *Annus Mirabilis*, and 'Of Heroic Plays, An Essay,' *Essays of John Dryden* ed. W.P. Ker (Oxford 1900), I 11, 152

35 See Ruth Nevo's discussion of the affinities between Cowley and Dryden in her *The Dial of Virtue* (pp.41, 73, 245, etc). In many respects her argument will gain additional support from the two previously unpublished books of *The Civil War*.

36 On one occasion, at least, Dryden suggested that the Civil War was a subject for epic treatment, declaring in the dedicatory epistle of *All for Love* that the honour and gallantry of the Earl of Lindsey, who died at Edgehill, was fit to adorn a heroic poem (Aden, p.94).

5

The Civil War and Cowley's Later Writings

After Cowley abandoned his intention of completing and publishing *The Civil War* he appears to have determined that his work on the poem should not be entirely wasted. In later years he quarried the poem, taking from it passages, lines, and phrases, which he incorporated in other works, especially in the *Davideis*.[1] If Sprat is right in stating that he had already written much of the *Davideis* while he was at Cambridge, influence may run from the *Davideis* to *The Civil War*, as well as from *The Civil War* to the *Davideis*, but internal evidence indicates that much of the latter poem was written or rewritten during the Commonwealth, in the years immediately preceding its publication in 1656.[2] During this period Cowley presumably salvaged material from *The Civil War* whenever he found that he could use it in the *Davideis*.

The most widely known and influential part of the *Davideis*, the description of Hell in Book I which opens 'Beneath the silent Chambers of the Earth,' makes an earlier appearance in Book II of *The Civil War* (ll.365-96).[3] In adapting the passage for the *Davideis* Cowley merely omitted two lines and made four minor verbal changes. This section of the *Davideis* was subsequently parodied by Dryden in *Mac Flecknoe*,[4] and it was

1 In his discussion of *A Poem on the Late Civil War*, Loiseau (pp.81, 403) noted a few of these parallels, but Books II and III of *The Civil War* provide examples much more striking than those that were known to him.

2 See the Introduction, part 4, note 3, p.38, above.

3 When exact references to the relevant passages of the *Davideis* are not given here, they will be found in the notes on the passages of *The Civil War* which are cited.

4 *Mac Flecknoe*, ll.72-85. See also A.L. Korn, '*Mac Flecknoe* and Cowley's *Davideis*,' *Huntington Library Quarterly*, XIV (1951) 99-127.

imitated by many poets. The suggestion has sometimes been made that Milton in *Paradise Lost* was influenced by Cowley's description of Hell in the *Davideis*.[5] If this is so, there is a curious irony in the fact that the great Puritan poet was drawing upon material which had in part been composed for a poem attacking his own party, a poem that may even contain an attack on himself.

No other passage from *The Civil War* so lengthy as this one is incorporated in the *Davideis*, but many individual couplets, lines, phrases, and images from the abandoned poem are re-used, including details from accounts of military actions. Cowley's description of the position of the opposing armies at the opening of the Battle of Edgehill (I 207-8) is adapted in his description of the Israelite and Philistine armies as they watch the combat between Samson and Goliath. Lines that he had used to describe incidents in the Battle of Newbury (III 341-2, 483-4, 510) are employed in the descriptions of battles in the *Davideis*. A line from his account of the death of Stane at Newbury, 'The parted head hung downe on ether side' (III 404) describes the death of one of Saul's opponents in the later poem, with the change of a single word. His description of the siege of Lichfield,

> Some with huge stones are crusht to dust beneath,
> And from their hasty *Tombes* receive their *Death* (II 109-10),

provides an earlier version of a conceit that drew Samuel Johnson's attention[6] when it appeared in the *Davideis*, applied to Cain's slaying of Abel:

> I saw him fling the *stone*, as if he meant,
> At once his *Murder* and his *Monument*.[7]

In a similar fashion, Cowley took lines and phrases from his elegies and eulogies of Royalist heroes in *The Civil War* and applied them to biblical heroes, especially to Jonathan, in the *Davideis*. His praise of Jonathan as one equally fit for both war and peace echoes his similar praise of King Charles (I 75-8), and his statement that Jonathan is 'All that kind *Mothers* wishes can containe' is taken *verbatim* from his panegyric on Jermyn (III 218). His description of Falkland, 'How good a Father, Husband, Master, Friend!' (III 599), is applied with a little variation to Jonathan. In many respects, indeed, the portrait of Falkland at the conclusion of *The Civil War* appears

5 This argument has perhaps been most fully developed in Rudolph Kirsten's *Studie über das Verhältnis von Cowley und Milton* (Meiningen 1899), pp.51-9.
6 'Cowley,' *Lives of the Poets* ed. G.B. Hill (Oxford 1905), I 51
7 Book I (*Poems*, p.247)

to be the prototype for the portrait of Jonathan in the *Davideis*: in both Cowley emphasizes the combination of magnanimity, wit, judgment, eloquence, learning, and friendship. He describes both as 'God-like,'[8] and both stand for him as the pattern of the ideal man. It seems likely that he developed his ideal partly through his knowledge of Falkland, and that the Jonathan of the *Davideis* is associated in his mind with the memory of Falkland, just as the battles of the biblical epic are associated with the battles of the Civil War.

Cowley's use of material from *The Civil War* is not confined to the *Davideis* but appears also in other work first published in his *Poems* in 1656. The ode 'To Mr. Hobs' provides a particularly remarkable instance of his transfer of a conceit from a totally different context in the earlier poem. In the ode he employs an image, derived ultimately from Claudian, to represent the combination in Hobbes of old age with wit:

> So *Contraries* on *Ætna*'s top conspire,
> Here hoary *Frosts*, and by them breaks out *Fire*.
> A secure *peace* the *faithful Neighbors* keep,
> Th'emboldned *Snow* next to the *Flame* does *sleep*.[9]

These lines had appeared in a slightly different form in *The Civil War* (II 333-6), where they expressed the paradoxical adjacency of the elements of fire and water in a battle on the river in the siege of Exeter.

Although Cowley gave the impression in his preface of 1656 that he had destroyed his manuscript of *The Civil War*, it seems evident that the poem was still in his possession, whether in his mind or in an actual copy, during the last years of his life. In Book VI of the *Sex Libri Plantarum* (1668) he gives a relatively short account of the Civil War, which derives partly from the earlier poem. In *The Civil War*, for example, Charles' purchase in 1640 of a truce with the Scots is described in the image of a golden shower and as a way of conquest unknown to our ancestors (I 103-6); in the *Libri Plantarum* it is described as a silver shower: 'argenteus imber,/Ignotum genus Armorum, pugnacibus olim/Parcisq; *Angligenûm* proavis.'[10] In the later poem Cowley continues the history of the Civil War to its end, as well as moving beyond into the Restoration. Thus Book VI of the *Libri Plantarum*

8 *The Civil War*, III 525, *Davideis* III (*Poems*, p.339)
9 *Poems*, p.190
10 *Poemata Latina* (1668), p.343. The similarities between the two passages are more extensive than I have attempted to illustrate here, and many other passages in the two poems provide parallels that are equally close.

provides in its different and more condensed form a completion of the design of a poem on the Civil War that Cowley had left unfinished more than twenty years before.[11]

11 The nature of Book VI as a poem that gives heroic treatment to seventeenth-century history is emphasized in the title given in 1683 to a translation of passages selected from it: *An Heroick Poem. Upon the Late Horrid Rebellion, His Majesties Happy Restauration: and the Magnanimity and Valour of His Royal Highness James Duke of York, in the late Dutch War.*

6

The Text

I THE COWPER MANUSCRIPTS

THE EARLIER and more important of the two Cowper manuscript copies of *The Civil War* (Panshanger MS D/EP/F.48) consists of three booklets, each of which contains one book of the poem. The booklets are made up of leaves about 6 by 7¾ inches, which are sewn together, nine leaves in the first, ten in the second, and thirteen in the third.[1] In each the first leaf and the verso of the final leaf are blank, except for a few short inscriptions,[2] and the poem is closely written on both sides of the other leaves.

In this manuscript (henceforth referred to as C1) the poem is transcribed in three apparently different hands, Book I in the first hand, Book II and lines 1-44 of Book III in the second, and the remainder of Book III in the third. All three hands are predominantly Italian. The third hand is larger, more carefully formed, and more modern in its characteristics than the second, but the second and third have more in common with each other than either has with the first. Book I contains a number of minor alterations and additions in a hand or hands different from that in which the book was originally copied.

1 Sheets (or half-sheets) of paper have sometimes been folded in two and sometimes cut in order to form these leaves. There are a number of watermarks, each booklet having different ones from the other two, but parts of them all have been hidden by sewing or removed by cutting. I have not succeeded in dating any of them.

2 The following inscriptions are written in an unidentified hand on the verso of the final leaves of the three booklets: 'Civil Warr'; '2d part of the Civil Warr.'; Civil War 3d Book'.

Identification of the revising hand or hands is difficult because most of the revisions involve no more than a single word, but the most substantial addition, the marginal insertion of a couplet (ll.511-12), is evidently in the third hand, and some of the other alterations are probably in that hand also, although there are others which may be in the second hand. There are some alterations also in Books II and III, but they are less numerous than those in Book I, and they seem to be in the hands of the persons who transcribed the parts of the poem in which they appear.

The question naturally arises whether any of these hands is Cowley's own. A comparison with the surviving examples of the poet's holograph writing makes it immediately clear that the first hand is not. The second hand, however, has some similarity with the poet's, and the third hand has a very close similarity. There are slight differences between this last hand and Cowley's as it appears elsewhere, but they may be accounted for by the fact that all the other surviving specimens (those at least that are known to the present writer) are some years later in date than *The Civil War*.[3] On the basis of the available evidence the probability that the third hand is the poet's seems strong. It is not altogether impossible, furthermore, that the second hand may actually be another version of Cowley's hand, less careful and less formal than that which he used in the later part of the poem, but this cannot perhaps be settled unless some additional specimens of the poet's hand, particularly from his earlier years, come to light.[4]

Even if it did not appear probable that part of the manuscript is in Cowley's own hand, there would be good reason to suppose that C1 provides a quite accurate copy of the poem, especially in Books II and III. There are some evident scribal errors in Book I, which presumably escaped the attention of the person or persons responsible for the later alterations in this part of the poem, but there appear to be few errors in Books II and III, and those

3 Among the specimens of Cowley's hand which show a strong similarity to the third hand of C1 (illustrated in the frontispiece) are the poet's letter of 20 April 1646 in the Bodleian, MS Clarendon 27, f.147 (the earliest example of his holograph writing I have seen), and the ode, 'The Book Humbly presenting it selfe to the Universitie Librarie at Oxford,' which he inscribed in the copy of his *Poems* (1656) that he gave to the Bodleian. Miss Margaret Crum of the Bodleian Library has been kind enough to examine the third hand of C1 together with some of the known examples of the poet's hand, and she concurs with me in considering that the third hand is probably Cowley's own. I do not, however, claim such authoritative support for my speculation that the second hand may also be Cowley's.

4 There is evidence that Cowley had some ability to alter and adapt his hand in accordance with his immediate purpose or occasion, but all the relatively early surviving specimens are of his writing on occasions which required carefulness and formality. The letter of 20 April 1646 is part of his official Royalist correspondence as secretary to Lord Jermyn.

that occur are relatively trivial. One indication that the copyists of Books II and III took pains to achieve accuracy is the fact that the marks of elision common in Cowley's writing are faithfully preserved in these later books, although the scribe of Book I may have been less scrupulous in reproducing them, for they appear less frequently in Book I than in the other two books in this manuscript.

Spellings in C1, especially in the second and third books, correspond closely with the spellings in Cowley's holograph writing, more closely indeed than one would expect in any copy not in the poet's hand. Cowley's letters show that he tended to write 'yow' for 'you' and 'thow' for 'thou', and that he favoured the spellings 'theise' for 'these', 'hast' for 'haste', and 'woeman' for 'woman', to give only a few examples;[5] these are the spellings that predominate in C1. There can be little doubt that the latinate spellings, which appear with special frequency in the second and third hands of this manuscript, are Cowley's own, even though spellings of this type were rarely reproduced in his printed works: 'Hæresies', 'tædius', 'Trophæs', 'præpared', 'repræsenting'.[6] The versions of proper names in C1 ('Brainford' for 'Brentford', 'Burlington' for 'Bridlington', 'Auburne' for 'Aldbourne') may sometimes appear eccentric to the modern reader, but they were in fact quite usual among writers of the highest literacy during the period to which the poem belongs. Frequently they are the forms Clarendon employs. There is no reason to doubt that these versions of names are the ones Cowley himself used.

This manuscript probably has the special value of preserving some records of authorial revision. For example, in III 422 'Spirit' is written (seemingly in the third hand) in the margin, evidently as a possible substitute for 'Soule', which is marked with a cross but not deleted, as if the poet had not fully made up his mind between the two alternatives. Some of the alterations in Book I (which are discussed below) appear to be authorial revisions of the text, and there are some deletions in Books II and III that seem more likely to have been made by the poet himself than by any other person.

5 See, for example, the letter of 8 January 1648-9, in the British Museum, Additional MS 19399, f.49, and the letters from the Cowper MSS printed in *RES*, n.s. XVIII (1967) 253-63.

6 Such spellings were occasionally retained by Cowley's printers, for example, '*Præcipice*' and '*Inhærence*' in the *Poems* of 1656 (*Pindarique Odes*, p.49; *Davideis*, p.47), but there is evidence that they appeared more frequently in his holograph writing than in print. In the fourth stanza of the ode 'The Book Humbly presenting it selfe to the Universitie Librarie at Oxford' Cowley writes 'Prædestination' in the holograph copy, while the printed texts have 'Predestination'. Similarly, Ben Jonson's printers frequently dropped spellings of this type that occur in Jonson's holograph writing. See C.H. Herford and P. and E. Simpson, *Ben Jonson*, VII 273.

One can only conjecture concerning the circumstances in which this copy of the poem was made. If the third hand is the poet's and the other two are not, Cowley may have employed two of his friends to transcribe the earlier parts of the poem, and then completed the copy himself, perhaps at the same time making those revisions in Book I that appear to be in the third hand. He cannot have chosen these two friends, if friends they were, for their calligraphical skill, because neither wrote in a hand as well formed and as legible as his own in the later part of the poem. Fortunately the second of the two writers seems to have had a meticulous concern for accuracy, although the first probably made his transcription with no more than ordinary care.

The commonplace book of Sarah Cowper that contains the second copy of *The Civil War* is a thick vellum-bound volume (Panshanger MS D/EP/F.36; hereafter referred to as C2). On the first leaf is the title, 'Poems Collected at Several/Times from the year 1670'. The second leaf contains a short prose description of Holland. *The Civil War* begins on the third leaf and occupies both sides of 45 leaves, which are numbered as pages 1 to 90. It is followed by many poems and a few short prose works, most of which belong to the Restoration period, although the last items transcribed extend in date to at least 1705. The first item after *The Civil War* is Thomas Flatman's song, 'Death' ('Oh the sad day'),[7] which is here incorrectly ascribed to 'Andrew Merveil', and the next are poems by Sir Charles Sedley. Later items include 'A Poem at Tunbridge', which is usually attributed to Rochester but is here assigned to Robert West.[8] Separated from this collection by a number of blank leaves, there is a second section, titled 'Collections of Several things out of History. begun about the year 1670', which commences on the last leaf of the volume and runs back toward the centre.

Most of the items in the commonplace book are copied in a sloping, quite unprofessional hand, which can be identified as Sarah Cowper's by a comparison with other specimens of her writing among the Panshanger MSS. In the upper right hand margin of the first page of *The Civil War* she wrote the ascription: 'By Abraham Cowley'. The text of Cowley's poem, however, is in a large, clear, regular Italian hand, with calligraphic features such as

7 Published in a slightly different version in Flatman's *Poems and Songs* (1674), pp.49-50.

8 This attribution is probably as erroneous as that which gives Flatman's poem to Marvell, but it has possible interest. Alexander Pope denied Rochester's authorship of the poem (usually titled 'Tunbridge Wells'), without giving any author's name. No evidence supporting his statement seems previously to have come to light. See D.M. Vieth, *Attribution in Restoration Poetry: A Study of Rochester's Poems of 1680* (New Haven and London 1963), pp.273-81.

ornate capitals that suggest the work of a professional scribe. It seems likely that *The Civil War*, copied by a scribe employed by Sarah Cowper, was the first item to be written in the commonplace book, and that Sarah subsequently copied other items that interested her, using not only the empty later part of the book but also the second leaf, which the scribe had left blank.

This manuscript of *The Civil War* is obviously a copy made from C1, and it is not a highly accurate copy. The scribe, as one might expect, frequently altered the spellings of the original, no doubt employing the forms habitual to him; more surprisingly, he introduced a large number of quite illogical and misleading marks of punctuation that do not appear in the original. He made his share of all the errors to which scribes are prone. Sometimes he omitted a word, and sometimes he copied the same word twice. He misread a substantial number of words, writing 'miur'd' for 'iniur'd' (I 60), 'rays' for 'rags' (I 217), 'great *Fire*' for 'bright *Pire*' (II 86), 'misted' for 'misled' (II 247), 'scenter' for 'Scepter' (II 466), and 'must' for 'most' (III 45). He had special difficulty with proper names, giving '*Dreins*' for '*Decius*' (I 467), '*Duine*' for '*Duina*' (II 99), '*Lay*' for '*Say*' (II 222), '*Prevation*' for '*Trevanion*' (II 249), and '*Sanon*' for '*Saxon*' (II 281).

The explanation of many of the scribe's errors is to be found in obscurities in the writing in C1. For example, in C1 the 'T' of '*Trevanion*' is easily mistaken for a 'P', and the middle part of the word is obscured by a blot. In the second and third hands of C1 the majuscule 'F' is easily misread as more than one other letter: the scribe of C2 produced the reading '*Bates*' for '*Fates*' (II 50), and '*Iuries*' for '*Furies*' (III 365). Many of the apostrophes that appear in C1 as marks of elision are placed close to the line of verse above the word to which they belong. The scribe of C2 frequently mistook these apostrophes for commas in the line above, and this provides the explanation of much of his highly erratic punctuation. In one instance he attached the brackets of a deleted phrase to the correction written above it in C1, producing the reading: '(With the shrill) Trumpetts brighter accent runs' (III 344).

It seems quite evident that C2 possesses no authority independent of C1, that the variants it contains are all scribal, and that they are errors, with the exception of a very few possibly acceptable conjectural emendations of deficiencies in C1. The scribe probably made his copy in some haste. He did not check his transcript with much care but allowed his own corruptions to stand even when they produced nonsensical readings, although he could easily have corrected them by re-examining the original. Since no text of the poem based on this copy could be very satisfactory, it is particularly fortunate that the original from which the copy was made has been preserved.

II THE TEXTS OF BOOK I

Only the two Cowper MSS provide the final lines of Book I, but most of the book exists in two other manuscripts that have been located, British Museum, Additional MS 36913 (referred to below as A), and Bodleian, Douce MS 357 (referred to as D), as well as in the text first published in 1679 as *A Poem on the Late Civil War* (referred to as P), which was subsequently reprinted in the *Miscellany Poems*. The printed text concludes with line 566, while the Additional and Douce MSS conclude with line 568. These three texts provide numerous readings that differ from those of the Cowper MSS, many of the variants being minor but some having importance. Each of the three deserves some consideration.

A general description of MS Add. 36913 is given in the British Museum's *Catalogue of Additions to the Manuscripts*. This is a volume of papers of the Aston family of Cheshire, most of which are concerned with official business and public affairs, extending in date from nearly the beginning to nearly the end of the seventeenth century. The papers have been bound together evidently in modern times, and Cowley's poem is placed at the end (fols. 311-20). It is headed, 'Of the Civill War suppos'd/ to be written by Abr: Cowly/ and that vpon very good/ ground tho' not in his printed/ workes'. The poem is transcribed in a clear Italian hand. Loiseau has suggested that this hand may be Cowley's,[9] but it does not in fact have any close resemblance to the definitely identified speciments of the poet's holograph writing.

Descriptions of MS Douce 357 will be found in the Bodleian Library's *Summary Catalogue of Western Manuscripts* and in the *Catalogue of the Printed Books and Manuscripts Bequeathed by Francis Douce, Esq. to the Bodleian Library* (1840). The manuscript is a commonplace book containing a large collection of seventeenth-century poetry, principally on political and topical subjects. The collection may have been begun in 1642, a date which appears with the initials 'A P' on the binding of the volume. The poem on the Civil War (fols. 42-9) is preceded by other Royalist verse of the 1640s, including Cowley's *The Puritan and the Papist* (fols. 26-30), and the Prologue and Epilogue to the *Guardian* (mysteriously ascribed to 'ye Poet *Aquila*', who is identified in the margin as 'Pooly') (fols. 41-41^v). It is followed by a large body of Restoration verse, seemingly copied in a different hand, which begins with Marvell's 'The Loyal Scot,' in a version dated no earlier than 1671,[10] and includes other poems dated at least as late

9 *Abraham Cowley's Reputation in England* (Paris 1931), p.26n

10 See H.M. Margoliouth, *The Poems and Letters of Andrew Marvell* (second edition, Oxford [1952]), I 295-6.

as 1681. Cowley's poem on the Civil War has the same title or heading as appears in MS Add. 36913.

It does not seem possible to date either of these manuscripts of the poem with any precision. MS Add. 36913 includes the papers of Sir Thomas Aston (1600-45), a Royalist leader during the Civil War, but there are no definite grounds for associating the copy of Cowley's poem with him.[11] The heading which the poem has in the two manuscripts suggests that both texts may derive from a copy made between 1668, the date of the first edition of Cowley's *Works*, and 1679, the date of the first publication of *A Poem on the Late Civil War*, but this is not altogether certain. The word 'workes' (although it is capitalized in the Douce MS) may be intended not as a title but as a reference to such publications as Cowley's *Poems* of 1656.[12]

The two manuscripts are very closely related, as the common heading given to the poem in both suggests. They have the same number of lines, including a final couplet which the 1679 text lacks – one of the many proofs that they were not copied from that text. They very commonly agree with each other in accidentals where both the Cowper MSS and the 1679 text differ, for example in the spelling of proper names: both have '*Grenvile*', while C1 has '*Greenvill*', C2 has '*Greenhill*', and P has '*Greenvil*' (l.429). They agree with each other in a number of substantive readings not found in C1, C2, or in P (see, for example, the textual variants in lines 221 and 397); and they agree in introducing a number of errors and probable errors not found in C1, C2, or in P: for example, 'thirsty' for the correct 'Thrifty' (l.106), 'Arts' for 'Acts' (l.232), and 'Fears' for '*teares*' (l.430).

Variants between A and D are relatively few. Where these occur, the readings in A are usually superior to those in D. The latter introduces a numbers of errors not found in A, such as 'Servants' for '*Severnes*' (l.184). In some instances, however, D provides a more accurate text than A. If D was copied from A, then the copyist corrected some obvious errors, even though he introduced other errors of his own. There are some minor instances, however, when D agrees with C1 and C2 against A and P (ll.256, 294, 360),

11 The hand and paper (like the heading which is given to the poem) may suggest a date later than 1660 for this copy. The watermark of the paper is an elaborate version of the horn on the crowned shield, similar to (but not identical with) Heawood #2726, dated 1678.

12 It might also be argued that a date later than 1679 is not absolutely ruled out. Curtis' publication may not have been very widely known, and the poem was not included in any collected edition of Cowley during the next hundred years. As late as 1727 Tonson's title-page for the poem in *Miscellany Poems* carried the quite accurate statement: 'Not printed in any Edition of his [Cowley's] Works.'

or when D agrees with P against A, C1 and C2 (l.384), which suggest that D has some authority independent of A.

When Langly Curtis published *A Poem on the Late Civil War* in 1679 he gave no information about the manuscript upon which he based his text, apart from stating that he met with it 'accidentally.' It is evident, however, that his manuscript was closely related to A and D, although possessing some independent authority. In substantive readings his text sometimes agrees with C1 and C2 as opposed to A and D, but more often with A and D as opposed to C1 and C2. Line 550 is missing in his text as in A and D (but not in C1 or C2); and P, A, and D all have the error '*Stanning*' for '*Slaning*' (l.428), which is correctly given in C1 and C2. His text lacks the final two lines of A and D, but it is possible that these were in his manuscript and that he chose not to print them, for if he had included them his text of the poem would have ended in the middle of a sentence.

The 1679 text differs in many accidentals from A and D, as a result no doubt of an attempt made by Curtis (or his editor or compositor) to regularize and modernize spelling, and to provide the necessary punctuation, little punctuation being provided in A and D. Curtis chose to spell out in full many of the verbs in past tense which are given with elided endings in A and D; for example, he printed 'ventured' where A and D have 'venturd' and 'Ventur'd' (l.25). He replaced with initials or dashes the names of rebels vilified by Cowley, such as Hampden, Essex, and Wharton. In this he may have been motivated not only by the ordinary prudence that caused many publishers of his period to suppress proper names when they printed satire but also by some sympathy for the men whom Cowley had attacked. One of these men, Lord Wharton (d 1696), was still alive, and he was a prominent leader of the non-conformist cause to which Curtis was himself dedicated.[13]

Curtis was occasionally able to provide more accurate readings than those in A and D. He seems to have taken some pains to achieve accuracy, for collation of copies of his publication shows that some in-press corrections were made.[14] But he printed a number of errors that do not appear in A and D: for example, 'Blood' for 'Floods' (l.334), '*Capaneu*'s' for '*Capaneus*' (l.535),[15]

13 See G.F. Trevallyn Jones' study of Wharton's career, *Saw-pit Wharton* (Sidney 1967). On Curtis see the Introduction, part 1, note 12, p.6, above.

14 For example, some copies have the misprint '*Licencester's*', while others have the correct '*Circencester's*' (l.368). References in the present edition are to the British Museum copy, 1077.h.4, because it is one in which some formes of the text appear in a corrected state (although still far from free of error).

15 This trivial error has shown a remarkable persistence, being reproduced in the

and 'Readilier' (1.156), which is probably a corruption of 'rudelier', the form of A, D, C1, and C2. The introduction of these errors, whether the fault of Curtis or his manuscript, is particularly unfortunate, because for nearly three hundred years Cowley's poem has been printed only in Curtis' text or in texts deriving from his, and some of the errors and doubtful readings of his edition have remained uncorrected in all subsequent editions.

The text of the poem that Jacob Tonson printed in his *Miscellany Poems* in 1706, 1716, and 1727 clearly derives from the 1679 publication. In these three editions the work is given a new title, printed on a separate page, 'A Poem on the Civil War, Begun in the Year 1641', but Curtis' title, 'A Poem on the Late Civil War' appears at the head of the first page of the text, and his (unsigned) prefatory epistle, 'The Publisher to the Reader' is included. The 1706 edition carries further the attempt that Curtis had made to modernize spelling and to rationalize punctuation, but it restores many of the elisions found in A and D that he had eliminated, and it introduces other elided forms not found in those manuscripts. The effort to provide a text of the poem that had the metrical smoothness and regularity so much valued during this period was continued in 1727, when the number of elisions was again increased. Much of this emendation or improvement was no doubt conjectural, and much of it might have been avoided if a manuscript had been available which preserved Cowley's own system of elisions to the degree that C1 evidently does even in Book I.

Tonson's editors in 1706 and 1716 altered the text of 1679 in other ways also. The names of Essex, Marten, and Pym, which had been replaced by dashes or initials in 1679, were restored in 1706, although Wharton's name was given only as 'W – n', Brooke's as 'B – k', and Hampden's as 'H – n', while Waller's remained 'W – ', and Sandy's remained a dash. These restorations are such as an editor who had some knowledge of the historical context might make without reference to the manuscripts; but the 1716 editor must either have had access to a manuscript similar to A and D, or have possessed some skill in textual emendation, for he corrected several errors in the 1679 text which had been carried into the 1706 edition, in each case restoring the readings that appear in the manuscripts. For example, he emended 'Blood' to 'Floods' (1.334), and 'continu'd' to 'contriv'd' (1.387), although he did not succeed in correcting all the errors which had appeared in 1679 or the deficiencies that edition shared with the manuscripts A and D,

most recent edition of the poem, A.R. Waller's. A mistaken effort at correction was made in the 1716 edition of *Miscellany Poems*, when the "s' was dropped, producing the reading: '*Capaneau*, two Armies'. The proper correction was made in *The Works of the English Poets* (1779).

such as the spelling '*Stanning*' for '*Slaning*' (1.428), and the omission of line 550. The corrections he made were incorporated in few later editions of the poem. Grosart reprinted this text,[16] but other editors failed to recognize that it was in some respects more accurate than the texts of 1679 and 1706.

It is possible that one of the Tonson's editors had access to a manuscript of the kind represented by A and D, but there is nothing to suggest that any of them had access to a manuscript which presented a text of Book I resembling that of the Cowper MSS. All the printed texts of the poem may be grouped with the manuscripts A and D as representing a version of Book I distinct from that of the Cowper MSS, for, despite the differences between them, the two former manuscripts and the printed texts have far more in common with each other than with the Cowper MSS. The Cowper MSS have a large number of substantive readings that appear in none of the other texts; most of them involve a single word but some involve several words or a phrase of moderate length. Some of these variants are almost certainly the product of authorial revision. It seems unlikely that anyone but Cowley himself could be responsible for two such different readings as occur in line 302: 'and so vail their shame' (P, A, D) and 'given their rayes by Fame' (C1, C2).[17]

There can be little doubt that the version of the text found in P, A, and D is the earlier or unrevised one, and that the text found in the Cowper MSS is the later or revised one. On the whole, readings in the Cowper MSS appear to be superior to those of P, A, and D, although there are many instances in which there seems to be little to choose between one reading and another, and there are some instances in which the readings in the Cowper MSS appear inferior. Most of the inferior readings, however, are easy to account for as scribal errors, while the superior readings are frequent enough and decisive enough in their superiority to suggest that the version of the text represented by the Cowper MSS benefited from some authorial revision which did not affect P, A, or D.[18]

This revision apparently occurred in more than one stage. Most of it had evidently already taken place before Book I was first transcribed in C1, for by far the larger number of the variants appear in the text as it is copied in

16 Grosart's choice of this text may have been accidental. He gives no reason for it, and there is nothing to indicate that he undertook any collation.

17 If P, A, D is the earlier and C1, C2 the revised version, as I suspect to be the case, the purpose of this alteration may have been clarification, to make it plainer than in P, A, D that the allusion here is to the influence attributed to the stars.

18 For example, words which in P, A, and D have little function but to fill out the metre are replaced in C1 by words which carry a greater weight of meaning: 'do' by 'faire', and 'which' by 'kind' (ll.335, 363).

the first hand of that manuscript. Later revisions, however, were incorporated by the other hand or hands that appear in this book in C1. These alterations not uncommonly consist in the deletion of a word that is retained by P, A, and D, and the substitution of another in its place. For example, 're-turn'd', which is the reading of P, A, and D, is deleted and replaced by 're-nu'ed' (I.81), and '*Heath*', the reading of P, A, and D, is replaced by '*Downe*' (I.471). In line 371 'Not' has evidently been formed by overwriting 'Nor', which is retained by P, A, and D. In line 116 C1 originally read: 'We know the *Plague* driues all *Diseases* out'; this has been altered in another hand to: 'The *Plague* will driue all lesse *Diseases* out'. P, A, and D remain closer to the first than to the second version; they have: 'The Plague we know, drives all Diseases out'.

There is, of course, the possibility that these changes are merely the corrections of scribal errors, as some of the other alterations undoubtedly are, or even conjectural emendations. If they are the corrections of scribal errors, however, it is surprising that these errors are found also in P, A, and D, which in other respects differ so much from C1.[19] Furthermore, none of them is a self-evident error (with the possible exception of the one in line 471); they are readings that are acceptable in their context. Even if one leaves aside the evidence that some at least of the alterations in this book may be in the poet's own hand, it seems reasonable to suppose that the authority of the poet lies behind them. If they were not made by Cowley himself, they may well have been made by someone who had access to a manuscript of the poem that contained authorial revisions not present in the manuscript or manuscripts from which A and D were copied, in that from which C1 was originally copied, or in that from which P was printed.

The hypothesis may be suggested that the A and D manuscripts and the printed texts derive ultimately from an early manuscript draft of Book I which Cowley allowed some circulation, perhaps among Royalists in Oxford, and perhaps even while he was still engaged in writing Books II and III, just as during his Oxford period he seems to have allowed the circulation in manuscript of various drafts of *The Puritan and the Papist*.[20] The final lines of Book I of *The Civil War*, which are preserved only in the Cowper MSS, may still have been unwritten when this draft entered circulation, although the fact that A and D break off in the middle of a sentence makes it more

19 This is not to deny that hypotheses can be framed to account for the presence of such scribal errors in all four manuscripts. For example, P, A, and D may derive from a manuscript, X, copied from C1 in its unrevised state. In this case, however, the scribe of X must have been not only careless but inventive.

20 See Sparrow, *Anglia*, LVIII 78-102.

likely that the last leaf was torn away and lost as the manuscript passed around. Cowley may later have returned to Book I in order to revise it, and the book may have been first transcribed in C1 when this revision was already well advanced but not completed; hence the subsequent alterations that seem designed to incorporate later revisions. Whether or not this hypothesis is correct, it seems likely that the Cowper MSS are superior to the other copies of the poem not only because they alone provide a text of Books II and III but also because they provide a later version of Book I than is to be found elsewhere.

III THE PRESENT TEXT

The present text follows C1 closely in most respects, but an attempt has been made to emend errors and to present a more readable text than a strict facsimile would provide. The 1679 text and the Additional and Douce manuscripts have been used to correct some evident errors in Book I, and a number of changes and additions have been made throughout in punctuation. All these departures from C1 have been recorded in the textual notes. The letters, 'u', 'v', 'i', and 'j' have been normalized.[21] Words that are underlined in the manuscript are indicated by italicization.[22] When the first letter of the first word in a line is a minuscule, as is frequently the case in Book I, it has been silently altered to a capital. The initial 'ff' has been transcribed as 'F', and 'm̄' as 'mm'. Such contractions and abbreviations as the following have been silently expanded: & (and), y^{e} (the), y^{n} (than), y^{m} (them), y^{t} (that), w^{ch} (which), w^{th} (with), frō (from). The manuscript contains catchwords, but they reveal no irregularities and they have not been recorded. Line-numbering is supplied by the editor.[23]

The transcription of the manuscript has not presented many serious difficulties. The first and second hands are smaller and sometimes less legible than the third, but with careful examination obscurely formed words and letters of the kind that were misread by the scribe of C2 can almost always

21 In all the hands of C1 'j' is written as 'i' and the initial 'u' as 'v'. The medial 'v' is written as 'u' in the first hand but not in the second or third. This last practice does not occur in Cowley's holograph writing, but the others do.

22 It will be noted that this underlining occurs only in Book I and in lines 1-362 of Book II. This may conceivably be an indication that work was begun but not completed to prepare C1 for the press.

23 Although there is no line-numbering in C1, a stroke is placed beside every twentieth line in Book I and beside every hundredth line in Books II and III. The total of the number of lines is given beneath or beside the last line of each book: 576 in Book I, 616 (correctly 617) in Book II, and 648 in Book III.

be read with an accuracy that is beyond reasonable doubt. There are problems, however, in distinguishing between minuscule and majuscule letters; for some letters the copyists in C1 employ two quite different forms, but for other letters the only difference is in size, and there are so many gradations in the size of the 'p' and 'y' of the first hand, for example, that it is not always clear which form is intended. There are similar difficulties in reading the punctuation: in particular, commas and periods are not always clearly distinguished from each other.

In C1 Book I has no paragraph indentation, but the sign of a cross imposed on a circle appears beside lines that are evidently intended to begin verse paragraphs: these signs occur at places where there is indentation in P, A, and D. In the present text lines have been indented where these signs occur, and some additional verse paragraphing has been adopted in Book I from P, A, and D at places indicated in the textual notes. Other punctuation in C1 has been altered when it is plainly deficient or creates special difficulties, but complete normalization has not been attempted. In the later part of the poem, at least, the punctuation is probably Cowley's own, and it has an interest that compensates for occasional inconsistencies and slight obscurities.

One of the peculiarities of the punctuation of C1 is the presence of numerous apostrophes to indicate elision, frequently in words in which the silent vowel has been retained rather than dropped, such as 'vict'ory' or 'chac'ed.' There can be no doubt that these marks of elision originate with Cowley himself.[24] They are a common feature of his holograph verse and of such printed works as the *Davideis*. To modern eyes and ears some of them appear superfluous, but many of them are valuable as making clear the pronunciation of the words and the metrical scheme of the lines in which they appear. In the present edition these marks have been retained, but some discretion has been exercised in their exact placing. In the manuscript they are often placed directly above the vowel that is to be suppressed, but they are sometimes merely placed above the centre of a word or in the closest space left by the tails of letters from words in the line above. In the works Cowley printed in his lifetime these marks were most commonly placed in front of the vowel that was to be suppressed, and that practice has been adopted here, the editor following his own judgment in cases where the proper placing is not clear in the manuscript.

24 Cowley was evidently subjected to criticism even during his lifetime for the excessive use of elided forms, and Sprat considers it necessary to defend him against those 'who upbraid some of his Pieces with roughness, and with more contractions than they are willing to allow' ('Life,' sig. B1v).

A further problem is provided by the existence of cancellations and other alterations in c1. In four instances words or passages have been deleted without the provision of any substitute (II 138, 323, 468; III 482). In two of these cases it has been possible to read the deleted passages with reasonable certainty: the passages have been incorporated in the text but placed within square brackets. Where revision or correction has occurred in c1 the text is here printed in its revised state, but alterations that seem to have any importance or interest are recorded in the textual notes, and words that have been deleted and replaced by others are given there when they can be read.[25] Many of these deletions, however, were made too thoroughly to allow any certain reading.

In the introduction of readings from P, A, and D into Book I a conservative policy has been adopted. There could be little justification for following c1 where it is plainly in error when the means of correction exist: to do so would simply be to produce another patently faulty text of this part of the poem, which has suffered seriously from error in every edition in which it has previously appeared. On the other hand, it has seemed best to avoid the hazards of a fully eclectic text in view especially of two considerations. There is a likelihood that c1 represents a different state of the text of Book I, later than that represented by P, A, and D; and there is reason to believe that the copy of this book in c1 may have been seen and altered by Cowley himself, even though it is not transcribed in his hand. In the present edition, therefore, readings from P, A, and D have been adopted only when they serve to correct obvious or strongly probable scribal errors in c1. Cases of emendation that are not self-evident are discussed in the general notes. Substantive variants in P, A, and D that have not been adopted into the text are listed in Appendix A. These include some errors and probable errors but also readings of value. Some deserve consideration as being possibly superior to the readings of c1, although the case for their adoption has not seemed altogether conclusive. Others, which appear to belong to an earlier state of the text, are interesting for the light they may shed on Cowley's methods of revision.

25 The difficulty of identifying hands in alterations which usually involve no more than a single word is so great that I have not attempted in the notes to distinguish between the two possibly different revising or correcting hands in this book.

THE CIVIL WAR

The Civill Warre

What rage does *England* from it selfe divide
More then Seas doe from all the world beside?
From every part the roaring *Canon* play;
From every part *blood* roares as loud as they.
What *English* Ground but still some moysture beares
Of young mens blood, and more of Mothers teares?
What aires unthickned with some sighs of Wives!
And more of Mayds for their deare Lovers lives!
Alas, what *Triumph* can this vict'ory shew
That dyes us red in *blood* and *blushes* too!
How can we wish that *Conquest*, which bestowes
Cypresse, not *Bayes* uppon the conqu'ering browes!
  It was not so when *Henryes* dreadfull name;
Not *Sword*, nor *Cause*, whole Nations overcame.
To farthest *West* did his swift conquests run;
Nor did his glories set, but with the *Sun*.
In vaine did *Roderick* to his holds retreat;
In vaine had wretched *Ireland* calld him *Great*.
Ireland which now most basely wee begin,
To labour more to *loose*, then Hee to *win*.
  It was not soe, when in the happy *East*
Richard, our *Mars*, *Venuses* Isle possest.

9 Alas,] Alas C1
13 It was] It twas C1
21 *Indented in* A *and* D, *not in* C1

'Gainst the proud *Moon*, Hee th'*English Crosse* displaid,
Eclypst one *Horne* and th'other paler made,
When our deare Lives we ventur'd bravely there,
And dig'd our owne to gaine *Christs Sepulcher.*
That sacred *Tombe* which should we now enjoy,
We should with as much zeale fight to destroy!
The pretious signes of our dead Lord we scorne,
And see his *Crosse* worse then his *Body* torne!
Wee hate it now both for the *Greeke*, and *Jew*,
To us tis *Foolishnes* and *Scandall* too.
To what with Worship the fond *Papist* falls,
That the fond *Zealot* a curst *Idoll* calls.
So twixt their double madnes heres the odds,
One makes false *Devills*, t'other makes false *Gods.*
  It was not soe, when *Edward* prov'd his cause
By a Sword stronger then the *Salique Lawes*
Though fetcht from *Phar'amond*: when the *French* did fight
With *woemens hearts* against the *woemans right.*
The'affrighted *Ocean* his first Conquest bore,
And drove red waves to the sad *Gallick* Shore.
As if h'had angry at that *Element* bin,
Which his wide Soule bound with an *Island* in.
Where's now that Spirit with which at *Cressy* we,
And *Poyctier*, forc'd from fate a Victory.
Two Kings at once we brought sad Captives home;
A Triumph scarcely knowne to Ancient *Rome.*
Two forraine Kings, but now, alas, we strive
Our owne, our owne good Sovereigne to captive.
  It was not soe when *Agin Court* was wonne,
Under great *Henry* serv'd the *Raine* and *Sun.*
A Nobler fight the *Sun* himselfe nere knew,
Not when he stopt his Course a fight to view.
Then *Death*, old *Archer*, did more skilfull grow;
And learnd to hit more sure from th'*English Bow.*
Then *France* was her owne Stories sadly taught,
And felt how *Cæsar*, and how *Edward* fought.
  It was not soe when the vast Fleete of *Spaine*

34 *Idoll*: *marginal correction in* C1
45 we,] we C1
59 *Indented in* P, A, *and* D, *not in* C1
Spaine] *Spaine*; C1
37 *Indented in* P, A, *and* D, *not in* C1
51 *Indented in* P, A, *and* D, *not in* C1

Lay torne and scatter'd ore the injur'd *Maine.*
Through the proud world a *Virgin* Terror strooke,
The *Austrian* Crownes and *Romes* seaven *Hills* she shooke.
To her great *Neptune* homag'd all his Streames,
And all the wide strecht *Ocean* was her *Thames.*
Thus our *forefathers* fought, thus bravely bled,
Thus still they live, whilst we alive are dead.
Such Acts they did as *Rome* and *Cæsar* too
Might envy those whom they did once subdue.
We'are not their *ofspring* sure, our *Heralds* ly;
But *borne* we know not how, as now we *dy.*
Their Pretious Bloud we could not venture thus;
Some *Cadmus* sure sow'd *Serpents* Teeth for us.
We could not els by mutuall fury fall,
Whilst *Rhene* and *Sennen* for our Armies call.
Choose that, or Peace; yee have a *Prince*, ye know,
As fitt for both, as both are fitte for you:
Furious as *Lightning* when Warrs *Tempest* came,
But Calme in *Peace*, calme as a *Lambent flame.*
  Have we forgot those happy Yeares of late
That saw nought ill, but us who were *Ingrate*?
Such Yeares as if earths Youth renu'ed had bin,
And that old *Serpent Time* had cast his Skin.
As gloriously, and gently did they move,
As the bright *Sun* that measur'd them above:
Then onely'in *Bookes* the *learn'd* could mis'ery see,
And the *unlearn'd* ne're heard of Miserie.
Then happy *James* with as deepe quiet raign'd,
As in his heavenly throne by Death he gain'd
And lest this blessing with his life might cease,
He left us *Charles*, that pledge of future Peace.
Charles under whom with much adoe no lesse
Then Sixteene Yeeres we endur'd our Happinesse:
Till in a Moment from the *North* we find
A *Tempest* conjur'd up without a *Wind.*
So soone the *North* her Kindnesse did repent,
First the *Peace maker*, and next *War* she sent.

77 *Tempest*: *marginal correction in* C1 79 *Indented in* P, A, *and* D, *not in* C1
80 who: *written in* C1 *above* that *deleted*
81 renu'ed: *marginal substitute in* C1 *for* return'd *deleted*

Just *Tweed*, that now had with long rest forgot
On which side dwelt the *English*, which the *Scot*,
Saw glittering Armes shine sadly on his face,
Whilst all th'affrighted fish sunke downe apace.
Noe bloud did then from this darke Quarrell flow:
It gave blunt wounds that bled not out till now;
For *Jove* who might have us'd his thundering power
Chose to fall calmely in a golden shower.
A way we found to conquest which by none
Of all our *Thrifty Ancestors* was knowne.
So strangely prodigall of late we are,
We there buy *peace*, and here at home buy *warre*.
  How could a *warre* so sad and barbarous please
But first by slandring those blest Dayes of *peace*?
Through all the *excrements* of state they pry,
Like *Emprickes* to find out a *Malady*.
And then with desperate Boldnesse they endeavour,
Th'*Ague* to cure by bringing in a *Feaver*:
This way is sure to'expell some ills; noe doubt;
The *Plague* will drive all lesse *Diseases* out:
What strang wild Feares did every morning breed?
Till a strang *fancy* made us sicke indeed;
And *Cowardize* did *Valours* part supply,
Like those that *kill* themselves for feare to *die*.
What frantick diligence in these men appeares,
That feare all ills, and act or'e all their *feares*?
Thus into War we scar'ed our selves, and who
But *Arons* Sonnes that the first *Trumpet* blew!
Fond men! who knew not that they were to *keepe*
For *God*, and not to *sacrifice* their *Sheepe*.
The *Churches* first this murd'erous doctrine sow,
And learne to *kill* as well as *bury* now.
The Marble *Tombes* where our *forefathers* ly,
Sweated with Dread of too much Company.
And all their Sleeping Ashes shooke for feare,

105 none] none, C1
109 *Indented in* P, A, *and* D, *not in* C1
116 The *Plague* will drive all lesse: *altered in* C1 *from* We know the *Plague* drives all
118 strang] strange PD; straing A; strong C1
125 who PAD] that C1
that PA] y^t D; yet C1
130 too PD] to C1

Lest thousand *Ghosts* should come and crowd them there.
  Petitions next for every *Towne* they frame,
To be restor'd to those from whom they came.
The same stile all and the same sence does pen,
Alas, they'allow set *formes* of *Prayer* to *men.*
O Happy we! if nether *men* would heare
Their studied *formes* nor *God* their sudden *Prayer*!
They will be heard and in unjustest wise
The many-mouthed *Rout* for *Justice* cries.
They call for *blood* which now I feare do's call,
For *bloud* againe much louder then them all.
In sencelesse Clamours and confused Noyse,
We lost that rare and yet unconquered *voice.*
So when the sacred *Thracian Lyre* was drown'd
In the *Bistonian Woemens* mixed Sound,
The wondering *stones*, that came before to heare,
Forgot themselves and turn'd his *Murderers* there.
The same lowd storme blew the grave *Miter* downe,
It blew downe that, and with it shooke the *Crowne.*
Then first a *State* without a *Church* begun;
Comfort thy Selfe, deare *Church*, for *then* twas donne.
The same rude Storme to Sea great *Mary* drove,
The *Sea* could noe such dangerous *tempest* move.
The same drove *Charles* into the *North*, and then
Would rudelier farr have driven him backe agen.
To fly from *Noyse* and *tumults* is noe shame,
Nere will their *Armies* force him to the same.
They all his *Castles*, all his *Townes* invade,
Hee's a large *Prisoner* ore all *England* made.
He must not passe to *Irelands* weeping shore,
The wounds theise *Surgeons* made, must yeeld them more.
He must not conquer his lewd *Rebells* there,
Lest he should learne by that to doe it here.
The *Sea* they subject next to their Commands,
The *Sea* that Crownes our *Kings*, and all their *Lands.*
Thus poore they leave him, their base *Pride and Scorne*;

133 *Indented in* P, A, *and* D, *not in* C1
152 *Church,*] *Church* C1
donne.] donne, C1
159 *Castles,*] *Castles* C1
146 Sound,] Sound. C1
165 next: *written in* C1 *above* make *deleted*

As poore, as these, now mighty men, were borne.
When straight whole *Armies* meete in *Charles* his right,
How noe man knowes; but here they are, and fight:
A Man would sweare that saw his alter'd state,
Kings were call'd *Gods* because they could *create.*
Vaine men! tis heaven this swift assistance bringes;
The same is *Lord* of *Hosts*, thats *King* of *Kings.*
Had men forsooke him, *Angells* from above
(The *Assyrian Host* did lesse their Justice move)
Would all have muster'd in his righteous ayd,
And *thunder* 'gainst your *Canon* would have playd.
It needes not soe; for man desires to right
Abusd *Mankind*; and, Wretches, yee must Fight.
Worc'ester first saw't, and trembled at the View,
Too well the ills of *civill warr* she knew.
Twise did the flames of old her towers invade,
Twise cal'd she in vaine for her owne *Severnes* Ayd.
Here first the *Rebell windes* began to roare,
Broke loose from those just fetters which they bore.
Here mutinous waves above their shores did swell,
And the first storme of this dire *Winter* fell:
But when the two great *Bretheren* once appear'd,
And their bright heads like *Leda's ofspring* rear'd,
When those sea-calming *Sonnes* of *Jove* were spi'd,
The *Windes* all fled, the *Waves* all sunke, and dy'd.
How fought great *Rupert*! with what rage and skill?
Enough to have conquer'd had his *cause* bin *ill.*
Comely young man! and yet his dreadfull sight,
The *Rebells* blood to their faint hearts does fright.
In vaine alas it seekes soe weake defence;
For his keene *sword* brings it againe from thence.
Yet greives he at the *lawrell* thence he bore,
Alas, poore *Prince*, they'le fight with him noe more,
His *Vertue* will bee'ecclipst with too much *fame*;
Hencefoorth not *he* will conquer, but his *name.*
Here *Sands* with tainted blood the fields did staine,
By his owne *Sacriledge* and *Kents* Curses slaine.
The first *Commander* did heavens Vengeance show,
And led the Rebells *Van* to Shades below.

178 your PAD] their C1
179 right] right, C1
190 rear'd,] rear'd. C1
205 The PAD] He C1

On two faire *Hills* both Armies next are seene,
Th'affrighted *Valley* sighes and sweats betweene.
Here *Angells* did with faire expectance stay
And wisht good thinges to a *King* as mild as *they*.
There *Fiends* with hungry waiting did abide;
And curst both but spur'd on the guilty side.
Here stood *Religion*, her lookes gently sage;
Aged, but much more comely for her *age*.
There *Schisme*, old *Hag*, but seeming young appeares,
As *snakes* by casting skin renew their yeares.
Undecent rags of severall dies she wore
And in her hands torne *Liturgies* she bore.
Here *Loyalty* an humble *Crosse* displaid,
And still as *Charles* past by she bowd and prayd.
Sedition there her crimson *Banner* spreads,
Shakes all her Hands, and roares with all her Heads.
Her knotty haires were with dire *Serpents* twist,
And all her *Serpents* at each other hist.
Here stood white *Truth* and her owne *Host* do's blesse,
Clad with those *Armes* of *Proofe*, her *Nakednesse*.
There *Perjuries* like *Canon* roar'd alowd,
And *Lies* flew thicke like *Cannons* smoaky *Clowd*.
Here *Learning* and th'Arts met; as much they fear'd,
As when the *Huns* of old and *Goths* appear'd.
What should they doe? unapt themselves to fight,
They promised noble pens the Acts to write.
There *Ignorance* advanc'd, and Joyd to spy,
Soe many that durst fight they knew not why.
From those who most the slow-sould *Monkes* disdaine,
From those she hopes for th'old *Monks* Age againe.
Here *Mercy* waits with sad but gentle looke
(Never, alas, had she her *Charles* forsooke).
For *Mercy* on her *friends* to heaven she cries
Whilst *Justice* pluckes downe *Justice* from the Skies.
Oppression there, *Rapine* and *Murther* stood,
Ready as was the Field to drinke their blood.

210 *they*.] *they* c1
213 *Religion*,] *Religion* c1
215 appeares,] appeares. c1
225 her owne: *written in* c1 *above a deletion*
229 met;] met c1
235 the PAD] y^{t} c1
236 Age: *inserted in margin in* c1
238 forsooke).] forsooke) c1

A thousand wronged Spirits amongst them moand,
And thrice the *Ghost* of mighty *Strafford* groand.
Now flew their *Canon* thicke through wounded Aire,
Sent to defend and kill their *Sovereigne* there.
More then *Hee* them, the *Bullets* fear'd his head,
And at his feete lay innocently dead.
They knew not what those men that shot them ment,
And acted their *pretence*, not their *intent*.
   This was the day, this the first day that show'd,
How much to *Charles* for our long *peace* we ow'd.
By his Skill here and spirit we understood,
From *Warre* nought kept him but his *Peoples good*.
In his great lookes what cheerfull anger shone!
Sad *warre* and joyfull *Triumph* mixt in one.
In the same beames of his *Majesticke* Eye,
His owne men *life*, his Foes their *Death* espie.
Great *Rupert* this, that wing brave *Wilmot* leads,
White-feather'd Conquest flies o're both their heads.
They charge as if alone they'd beate the foe,
Whether their *Troopes* follow'd them up or no.
They follow close, and hast into the fight,
As swiftly as the *Rebells* make their flight.
Soe swift the *Rebells* fly, as if each *Feare*,
And *Jealousie* they fram'd, had met them there.
They heard *warrs Musicke* and away they flew,
The *Trumpets* fright worse then the *Organs* doe.
Their *Soules* which still did new by-wayes invent,
Out at their wounded *Backes* perversely went.
Pursue noe more, yee noble *Victors* stay,
Least too much Conquest loose so brave a day.
For still the Battle sounds behinde, and fate
Will not give all, but sets us here a rate.
Too deare a rate she sets, and we must pay,
One honest man for ten such slaves as they.
Streames of blacke tainted blood the field besmeare,
But pure wel-colour'd Drops shine here and there.
They scorne to mixe with floods of baser veines,
Just as th'ignobler Moistures *Oyle* disdaines.

251 *Indented in* P, A, *and* D, *not in* C1
273 fate] fate, C1
279 veines,] veines C1
280 disdaines.] disdaines C1

Thus fearlesse *Lindsey*, thus bold *Aubigny*
Amidst the Corps of slaughterd *Rebells* lie,
More honour'ably then *Essex* ere was found,
With Troopes of living Traytors circled round.
Rest to your valiant Soules, ye sacred paire,
And all whose deaths attended on yee there.
Yow're kindly welcom'd to heavens peacefull coast
By all the reverend *Martyrs* noble Host.
Your soaring Soules they meete in triumph all,
Led by great *Stephen* their old *Generall.*
Goe *Wharton* now, prefer thy flourishing state,
Above these murther'd *Heroes* dolefull fate.
Enjoy that life which thow durst basely save,
And thought a *Sawpit* nobler then a *Grave.*
Thus many sav'd themselves, and *Night* the rest,
Night that agrees with their blacke Actions best.
A dismall Shade did Heavens sad face oreflow,
Darke as the Night slaine *Rebells* found below.
Noe gentle *Starres* their chearfull glories rear'd,
Ashamd they were at what was donne, and fear'd:
Lest wicked men their bold excuse should frame
From some strong *Influence* given their rayes by Fame.
To *Duty* they, *Order* and *Law* incline,
They who nere err'd from one æternall Line,
As just the ruine of these men they thought,
As *Sisera's* was, 'gainst whom themselves they fought.
Still they Rebellions end remember well,
Since *Lucifer* the *Great*, that shining *Captaine* fell.
For this the *Bells* they ring, and not in vaine,
Well might they all ring out, for Thousands slaine:
For this the *Bonfires* their glad brightnes spread,
When *funerall flames* might more befitt their Dead:

282 slaughtered: *written in* c1 *above a deletion*
lie,] lie. c1
285 to your: *inserted in margin in* c1
286 there.] there c1
289 in: *written in* c1 *above a deletion*
291 state,] state. c1
293 durst: *marginal substitute in* c1 *for* didst *deleted*
295 rest,] rest c1 296 best.] best c1
302 From: *marginal correction in* c1

For this with solemne *thankes* they *vex* their *God*,
And whilst they *feele* it, mocke th'*Almighties* Rod.
They proudly now abuse his *Justice* more,
Then his long *Mercies* they abus'd before.
Yet theise the men that true *Religion* boast,
The pure, and *Holy*, *Holy*, *Holy*, *Hoast*.
What great reward for so much zeale is given?
Why, *Heaven* has thankt them for't, as they thank't *Heaven*.
Witnesse thow, *Brainford*, say thow ancient *Towne*,
How many in thy streets fell groveling downe?
Witnesse, the *Red Coates* weltring in their gore,
And dyed anew into the Name they bore.
Witnesse those men blowne high into the Aire,
All *Elements* their ruin Joy'd to share.
In the wide *Aire* quick *flames* their bodies tore,
Then drown'd in *Waves* they're tost by *Waves* to *Shore*.
Witnesse thow *Thames* who wast amaz'd to see
Men madly runne to save their lives in thee,
In vain; for Rebells lives thow wouldst not save,
And downe they sunke beneath thy conquering wave.
Good, reverend *Thames*, the best belov'd of all
Those Noble *floods* that meete at *Neptunes* Hall,
Londons proud Towers which thy faire head adorne
Move not thy *glorie* now (but *griefe* and *scorne*).
Thou griev'st to see the *white-nam'd pallace* shine,
Without the Beames of its owne *Lord* and *Thine*.
Thy *Lord*, who is to all as good and free,
As thow, Kind *Flood*, to thine owne Banks canst bee.
How do'es thy peacefull backe disdaine to beare,
The rebells busie Pride from *Westminster*?
Thow who thy Selfe, dost without Murmur pay
Æternall *Tributes* to thy *Prince*, the *Sea*!
To *Oxford* next great *Charles* triumphant came,
Oxford the *British Muses* second Fame.

317 boast,] boast. c1
318 *Holy, Holy, Holy,: scored through but not heavily deleted in* c1
320 Why,] Why c1
331 save,] save. c1
333 *Thames*,] *Thames* c1
all] all, c1
334 Hall,] Hall c1
336 *scorne*).] *scorne*) c1
346 Fame.] Fame c1

Here Learning with some state and reverence lookes,
And dwells in *Buildings* lasting as her *Bookes*.
Both now æternall, but they'had *Ashes* bin,
Had these *Religious Vandalls* gott but in.
Not *Bodleys* noble worke their rage would spare,
All *Bookes* (they know) the chiefe *Malignants* are.
In vaine they silence every Age before;
For *Pens* of times to come will wound them more;
The *Temples* decent Wealth, and modest State,
Had sufferd, that their *Av'arice*, this their *Hate*.
Begg'ary and Scorne into the *Church* they'd bring,
And make *God glorious*, as they made the *King*.
O Happy Towne to whom lov'd *Charles* his sight,
In these sad times gives *safety* and *delight*!
Thee fate with *Civill Warre* it selfe does blesse,
Scarce wouldst thou change for *peace* this *Happinesse*.
'Midst all the Joyes kind heaven allowes thee here,
Thinke on thy *Sister*, and shed then a *Teare*.
   What fights did this bad *Winter* see each day?
Her winds and Stormes came not so thick as they.
Yet nought these farr-lost Rebells could recall,
Not *Marlebroughs* fate, nor *Cirencesters* Fall.
Still, still for Peace the *gentle Conquerour* sues,
By's *Wrath* they perish, yet his *Love* refuse.
Not yet is that Plaine *Lesson* understood,
Writ by kind heaven in *Brookes* and *Hambdens* blood.
Chad and his *Church* saw where their *enemy* lay,
And with just *Red* new markt their *Holiday*.
Fond man! this blow the injur'd *Crozier* strooke;
Nought was more fitt to perish, but thy *Booke*.
Such fatall vengeance did wrong'd *Chalgrove* shew,
Where *Hambden* both *began*, and *ended* too,
His curst Rebellion; where his Soules repayd,
With *Separation* great, as that he made.

356 sufferd,] sufferd C1
362 thou change: *inserted above the line in* C1
363 kind: *marginal correction in* C1   370 By's: *altered in* C1 *from* By his
371 Not: *seemingly altered in* C1 *from* Nor
376 Nought was ADP] Was nought C1
thy PAD] his C1
378 too,] too. C1

Hambden whose *Spirit* mov'd o're the goodly frame
O'the *British world*, and out this *Chaos* came.
Hambden a man that taught *Confusion, Art*;
This *Treasons* restlesse, and yet noiseless *Heart*.
Hambden whose Braine like *Ætnas* Shop appear'd,
Where *Thunder's* forg'd, yet noe sound outwards heard.
Twas he contriv'd what ere bold *Martin* said,
And all the *Popular Noise* that *Pym* has made.
Twas he that taught the Zealous Rout to rise,
And be his *Slaves* for some faind *Liberties*.
Him for this great designe Hell thought most fitt;
Ah, wretched *Man*! curst by *too good a Wit*!
  If not all this your stubborne hearts can fright,
Thinke on the *West*, thinke on the *Cornish* might.
The *Saxon* fury to that farre-stretcht place,
Drove the torne reliques of great *Brutus* race.
Here they of old did in long safety ly,
Compast with *Seas*, and a worse *Enemy*.
Nere till this time, nere did they meet with foes,
More cruell and more Barbarous, then those.
Yee noble *Brittaines* who so oft with blood
Of *Pagan Hosts* have dyed old *Tamars Flood*.
If any drop of mighty *Uther* still,
And *Uthers* mightier *Sonne*, your veines does fill,
Show now that Spirit, till all men thinke by you,
The doubtfull tales of your great *Arthur* true.
Ye'have showne it, *Brittaines*, and have often donne,
Things that have chear'd the weary setting *Sunne*.
Againe did *Tamar* your dread Armes behold,
As just and as successfull, as of old.
Hee kist the *Cornish* Banks and vow'd to bring,
His richest waves to feed th'ensuing Spring.
But murmur'd sadly and almost denide,
All fruitfull Moisture to the *Devon* side.
Ye *Sonnes of Warre*, by whose bold Acts we see,
How great a thing *exalted man* may be.

381 frame] frame, c1
382 *world*,] *world* c1
392 Ah,] Ah c1
too] too PAD; *so* c1
395 that: *seemingly altered in* c1 *from* this
farre-stretcht] farre-strectcht c1
401 blood] blood, c1
404 *Sonne*,] *Sonne* c1
fill,] fill. c1
408 weary PA] wary D; wearied c1

The *world* remaines your debter that as yet,
Ye have not all gone forth, and conquer'd it.
I knew that Fate some wonders for you meant,
When matchlesse *Hopton* to your Coast she sent.
Hopton so *Wise* he needes not *fortunes* Ayd,
Soe *fortunate* his *wisdomes* uselesse made.
Should both those two, his tryd *Companions* faile,
His *Spirit* alone and *Courage* would prevaile.
Mirac'ulous man! how would I sing thy Praise,
Had any *Muse* crown'd *me* with halfe the *Bayes*
Conquest has given to *thee*, and next thy name,
Should *Barkley, Slaning, Digby* presse to fame.
Godolphin thee, thee *Greenvill* I'de rehearse,
But *teares* breake off my verse.
How oft has vanquisht *Stamford* backwards fled,
Swift as the parted Soules of those hee led.
How few did his huge multitudes defeate?
(For most are *Cyphers* where the *Numbers* great)
Numbers alas of men that made noe more,
Then hee himselfe ten thousand times told o're.
Who heares of *Stratton* fight but must confesse,
All that he heard or read before was lesse?
Sad *Germany* can no such Trophy boast,
For all the Blood these twenty yeares she'has lost.
Vast was their *Army* and their *Armes* were more,
Then th'Host of *Hundred-handed Gyants* bore.
Soe strong their *Campe* it did almost appeere
Secure, had neither *Armes* nor *men* bin there.
In *Hopton* breaks, in breake the *Cornish* Powers,
Few and scarce armd, yet was th'advantage ours.
What doubt could bee their outward strengths to winne,
When we bore *Campes* and *Magazeens* within?
The violent *Sword* outdid their *Muskets* ire,
It strucke the bones, and there gave dreadfull Fire.
Wee scorn'd their *Thunder*, and the reeking *Blade*
A thicker Smoake then all their *Canon* made.

419 that Fate PAD] the fates C1
421 needes: *inserted in margin in* C1
427 to: *inserted above the line in* C1
428 *Barkley, Slaning,*] *Barkley Slaning* C1
429 rehearse,] rehearse. C1
430 verse.] verse C1
435 *Numbers*] Numbers PAD; *Number* C1
443 appeere] appeere, C1
448 within?] within, C1

Death and loud *Tumult* fill'd the Place around,
With fruitlesse rage falne Rebells bit the Ground.
The *Armes* we gain'd, *Wealth*, *Bodies* of the Foe,
All that a full-fraught Victory could bestow.
Yet stayes not *Hopton* thus, but still proceeds,
Persues himselfe through all his glorious Deeds:
With *Hartford* and the *Prince* he Joyn'd his fate,
(The *Belgian* Trophies on their *Journey* waite.)
That *Prince* who oft had checkt Proud *Wallers* Fame,
And foold that *flying Conquerours* empty name.
Still by his losse this fertill *Monster* thriv'ed,
This *Serpent* cut in Parts rejoyn'd and lived;
It liv'd and would have stung us deeper yet,
But that bold *Greenvill* its whole fury met.
Hee sold like *Decius* his devoted breath,
And left the *Commonwealth* Heyre to his *Death*.
Haile, mighty *Ghost*, looke from on high and see,
How much our Hands and Swords remembred thee.
On *Roundway Downe*, our rage for thy great fall,
Whet all our Spirits, and made us *Greenvills* all.
One thousand Horse beat all their Numerous Power,
Blesse me! and where was then their *Conquerour*!
Coward of *Fame*! he flies in hast away,
Men, *Armes* and *Name* leaves as the victors prey.
What helpt these *Iron Regiments* which he brought?
That mooving *statues* seem'd, and so they fought.
Noe way for *death* but by *disease* appear'd,
Canon and *Mines*, a *Siege*, they scarcely feard.
Till 'gainst all hopes they prov'd in this sad fight,
Too weake to *stand* and yet too slow for *flight*.
The *Furies* howl'd aloud through trembling Aire,
Th'astonnisht *snakes* fell sadly from their Haire.
To *Luds* proud *Towne* their hasty flight they tooke,
The *Towers* and *Temples* at their Entrance shooke.
In vaine their losse they'attempted to disguise,
And musterd up new *Troopes* of fruitlesse *Lies*.

453 *Tumult*: *altered in* C1 *from* '*Tumults*'
458 Persues: *marginal substitute in* C1 *for* Presses *deleted*
471 *Downe*,] *Downe*; C1. '*Downe*' *is a marginal substitute in* C1 *for* '*Heath*' deleted.
477 which PD] wth C1; whith A
480 *Mines*, a *Siege*,] *Mines* a *Siege* C1 485 hasty: *marginal correction in* C1

God fought himselfe, nor could th'Event be lesse,
Bright *Conquest* walkt the fields in all her Dresse.
Could this white *day* a gift more gratefull bring?
O yes! it brought blest *Mary* to the *King*.
In *Keinton* field they meete, at once they view,
Their former *victory* and enjoy a *New*.
Keinton the Place that Fortune did approove,
To bee the noblest *Scene* of *War* and *Love*.
Through the glad vale ten thousand *Cupids* fled,
And chac'ed the wandring *Spirits* of *Rebells* dead.
Still the lowd sent of *powder* did they feare,
And scatterd *Easterne Smells* through all the Aire.
Looke, happy *Mount*, looke well for this is *shee*,
That toyld and travaild for thy *victory*.
Thy flourishing head to her with rev'erence bow,
To her thow ow'st that Fame that crownes thee now.
From farr stretcht Shores they felt her spirit and might;
Princes and *Gods* at any *distance* fight,
At her *returne* well might she a Conquest have,
Whose very *absence* so much Conquest gave.
This in the *West*; nor did the *North* bestow
Lesse cause their usuall *gratitude* to show.
With much of state brave *Cav'endish* issu'ed forth,
As swift and feirce as *Tempests* from the *North*,
Ca'ndish whom every *grace* and every *Muse*,
Kist at his birth, and for their owne did choose.
Soe good a *Wit* they meant not should excell
In *Armes*; but now they see't, and like it well.
So large is that rich *Empire* of his heart,
Well may they rest contented with a part.
How soone forc'd Hee the *Northerne Clouds* to flight?
And strooke *Confusion* into *Forme* and *Light*.
Scarce did the *Power divine* in fewer Dayes,
A peacefull *World* out of wilde *Chaos* raise.
Bradford and *Leeds* propt up their sickly Fame,
They brag'd of *Hosts* and *Fairfax* was a *Name*;

496 *Love*.] *Love* c1
498 chac'ed: *marginal correction in* c1
511–12 *These two lines are inserted vertically in the margin in* c1.
511 state PAD] fate c1
512 *North*,] *North* c1
515 excell] excell. c1

Leeds, Bradford, Fairfax's powers are all his owne,
As quickly, as they *Vote* men overthrowne.
Böötes from his *Waine* look't downe below,
And saw our *Victories* move not halfe so slow.
I see the gallant *Earle* break through his foes,
In *dust* and *sweat* how gloriously he showes!
I see him lead the *Pikes*! what will he doe?
Defend him *God*! Ah whether will he goe?
Up to the *Canon* Mouth he leads; in vaine,
They speake lowd *Death*, and threaten till they're t'ane.
Soe *Capaneus* two *Armies* fil'd with wonder,
When he Charg'd *Jove* and grappled with his *thunder*.
Both *Hosts* with *Silence* and pale Terrour shooke,
As if *they* all, not *He*, were *Thunder-strooke*.
The *Cowrage* here and boldnesse was noe lesse,
Onely the *Cause* was better and *successe*.
Heaven will let nought be by their *Canon* donne
Since at *Edg-hill* they sinn'd and *Burlington*.
  Goe now, your silly Calumnies repeate,
And make all *Papists* whom yee cannot beat.
Let the World know some way with whom you're vext,
And vote them *Turkes* when they ov'erthrow yee next.
Why will yee die, fond men! why would ye buy
At this deare Rate your *Countries slavery*?
Is't *liberty*? what are those threats we heare
From the base rout? can *liberty* be there?
Why doe yee thus th'old and new *Prisons* fill?
When thats the onely why, because you will!
Fain would you make God to thus *Tyrannous* be,
And damne poore men by such a *stiffe decree*.
Is't *Property*? why doe such numbers then
From *God* begg *vengeance*, and *reliefe* from men?

525 *Bradford, Fairfax's powers* are all his owne,] Bradford, *Fairfax powers* are all his owne. C1; *Bradford, Fairfax* Powers are strait their own, P; Bradford Fairfax's powers are streight theire owne A; Bradford, Fairfax's powers are Stright theire owne D

534 they're] thei're C1
538 *He*,] *He* C1
543 now,] now C1
549 Is't] Ist C1
550 there?] there. C1
552 why,] why C1
553 thus: *written in* C1 *above a deleted word*
555 then] then. C1
556 men?] men. C1

Why are th'*Estates* and *goods* seisd on of all
Whom *Covetu'ous* or *Malitious* men Miscall?
Whats more our owne then our owne lives, but, oh,
Could *Yeomans*, or could *Bourchier* find it soe?
The *Barbarous Coward*, alwayes us'd to fly,
Did know noe other way to *see* men dy.
Or is't *Religion*? what then meane your *Lies*,
Your *Sacriledge* and pulpit *Blasphemies*?
Why are all *Sects* let loose, that ere had birth
Since *Luthers Noyse* wak'd the *Lethargicke Earth*?
Tis *Madnesse* onely; which thow *Powers* above,
Father of *Peace*, mild *Lamb*, and gaullesse *Dove*,
Gently allay, restore to us our sight,
And then, oh, say once more, *Let there bee Light.*
Speake to the restlesse *Sword*, and bid it stay,
Stop *Plague* and *Famine* whilst they're yet o'th'way.
But if that still their stubborne *Hearts* they fence,
With new *Earth-workes* and shut thee out from thence,
Goe on, great *God*, and fight as thou has fought.
Teach them, or let the *world* by them be taught.

560 *Bourchier* c2. *Seventh and eighth letters lacking in* c1 *because of disintegration of paper.*
563 *Lies,*] *Lies* c1
564 *Blasphemies*?] *Blasphemies.* c1
567 above,] above. c1
568 gaullesse: *marginal correction in* c1 *Dove,*] *Dove.* c1
572 o'th'way] o'th way c1
574 thence,] thence. c1
575 on, great *God*,] on great *God* c1

The second Booke.

Thus like a *Deluge War* came roaring forth,
The bending *West* orewhelm'd, and riseing *North.*
A *Deluge* there; and high red *Tides* the while
Oreflowd all parts of *Albions* bleeding *Ile.*
For dire *Alecto*, ris'en from *Stygian* strand,
Had scatterd *Strife* and *Armes* through all the Land.
In a black hollow Clowd, by ill Windes driven,
Shee sat; oreshadow'ed *Earth* and frighted *Heaven.*
Thus like *Triptol'emus* through wide aire shee rode;
And all the fertill glebe with discords sow'ed.
The fatall seede still dropt shee as shee went,
And her owne clowds with a shrill *Trumpet* rent.
Great *Brittaines* aged *Genius* heard the sound,
Shooke his gray head, and sunck into the ground.
The'astonisht *Plowmen* the sad noyse did heare,
Look'ed up in vaine, and left their worke for feare.
Pale *woemen* heard it from afarr, and prest
The crying *Babes* close to their panting brest.
The nightborne *Virgin* stopt on *Hopton* heath;
Thrice filld the balefull *Trumpe* with deadly breath;
Scarce had the fatall sound thrice strooke the aire,
When strait her owne deare *Gell* and *Brereton's* there.

7 driven,] driven c1

Men whom shee lov'ed, and twice had sav'ed before
From *Hastings* sword, when thowsand fates it bore
On the keene point; when from his dropping blade
Warme *Soules* reek'd out, and *mists* around him made.
Just as the Sword raisd it selfe up to'his pray,
In a blind Clowd shee snatcht them both away.
Let now (said Shee) lesse villaines fill their roome,
Theise have a *Race* of *Mischeifes* still to come.
They have; and now meet here by her drad call,
To beare the *Curse* of great *Northamptons* fall.
Up marcht the loyall *Earle*, and joy'd to see
Their *Numbers*, and vaine *Odds* for *Victoree*.
Still as hee march'd gay *Conquest* neere him kept;
But still (Ah mee!) shee *Sighd*, and still shee *Wept*.
Up to their Horse our Troopes advance; and see
The power of *Custome*! at first charge they flee.
Their proud-mouthd *Canon* all forsaken lay;
Gap'ed with wide horrour, but had nought to say.
Why doe the conquering Troopes soe farr persue,
And *Edgehills* almost-*Victory* renew?
Whilst the brave *Earle* engaged with Enemies round,
Still *gives* a *Death*, and still *receives* a *Wound*?
O *God*! his Horse is shot; it falls, and throwes
The noble burden into'a Crowd of Foes.
Yet still hee fought, till hee on every side
With slaughter'ed corps had almost *fortified*
The place hee stood in; for each blow hee strooke,
Cut out a *Life* and *Name* from *Fates* large *Booke*.
At last hee groanes and reeles with many'a stroake;
The *Brambles* round all dread the tottering *Oake*.
They proffer *Life*, but hee to them disdaines
To owe one drop in all his generous veines.
Hee scornes to'accept the safety of his *Head*
From *Villaines*, who their owne had forfeited.
The fetterd Soules below of those hee slew,
Curst his free *Spirit*, whilst up through aire it flew.
Looke back, great *Spirit*, as thow doest mounting goe;
And see *thyselfe* againe i'the feild below.
Midst the lowd Throng behold thy gallant *Sonne*,
Cut out his way to *Fame* as *thow* hast donne.

Like thee, in all but *Death*, the brave *Youth's* found,
In that too, comes too neere *Thee* by a *Wound*.
O stay, bright *Planet*, stay a while, and veiw,
Our just revenge set more in *red* then *Yow*.
'Tis gonne, and Shades drop downe on all; by *Night*
The Rebells *now* are sav'ed; at *Morne*, by *Flight*.
  Yee bold *Cornavian* race, from hence begin
Your *Lesson*, from hence dread th'Effects of *Sinne*.
Ope wide your gates; great *Rupert* is come downe;
What wilt thow doe, black *Vulcans* noysy *Towne*,
Old *Bremigham*? lowd Fame to thee affords
A title from the *Make*, not *Use* of *Swords*.
Did ere *Pyracmon* and big *Brontes* prove
The new-made *Thunders* force against their *Jove*?
The high borne *Welch* disdaine a stop soe base;
Downe falls the barbarous *Cyclops* sooty race.
They knock the Earth, and every cave around
Ecchoes as lowd, as to their *Anviles* sound.
How bravely there the noble *Denby* lead?
Till, oh, wide *Death* gap'ed in his wounded Head.
An old and youthfull Souldier! O sad sight!
The crimson streame all staines his reverent *White*!
Goe burne the wicked *Towne*, and let it all
Bee one bright *Pire* for his great *Funerall*.
Into one glowing *Forge* the whole streets turne;
Soe *Ætna*, *Vulcans* other *Shop*, does burne.
Too late the foolish Rebells peace desire;
Like *Paris* Lust quencht when his *Troyes* on fire.
The *Ghosts* see flames beneath, as they drop downe,
And wondring thinke that still they veiw their *Towne*.
The neighboring *Rea* starts back with pale affright,
To see his waves peirc'ed through with dreadfull Light.
  Lichfeilds strong *Close* beheld this light afarre;
Beheld in vaine, and still præpar'ed for *Warre*.
Hence, yee profane; this is a sacred place;
Long hallow'ed by the peacefull *Miter'ed* race
Of reverent *Duina*; feare t'offend this *Sea*,
Founded at first, and built by *Victoree*.
Not here, oh, doe not here proud Ensignes spread,
To'affright the *Ghost* of *Canonized Ced*.

67 'Tis: *marginal substitute in* c1 *for a deleted word, perhaps* Hee's

The soules of thowsand *Bishops* midst yee stand,
And with heard prayers adde strength to *Ruperts* hand.
Rupert is come, and the place stormed round;
All shapes of active mischeife fill the ground.
Some whilst the walls (bold men!) they'attempt to scale,
Drop downe by'a leaden storme of deadly haile.
Some with huge stones are crusht to dust beneath,
And from their hasty *Tombes* receive their *Death.*
Some leave their parted hands on th'highest wall,
The joynts hold fast a while, then quake, and fall.
Nature and *Art* did *Cowrage* overpower,
And the proud *Wall* at last grew *Conquerour.*
The'unwearied *Prince* scornes to bee conquer'd soe;
The labouring Spade and Pick-axe sound below.
With a dire noyse the earth and wall is rent,
High into aire th'unwilling Stones are sent.
Twice all about, the ground did tremble there,
First with the violent *shock*, and next with *Feare.*
The wicked *Guards* thought t'had some *Earthquake* binne,
Their Soules confest the guilt of *Korahs* Sinne.
A *Breach* is made, and enter'd; but, oh, stay;
Sell not your valours and high Fates for pray.
Whilst yee seeke that, behold our souldiers ta'ne,
The matchlesse *Digby* hurt, and *Usher* slaine,
The rest driven back by their despairing Steele,
Achilles like, our Vict'ory slaine i'the Heele.
Yet when their boyling veines did once begin
To coole and let some *Thought* and *Providence* in;
When *Ruperts* Spirit they weighd, a Spirit no lesse
Driven on by *Ill*, then spurd by *good successe*,
They yeild the place and their *Lives forfeit* save;
Reserv'd by Fate for some *lesse hallow'ed Grave.*
Unhappy men! who can your curses tell?
Damn'd, and infam'ed for fighting *ill soe well*!
Such fate and edge did Lincolne Rebells feele
[ ] flameing Steele.
Oft did the noble *Youth* whole Armies chase;
Hector in his *Hands*, and *Paris* in his *Face.*

125 behold our souldiers t'ane: *marginal substitute in* c1 *for a deleted phrase ending* t'ane
126 slaine,] slaine. c1 132 *successe*,] *successe.* c1
138 *The earlier part of the line is deleted in* c1, *and blank in* c2.

Oft from his sword the vanquisht *Parham* fled;
The *Man* lookd big, and joyd when hee was dead.
At last old *Gainesbrow* his sad fall beheld;
And all along *Trents* mournfull waters swelld.
Too few the teares of its owne *Spring* hee thought,
Too few the waves that thirty *Rivers* brought.
The sullen Streame crept silent by his shore,
Mute as the *Fish* his populous current bore.
Whilst Hee, with thowsand foes strow'ed lifelesse by,
In all the *triumphs* of brave *Death* did ly.
Like some fair *Flowe*r, which *Morne* saw freshly gay,
In the feilds generall ruine mowne away.
The *Hyacinth*, or purple *Violet*,
Just languishing, his colourd *Light* just set.
Ill mixt it lies amidst th'ignobler *Grasse*;
The country *daughters* sigh as by'it they passe.
   Meanewhile the *Essexian Army* marcht about;
Their *Redding Blaze* by *Chalgroves storme* blowne out.
Downe towards their Campe avenging *Angells* move;
Before them *Clowds* of pale *Diseases* drove;
Faintnesse, and *Thirst*, *Madnesse*, and sickly *Heats*;
The brood *Gods wrath* joynd with *mans sinne* begets.
Armd with this strength *Death* sets at once on all
The *Quarters*; their proud boasts grow weake, and fall.
Oxford, a prisoner *King*, and wealthy *pray*,
(Bold, seely hopes) sunck into aire away.
A deadly dampe does their stiffe veines surprize,
And leaden fate sits in their fixed eyes.
The sacred flame wanes in their torturd heads,
From thence through all the bones and marrow spreads.
Their feeble hands the weapons burden hate,
And trembling knees deceive their bodies waight.
Some fell like sickly *Autumnes* yellowish Leaves,
Their *deaths* as silent *then*, as *now* their *Graves*.
Some madly talke, blaspheme, and rave about,
The *Feinds* and *Furies scourge* their *Spirits* out.
The pent-up *fire* in their wild heads does swell;
And their scorch'd *Soules* drop *roaring* into *Hell*.

151 freshly c2] fresly c1
169 wanes: *the third letter of the word is indistinct in* c1. c2 *has* wars

Great *God*, thine hosts from such a curse defend;
May none but *Rebells* lives soe sadly end!
Some whilst the watch and *sentinells* they keepe,
Nod into'a black and everlasting sleepe.
Some, as they move, their ranks and lives forsake,
And a quick march to'æternall *Quarters* make.
Their fellowes gaze around, amas'ed to'espy
Soe many fall, and yet noe *Rupert* nigh.
Th'*Essexian Ghosts* below all woundring stood,
To see whole *Troopes* come downe unstain'd with blood.
In vaine they oft remove, change oft the aire,
Up march the vengefull *Angells* in their Reare.
Infect'ions brought them in by every *wind*;
And *swarmes* of country *Curses* crowd behind.
Toward *Londons* frantick Towne the *tawny Host*
Retreats, and their sighs forth a fruitlesse boast.
Before from *Keinton* such torne pride they brought,
Then *God* and *Man*, but *God alone* now fought.
At the same time hee fought almost alone,
When *Wallers* boastfull powers were overthrown.
Both to their *Dens*, well worried both, retreat,
There snarle, and grinne, and brag which *lest* was beat.
When (loe!) two *Armies* by two *Princes* lead,
At *Bristow Walles* their conquering *Crosses* spread.
Where beawteous *Frome* weds *Avons* wealthy tide,
(*Avon* stout *Bridegroome*, *Frome* a lovely *Bride*)
Bristow, the goodly *Cyty*, stands alone;
And sees two *Countries*, but submits to none.
Herselfe alone a *Province* large and wide,
For what in *Land* shee wants, in *Sea's* supply'ed.
The farthest *Easterne* waves her *Armes* can tell,
And *Magellanick Fishes* know them well.
Noe where can *Thetis* her blew head upreare,
Noe where looke round, and not see *Bristow* there.
All *Nature* was her owne by wide commerce,
And her rich streets saw all the *Universe*.
Thus streames of Wealth flow'ed in with every *Tide*,
But in too rusht *Fulnesse* of *Bread*, and *Pride*.
Strait they the bonds of *frëest duty* broke,
And from their necks cast *Charles* his gentle yoake.

188 To c2] Too c1

Instead of him whom Heaven did highest place,
The *Sonne* of two great *Kingdomes* crowned race,
Whom did theise *sencelesse Sinners* choose to obey,
Whom but th'unworthy seed of factious *Say*?
At once their *Faith* and *Reason* they forsooke;
The *Devill* for *God*, and *Fines* for *Charles* they tooke.
In vaine their strong-built *Castle* makes them bold,
In vaine, though't boast a Pris'oner *King* of old.
In vaine, alas, they trust the workes they have made,
And thinke our *Sword* lesse powerfull then the *Spade*.
Should Fates againe give *Briareus* a birth
And all those great first *Rebells* of the *Earth*.
Should they assist your armes (as sure they'de doe)
And cast up workes of *Hills* on *Hills* for yow.
Not those would guard this cause in which yee fight,
Nor *Fines* guard them although his *Cause* were *right*.
Rupert this side, and *Maurice* that, assaile;
Nere yet did *Rupert*, nere did *Maurice* faile
In what their Swords were drawne for; at first sight
Of their keene blades did Fate our Victory write.
On this side *Maurice* with the nimble might
Of strong-limm'd *Westerne* Youth, begins the fight.
They scorne the grimmest dangers of the place;
Still *Lansdowne*, *Stratton* still's before their face.
They joy to *kill* their foes, they joy to *Dy*;
In the deepe *Trenches proud* and *gasping* ly,
Glad ev'en in *Death*, if they can *fill* them *soe*;
A streame of Enemies blood does downewards flow.
But, oh, what Devill misled those shot soe right;
And added *Fate* to their uncertaine flight,
By which they *Slaning*, and *Trevanion* found?
They could not sure have ment soe proud a wound.
Both hit, as if they'de both a mind to spare;
Both in the *Thigh*; but, oh, *Death* crept in *there*!
Both matchlesse men! and *Freinds* soe neerely growne,
That each felt least that wound which was his owne.
Meanewhile great *Rupert* by maine force possest
Their blood-dyed *workes*, and on to Vict'ory prest.

242 their: *written in* c1 *above* his (?) *deleted*

Into the streets they breake; and all around
The groanes of men, and shreikes of woemen sound.
There valiant *Lunsford*, there the *Hero* fell,
And with rich blood did their base *channels* swell.
The'accursed bullet his strong hart peirc'ed through;
Away his *Spirit*, swift as the *Bullet*, flew.
O sad! two minutes more had conquest showne;
Just now they beg their *lives*, and yeild their *Towne*.
They march unarm'ed away; the *Conqu'erours* give
A *Pardon*, but *Fate* onely a *Repreive*.
Then first did *Fines* his *Conscience* ake and smart,
Then first the vengefull *Serpents* stung his heart.
His guilty Soule shooke with each blast of winde;
The tread of *Rupert's* Horse still sounds behinde.
Still on each side his *Murthers* vex his sight,
Bourchier on th'*left*, and *Yeomans* on the *right*.
Halters and *brands* the angry *Figure* shakes;
The *palfry* starts, the *Rider* sweats and quakes.
Thus happy now was *Bristol* forc'ed to bee;
And *Charles* lay'd here fast hold uppon his *Sea*.
   From hence great *Maurice* with his westerne force,
To *Isca's* stubborne seidge turne back their course.
Isca an ancient, strong, and factious Towne;
Peace gave it *Wealth*, and often *Warrs*, *Renowne*.
Here did the race of *Saxon* triumphs stay,
Troyes fatall seed they drove from hence away.
Hether the *Danes* victorious *Poleaxe* came;
It felt great *Suenoes* rage in blood and flame.
Yet they the swelling *Norman* durst oppose,
Till *Heaven* it selfe, declar'ed which side t'had chose.
Downe at his feet, downe fell th'unbatterd Wall;
The *Cities Stones* did *Homage* first of all.
Strange was the sight; yet not soe strange a show
That they fell then, as that they fell not now.
Thrice since that time did they a Seidge sustaine;
First *Courtneys* wrath here tyr'ed it selfe in vaine.
In vaine did *Warbecks tragick Pageant* here,
With *Armes* as weake, as his false *clayme*, appeare.
The *Painted Rose* was here discern'ed too well,
All his false *Leaves* soone lost their hue and fell.

Much of white fame did this good action get;
And *Henries Sword* beares witnesse still of it.
Alas, thow wisest *King*, what hast thow donne?
They'le use it 'gainst thy best and greatest Sonne.
Againe they prove their faith, and nobly fight
'Gainst *Sword*, and *Famine*, and the *Cornish might*.
The *Cornish* then *rebell*, the *Cornish fall*;
Their strength (wee see) and boldnes is not all.
The *Causes* change now changes both their doomes;
Isca rebells, and *Cornwall* overcomes.
Warwick, the Publick *Pyrat*, brings them ayde,
And dares, like an high *Tyde*, the Land invade.
Hee seekes his prey both uppon *earth* and *Sea*;
Soe lives the doubtfull *Crocodile*, and *Hee*.
What dares not hee who can, like *Jonas*, sleepe,
In midst of his *Rebellion*, and the *Deepe*.
Who can a Mind constant in Sinne retaine,
Amidst those dreadfull *wonders* of the *Mayne*,
Who feares noe *Shipwrack*, which the *Stormes* foretell,
When mutinous *waves rise up*, and *Windes rebell*!
And yet on *Exes* streames hee learnt to feare,
There rose a new and deadlier *Tempest* there.
The *Canons* murthering blasts from ether shore,
Their canoas pride, and thin-built safety tore.
Here a tall Ship sunck by degrees below,
The decks yet seene, now masts, and nothing now.
[Here floate the Waves,] and there the *Men* about;
In rush the *Waves*, and crowd their wet *Soules* out.
Some feele hot wounds shot through the dashing flood,
They drinke in *Water*, and supply't with *Blood*.
Some, not yet slaine, are caught by *Fish* beneath,
And feele their painfull *Buriall* ere their *Death*.
Here on the *Streame* two Ships for *waters* call;
The *Streame* lookes on, and brings noe helpe at all.
A naturall hate though to the *Flame* hee bore,
Hee will not quench't; but hates the *Rebells* more.
Soe *Cold* and *Heat* on *Ætna's* top conspire,

299 Alas,] Alas. c1
307 *Warwick*,] *Warwick* c1
323 Here floate the Waves,: *deleted* in c1. c2 *reads* Here float the wares

Here *Frosts* ly bound, and by them breakes out *Fire*.
A secure peace the faithfull *neighbours* keepe;
Th'emboldned *Snow* next to the *Flame* does sleepe.
Some to avoyde the *fires* embrase a *wave*;
Some, burning planks, from *waves* there life to save.
What helpe, alas, could in this Change appeare?
Onely the death thats next them, that they feare.
Warwick beholds dead corps around him swimme,
And their last breath heard, when it cursed him.
Hee dares not longer his just fortune try;
In hast, but slow, the batterd *Vessels* fly.
How was the hopeing *Towne* that night dismayde,
When the next *Tide* cast up to them their *ayde*.
Thus happy *Charles* obtain'ed without the *Sea*
And without *Ships* a *Navall Victorie*.
This timely blow well broke th'*Excestrian pride*;
Nor could they long our feirce assaults abide.
With *Bristols* fate *Stamford* the *Towne* resignes;
Noe precedent soe fit for *Him*, as *Fines*!
Beware next, *Plymmouth*; for if future thinges,
Nere faile my prophesing *Muse*, in what shee sings,
Thy conquest soone fame from my pen shall git;
Meanwhile a sadder *Vict'ry* calls for it.
  Th'Imperiall Hoast before proud *Gloc'ester* lay;
From all parts *Conquest* did her beames display.
Feare, *Sadnesse*, *Guilt*, *Despaire* at *London* meete;
And in black Smoakes fly thick through ev'ery Street.
Their best Townes lost, noe Army left to fight!
Charles strong in *Power*, *invincible* in *Right*!
If hee march up, what shall theise wretches doe?
They're trowbled all; and Hell was troubled too.
  Beneath the silent Chambers of the Earth,
Where the Suns fruitfull beames give Metalls birth.
Where hee the growth of fatall Gold does see,
Gold, which above more Influence has then Hee.
Beneath the dens, where unflecht Tempests ly,
And infant Windes their tender voyces try.
Beneath the mighty Oceans wealthy caves;
Beneath th'æternall Fountaine of all waves,

370 infant: *written in* C1 *above* tender *deleted*

Where their vast Court the mother waters keepe,
And undisturb'd by Moones in silence sleepe.
There is a place, deepe, wondrous deepe below,
Which genuine night and horrour does oreflow.
Noe bound controules th'unwearied space; but Hell,
Endlesse as those dire paines which in it dwell.
Here noe deare glimpse of the Suns lovely face,
Strikes through the solid darknesse of the place.
Noe dawning Morne does her kind reds display;
One slight, weake beame, would here bee thought the Day.
Noe gentle Starrs with their faire drops of light
Offend the tyrannous and unquestion'ed Night.
Here Rebell Minds in envious torments ly;
Must here forever Live, forever Dy.
Here Lucifer, the mighty Captive reignes,
Proud midst his Woes, and Tyrant in his Chaines.
Once Generall of a guilded Hoast of Sp'rites,
Like Hesper, leading on the spangled nights.
But downe like Lightning, which him strooke, hee came,
And roar'd at his first plunge into the flame.
Myriads of Spirits fell wounded round him there;
With dropping Lights thick shone the singed aire.
Since then the dismall solace of their woe,
Has onely binne weake mankind to undoe.
Round the fond earth their thin-wrought nets they throw;
Worlds of mad Soules come crowding downe below.
But their deare Sinne, the Sinne themselves dare boast,
The Sinne they Love in man, and punish most,
Is proud Rebellion, their great Sonne, and Sire;
Which kindled first, now blowes the'æternall fire.
A tall and dreadfull Feind! with double Face,
One virgin like, and full of painted Grace.
Faire seem'd her hew, and modest seemd her guise;
Her Eyne cast up towards Heaven in holy wise.
From her false mouth kind words did alwayes fly,
Religion, Reformation, Liberty!
Oft sung shee Psalmes, and oft made zealous prayers;
All long and lowd, to cheat th'unknowing eares.
Her other face was grisly black of hew,
And from her stareing eyes feirce Lightning flew.

Her wicked Mouth spoke proud and bitter things,
Blasphem'ed Gods Church, and curst anoynted Kings.
Thowsand wild Lyes from her bold lipps there came;
Her Words were Bullets, and her Breath was Flame.
Thus as shee went, shee'enrag'ed the beastly rout,
And hurld unbounded ruine all about.
Like a rough Wind all rest and peace shee hates,
And joyes in th'Earth-quakes of well-grounded States.
Good God! what hoasts has this worst Feind of Death,
Sent mangled to th'unlovely Lands beneath.
There factious Korah and his murm'urers roare;
Still curse great Moses, but themselves much more.
Through gapeing gulfs thether alive they fell;
And skipt o're the first Death, with hast to Hell.
By them, an Hoast of plague-strooke Rebells lay;
Noe endlesse fires purge the raw sores away.
By them, the men, whose factious hisse and sting,
Did the just scourge of forked Serpents bring.
How did their new-come Soules start back with feare,
Meeting againe theire firy Serpents here!
Davids proud Sonne hangs up in flames by th'haire;
A thowsand Feinds stand round and wound him there.
Still with fresh darts his dropping limmes they tore,
As Joab, and the young men did before.
By him the Pol'itick wretch, soe fondly wise,
Forever hangs; and as hee dy'ed, hee dyes.
To them old Shimei from his stake does call,
And curses both, and Hell, and Heaven, and all.
By them still Sheba does his Trumpet sound;
Foole! for it calls the torturing Feinds around.
And there ly those, who cut old Jacobs Stemme,
And rent in twaine the Jess'ian Diadem.
What though the Tyr'annous King their prayers denide?
What though God spoake't, and Fate was on their side?
They who their Princes scourge disdain'd to beare,
Are by worse Tyrants lasht with Scorpions there.
There Baâshas head weares still a burning Crowne,
And Zimri, whose wild Spirit came smoaking downe.

421 Death: *written in* c1 *after* Hell *deleted*

In such feirce flames the Traytour now is fried,
That hee thinkes those scarce warme, in which hee died.
What Toung can all these dismall Starrs of Hell,
(As numberlesse, as those Heaven shines with) tell?
But of all Lands, (though all sende millions in)
More bountifull then Albion none hath bin.
There thowsand stubborne Barons fetterd ly,
And curse their old vaine noyse of Liberty.
They who their angry Soveraigne to oppose,
The hatefull yoake of France and Lewis chose.
A vaine pretence from Johns bad acts they bring;
John was a fond wild man, but yet their King.
Next them their Sonnes, who vext old Henries Crowne,
Blunted his Sword, and his high Throne pluckt downe.
Who lopt all branches from the royall Oake,
And into many parts the Scepter broke.
Montford the cheife, that falsest sonne of earth,
Till theise ungodly times gave [ ] birth.
They, who unhappy Edward cast soe low,
His wicked Queene, around whose head does grow
A Crowne of torturing Flame, that shines, and burnes;
Her Mortimer close by forever mournes.
Their scorching lusts, and all their hot desires,
Are now extinguisht quite by greater fires.
Th'unchristian Bishop too, who first did preach,
What now theise Bishop-haters boldlier teach.
Tormenting heats his subtle braine surprize,
Oh mine head akes, still, mine head akes, hee cryes.
But all the art and rage of Death, does still
Matrevers Sp'irit, and barb'arous Gourneys kill.
The paines that dying Edward felt before,
Would seeme his heav'en, if onely those they bore.
Nor did the second Richards dolefull end,
A lesser troope to theise black mansions send.
Hether his Lords, hether his Commons come;
Noe Priveledge can save them from the doome.
There Warwick lyes, who like a God awhile,
Raisd and pulld downe the Kings of Albions Ile.

456 bin.: *blotted in* c1, *which may read* bin?
468 *Penultimate word heavily deleted in* c1, *and represented by a blank in* c2

There Gloc'ester, whom noe sacred life withstood,
(Blood-thirsty man!) is drown'd in boyling blood.
The deform'd wretch grinning with paine does show,
Farr ouglier now then any Feind below.
There too an endlesse multitude is spread,
By Kets, and Cades, and Tylers thether lead.
Long darknesse now their Ign'orance does repay;
Blind, stubborne men, that hether groap'd their way!
Th'accursed powder-traitours there remayne,
(Ne're yet did Hell, nere shall such Sinners gaine)
Still by swift flames they're torne, and blowne up high,
Still those swift flames the nimbler Feinds supply.
But nere did the large Threshing-floore below,
A richer Crop then this yeares Harvest know.
At once whole feilds of ripened Traytours fell;
'Tis onely Peace breeds Scarcity in Hell.
Which that the Stygian Tyrant might prevent,
Hee calls below a dreadfull Parlament.
Deepe in a dismall den, Bel-zebubs Hall,
The Feinds all meet at their grimme Soveraignes call.
From every part of that wide Land they come;
The Soules awhile rest from their endlesse doome.
They rest awhile; but woe to man above!
For none but mighty ills theise Sessions move,
The change of a Religion or a State,
Mischeifes of greatest consequence, and weight.
Th'affaires of bleeding Brittaine calld them now;
Alas, unhappy Ile, what wilt thow doe!
They all set round, and from his direfull throne
Of burnisht Flames the Tyrant rose alone.
Much anger in his words, much in his looke;
The Feinds themselves, and all Hells Empire shooke.
My Freinds, and fellow Gods,
I need not, I suppose, the desperate state,
Of all our Brittish hopes to yow relate.
Yow'have heard and seene't, and are asham'ed, I know,
To see our bold Confœderates falne soe low,
Since coward Fines did from lost Bristoll flee,
Against those solemne Oaths to'his God and Mee.
Which shall wee'endure? shall wee sit tame and still,
Suff'ering a Cause soe'unjust to thrive soe ill?

Shall wee behold long sleepy peace againe,
The ills of Charles his dull and godly raigne?
Shall wee againe the Bishops pride behold,
Which sixteene hundred yeares hath us controul'd?
It must not bee; by my great selfe, I sweare,
Had I another Heav'en I'de venture't here;
The Cause is ours, ours the cheife gaine will bee;
Is Say, or Pym concern'd soe much as Wee?
Goe then, hast all to Luds seditious Towne;
Yee know, and love't, scarce Hell is more your owne.
There's nothing now your great designe to stay,
God, and his troubl'esome Spir'its are gonne away.
I heard the voyce, I heard it bid them goe;
'Twas a good sound! they left Jerus'alem soe!
Seeke first the men who our high bus'ines sway,
Saint-Johns, the Vanes, Kimbolton, Pym, and Say.
Without a noyse possesse their Soules, get in
As subtly, as the close Originall Sinne
Seazes the new-form'd Infant in the wombe;
And let your acts shew first that yow are come.
Urge their lowd Feares, unmaske their ougly Guilt;
Too shallow's yet the Streame of blood they've spilt;
Tell them they all on dang'erous Rocks are cast,
And some high Tide must bring them off at last.
Bid them rush on, breake through all sins their way;
Vengeance behind oretakes them if they stay.
With such bold deeds let them the world amaze,
That men shall find noe leysure to dispraise.
Tell them what mighty Names they're like to grow,
Whilst modest Catiline blushes here below;
With shame and envy their high acts hee sees,
And seemes a Cic'ero, when compar'ed with these.
Tell them how brave a Funerall they may have,
They, and three Kingdomes with them in one Grave.
When they shall say to Fate, yow owe us more,
Then all your Famins, and sick Yeares before,
When each shall publick ruine round him see,
And as hee falls, cry out, 'Twas donne by Mee.
Theyr gallant deeds (my Freinds) will ours excell;
Wee, wee our selves from Heav'en lesse nobly fell.

This at the worst; then brighter things suggest;
All the bold hopes that swell a Traytours brest,
Conquest with Slaughter (else 'twill make noe show),
The Crowne cast downe to Earth, the King more low,
The Churches Lands (alas, what's that? 'tis lesse,
Then will suffice their very Wantonnesse,
Much lesse their Av'arice), all the Kingdomes Wealth,
Theires, not, as now, by borr'owing, plunder, stealth,
But openly, confest, and by a Law;
For such shall Votes bee then, and such their awe.
Th'Estates and Lives shall bee theyr owne of all
Whom they by'unpopular Names but please to call,
Their rage and furious Av'arice shall appeare,
Boundlesse as Marius Sword, and Sylla's Speare.
If in their misty Soules there chance to shine
The smallest peacefull glimpse of Light divine,
Raise up new fogs, and thicken clowds apace,
Till all our Night of Hell confuse the place.
Next to their Preists; use here all art and care;
Bee yow to Them, what they to th'People are.
Their sordid soules with dull rewards enflame,
Large feasts, and larger Gifts and popular fame.
But sometimes shake the Halter and the chaine,
Shew them their Ilands, and new World againe.
Bid them now groane, and knock the pulpit more,
Pray longer, and preach lowder then before,
Bid them renew old blasphemies, and fling
All Texts of wicked Princes at their King,
Bid them their mouth-Granadoes cast about,
Till their owne fires ceaze all the catching rout.
Then into every street your force divide,
Swarme like the Plagues that scourgd old Pharaos pride,
Mens brests with thirst of blood, and fury fill.
Spare not, for 'twill bee thought Gods Spirit still.
Strengthen weake Rebells, and confirme the bold,
Adde fewell to the hot, flame to the cold.

572 Slaughter] Slaughter, c1
show),] show) c1

576 Av'arice),] Av'arice) c1

In different shapes to differing mindes appeare,
In shapes of hope, and zeale, and hate, and feare.
Learne this wise art from your grand en'emy Paul,
And to gaine some, doe yow turne all to all.
Pluck from their hearts each mild and sober thought,
Till warr and publick woe with joy bee bought
Ev'en by the Covetu'ous, till pale Cowards fight,
And all men crowd to ruine with delight.
Cease not, my Freinds, till yow their ensignes spy,
Advanc'ed 'gainst Charles his Army, and the Sky.
The rest, when once their banners spread yee see,
Leave to th'æternall Justice, and to Mee.

The third Booke.

Hee spoke, and what hee spoke was soone obeyd;
Hast to their London prey the Furies made.
The gapeing ground with naturall joy made roome,
For this old monstrous burden of her wombe.
In a long dismall line through earth they'arise;
Th'affrighted Night shuts close her trembling eyes.
It was the Noone of Cynthias silent course,
And sleepe all senses bound with gentle force.
The subtile Feinds themselves through London spread;
Softly, as Dreames, they steale into'every head,
There unawares the powres of Soule surprize,
Whilst each at rest, unarmd, and fearlesse lies.
The Will they poyson, and the Reason wound,
Leave the pale Conscience blinded, gagd, and bound,
All ornaments of Nature, Art, or Grace
(Like Zealots in faire Churches) they deface.
The rebell Passions they below unchaine,
And licence that wild Multitude to raigne.
Theyr busines donne, home fled the night and they;
But scarce could Natures selfe drive on the day.
Pale, as his Sisters lookes, the Sunne arose,
The sullen Morne a night-like garment chose.
What strang, wild madnesse this ill morning brought?
Soe soone in minds præpar'd Hells poyson wrought!

Up rose the mighty Traytours, in whose brests,
The guilt of all our ills soe tamely rests,
By sleepeing now they'advanc'ed our ruine more,
Then by long watchings they'had donne oft before.
Strait, like thick fumes, into their braines arise,
Thowsand rich slanders, thowsand usefull Lies.
A thowsand arts and thowsand slights they frame
T'avert the dangers of sweet Peaces name.
To Westminster they hast, and fondly there,
Talke, plot, conspire, vote, cov'enant, and declare.
New feares, new hopes, pretences new they show,
Whilst ore the wondring Towne their nets they throw.
Up rose their Preists (the viperous brood that dare
With their owne mouths their beawteous Mother tare).
Their walking noysy diligence nere will cease;
They roare, and sigh, and pray, and eate 'gainst peace.
Up rose the base Mechanicks, and the Rout,
And cry'd, Noe peace, th'astonisht streets throughout.
Here, injur'd Church, thy strong avendgment see;
The same noyse plucks downe Peace, that pluckt downe thee.
All strive who first shall goe, who most shall give,
Gloc'ester, and stiffe-neckt Massey to releive.
Their onely Sonns the frantick Woemen send,
Earnest, as if in Labour for their End.
The Wives (what's that, alas), the Maydens too,
The Maides themselves bid their owne dear ones goe.
The greedy Tradesmen scorne their Idol Gaine,
And send forth their glad Servants to bee slaine.
The bald and gray-hair'ed Gownemen quite forsooke
Their sleepy Furrs, black Shoes, and City looke,
All ore in Iron and Leather clad they come;
Poore Men that trembled earst at Finsburies Drumme!
Forth did this Rage all Trades, all Ages call;
Religions, more than ere before were All.
  Three thowsand hot-brained Calvinists there came;
Wild men, that blot their great Reformers Name.
Gods Image stampt on Monarchs they deface;
And 'bove the Throne their thundring Pulpits place.

38 tare).] tare) c1 49 alas),] alas,) c1

Goodmans, and firy Knoxes his brood, the men
Of bloody Inks, Ravillacs with their Pen.
To whose curst Zeale the Caledonians owe,
Their former Mis'eries, and Rebellions now.
Can yow, alas, the power from Tyrants take?
Why God himselfe yow the worst Tyrant make.
What's more unjust then Millions to create
For endlesse paines, and damne men for their Fate!
The Sinnes which by yow now on God are throwne,
Yow'le find at the great Triall all your owne.
If such foule Waters the fam'd Lake containe
Let's rather drinke old Tybers Flood againe.
Let our great Thames pay Homage as before,
Rather then new and worser streames adore.
If wee're resolv'd and fixt our Way to loose,
Let's some false Road before false By-wayes choose.
But rather let our Isle the Oceans Tyde,
As from the World, from the Worlds Faults divide.
Let other Lands love darknes; 'tis our Right,
Our Countries Priv'eledge to have lest of Night.
The Independents their two thowsand sent;
Who into Raggs the seamelesse Vesture rent.
In whose proud Churches may at once bee seene,
More Popes then have at Rome since Peter binne.
The dismall Hær'esy of wild Muncers crew,
Hether twelve hundred stout Mechanicks drew.
Those Christian Monsters! Wretches that begit
Confusion here, and must inherit it.
All things (they hold) to all must Common bee;
Are theise they who defend our Propertie?
Sure they'd renounce this Doctrine if they knew
That a great learnd Philos'opher thought soe too.
The number of their Wives their Lusts decree;
The Turkish Lawe's their Christian Libertie!
Sure th'Easterne Moone theise Champions would have had,
But that they found at home a Cause as bad.

72 owne.] owne c1
80 World,] World c1
79 Tyde,] Tyde c1
91 things: *inserted in margin in* c1

Noe things or places sacred they beleive;
But with their God himselfe in Common Live.
They scorne their wretched Infants to baptize;
(The unwasht Soule in black uncleannes lies)
Though they bee all borne and begotten, in
More then the Common staines of native Sinne.
The Civill Sword and temp'orall power they'orethrow;
Alas! who would not that offended soe?
Prophets and Inspirations they obey;
Governd by stormy Spirits, like the Sea.
Who take such helpes might well bring in the Scot;
Good God! is Munsters Story quite forgot?
With theise came thrice five hundred Brownists out,
Preachers, and Saints! a base and ign'orant rout!
All without Sinne or Haire! whose deepe-stampt Grace
Nor Murders, nor Adult'eries could deface,
Nor Sacr'iledge, nor Rebellion, nor all
Those Sinnes which theise the Marks of Christians call.
With theise five hundred Antinomians went;
(Noe doubt to fight for Law was their Intent)
The Tables writ by God they cast to ground;
(A nobler Cause in Moses Zeale was found)
Alas those Lawes were not by Christ orethrown;
They're cut more deepe in the great Corner Stone.
Novatus his seven-hundred joynd with theise;
(For against Truth Hell can yoake Contraries)
Ah cruell Wretch! who Heav'en to all denies;
Nether Mans Teares nor his Gods Blood does prize!
Unhappy Sect, in whom at first began
That odious, seely Name of Puritan!
With theise fower hundred beastly Monsters came,
Who falsely take great Loves and Adams Name.
What Adams guiltlesse inn'ocence made him doe,
Even that their Fall and Lusts perswade them to.
Naked they preach, repent, and Sinne, and pray;
They fight not soe; who now more arm'd then they?
Faire naked Truth from theise foule Gnosticks fled;
Blusht, and then coverd first her modest head.

110 forgot?] forgot. c1
116 theise: *inserted in margin in* c1 132 to] too c1

Pelagius Doctrine did fower hundred bring.
By'opposing Grace they learnt to'oppose their King.
Men that Resist not Grace, (soe others doe)
But take offensive Armes against it too.
Their Errours bring Mans weaknes to our sight,
And their owne Pens confute what they doe write.
The Arian Unbeleife (whose swelling course
Orewhelm'd the'old Church with swift and violent force,
Till that great Bishop who alone withstood
Hell and the World, forc'ed back th'impetuous Flood)
In a more dang'erous shape reveiv'd anew,
Five hundred men to this lewd Army drew.
The Jewish Malice was lesse proud and high;
Theise men the very Godhead Crucifie.
Others feirce Seidge batters the Churches Wall,
Theise undermine it quite, and blow up all.
If this bee true, then wretched man receives
Noe more from his Christs death then from the Theives.
Is this the thanks to his deare blood wee owe?
Ah, my great Saviour, can men use thee soe?
A thowsand Swords the Sect of Freedome brought;
Those sencelesse men here with most reason fought;
For such a Warre who would bee listed in,
But onely those who count noe action Sinne?
Some for this Cause old Hebrew dotage prest,
Two hundred which keepe still the ancient Rest;
An hundred Circumcis'ed; their Soules the Knife
Had slaine before, the Sword claym'd now their Life.
Three hundred Chiliasts, who hop'ed now to'advance
Their Paradise, their rare, divine Romance.
A temp'orall raigne of Saints they expect on Earth,
And this, this very Parl'ament gives it birth.
By this indeed wee guesse Christs Kingdome neare,
For Antichrist (wee know) must first appeare.
The rest who sent in lesser helpes to theise,
Was Marcion, Nestorius, Eutiches,
Montanus, Marcus, and Sabellius,
Donatus, frantick Manes, Audius,

162 *A deleted word, probably* old *precedes* ancient *in* c1.

Besides th'Apostolicks, and Encratites,
Angelicalls, Jovinians, Hieracites.
Paulists, Priscillians, Origenians,
Cerinthians, and Nicolaitans.
Wicleffians, Hussites, and the Zwinglian crew,
Hemerobaptists, and Sebaptists too.
Weigelians, Vorstians, and Suencfeldians;
With hundred more ill Names of Puritans.
With theise (ô strange!) five hundred joyn'd that hold
The papall Faith (soe mighty'a God is Gold).
What could the threatning Bulls of Conscience doe?
Rome hates all Sects, but Rome loves Money too.
  Theise are the loathsome Hæresies that sent
An Army forth for their deare Parlament.
And those are now whom wee a Synod call,
The Repræsenting Body of them all.
Such quarreling Sects, Spirits of soe different kind,
Nothing but loved Rebellion could have joynd.
Such was that Host, soe various to behold,
That quarterd in the mighty Arke of old.
Whilst they around the common danger see,
The Lions, Beares, Wolves, Tygers, all agree.
Each had a sev'erall forme, and sev'erall Name,
And when theise met, oh then the Deluge came.
  The matchlesse King to meet this wicked rout,
Quits Gloc'ester hopes, and drawes his Army out.
Unhappy Gloc'ester! whom fates cruell doome
Will not as yet permit to bee orecome!
So a young Lion with gay rage possest
Persuing to their dens some smaller beast,
A Fox or Wolfe; teares ope to them his way,
Nor earth nor stones defend the panting prey;
But if some Bull or rugged Beare appeare,
If their shape strike his eye or noyse his Eare,
Hee leaps from thence, and hasts t'a nobler fight;
The imprison'd Beasts peepe forth, and joy at sight.

182 Puritans.] Puritans c1 184 Gold).] Gold) c1
189 call,] call c1
190 *A deleted word, perhaps* truly, *precedes* Repræsenting *in* c1.
208 Eare,] Eare. c1

This saw the various Host and homewards drew,
Thought their worke donne when more they durst not doe;
Swiftly they fled; feare has the nimblest Feete;
But, oh, Gods wrath is Wing'd and farre more fleete.
At Auburne with sad eyes they veiw our Horse;
The valiant Jermin stops their hasty course,
Jermin in whom united does remaine
All that kind Mothers wishes can containe;
In whom Wit, Judgment, Valour, Goodnesse joyne,
And all theise through a comely Body shine,
A Soule compos'd of th'Eagle and the Dove;
Which all men must admire, and all men love.
What was an Host to him? hee charg'd it through;
With unfeard noyse the bullets round him flew.
Though causelesse was their hate in peace before,
He show'd in Warre none could deserve it more.
With him charg'd in the matchlesse Digby too;
And Vivevile, but with fates of different hew.
Digby on whom free Pallas did bestow,
All that her Armes can dare, and Wit can know;
In both has gain'd her Gorgons pow'er ore men,
By's Sword struck dead, astonisht by his Pen.
They force their passage through an Host, and strow
The way with groaning Rebells as they goe;
Onely young Vieuville whilst hee well did tread
The dangerous path to Fame theise Heroes led,
Opprest by Numbers, and ill Starres, was ta'ne,
Revil'ed, and mockt, and in coole Malice slaine.
Soe when the Canniballs on some stranger ceaze,
(The onely race more barbarous then theise)
They dance about their Pris'oner, and around,
Their shouts, and laughters, and wild Musicks sound,
Such is their wanton furies tragick play;
They bait it first, before they kill their prey.
Gallant young man! well worth a gentlier doome,
Then by base hands to fall soe farre from home!
How has thy fate transgrest thy freinds intent!
And sent thee, ah, much farther then they ment!
Thy wretched parents Hope, whilst they should Mourne;
And marke in vaine all Winds for thy returne.

This wel-struck blow disorders much their flight;
And soone the royall Host appeares in Sight.
His Troopes to Hills and Hedges Essex drawes;
Wisely they doubt their Valour and their Cause.
Ruthen, the faithfull Scot, on th'other side,
(That reverend Oake whose strength does still abide,
Though all the bowes around old Trophæs beare;
Ruthen, whom Thames, noe lesse then Rhene, shall feare)
With ready skill orders and ranckes his force,
Whilst the great Prince brings up the joyfull Horse.
Charles rides about with wise and comely care,
And like his God seemes almost ev'ery where,
Præpares all helpes that Conquest could require,
And as hee rides to all adds Soule and Fire.
The gallant Beast knew well his sacred load,
And much disdain'd the ground ore which hee troad.
Such was that Horses Colour, such the shape,
God Saturne tooke to hide his pleasant rape.
Such was his pace, soe proud a maine hee spread;
With such sharp neighs from jealous Ops hee fled.
Such was that horse which tooke his wondrous birth
When the great Trident strooke the teeming earth.
Soe foam'd, soe pranc'ed, as if hee scornd to bee
Thought of lesse Worth then the fat peacefull Tree.
Things well dispos'ed; thus in his Armyes Head
The King began; Truth was in all hee said.
Whilst yow, my Lords and Gentlemen I veiw,
The choyse of all that Peace or Warre can shew,
(Whose presence here confutes th'usurped Name
Which our bold foes to their small Faction clayme)
With words (meethinkes) 'tis vaine your zeale to stay;
More then wee can, your Worths and Wrongs will say.
Nor can I doubt th'event when to my thought
The diff'erence twixt your foes and yow is brought.
A battaile Fame nere knew with greater odds,
Since the base Sonnes of earth oppos'd the Gods.
Yow by just power are hether calld, and met
As lawfully, as Parlaments can set.

262 where,] where. c1

They are but formall Tumults, and noe more
Have warrant for their Swords then Clubs before,
Yow fight things well establisht to defend;
All ages past your pious armes commend;
They for wild dreames which from sick Fancies flow;
Which, may they'orecome, if yet themselves doe know.
Yow all one Church binds close, I'me sure the most;
More Sects then Squadrons fill their spotted Host.
Your births command yow to orecome or dy;
They their Forefathers wrong unlesse they fly.
In this dread way your spirits have oft binne showne;
To many'an Hill and many a Plaine they're knowne.
They're new unskilfull Men, and in their Mind
Deepe stick the Wares and Wives they'have left behind.
Men that in Finsb'ury with much terrour heare
The noyse of their owne Muskets once a yeare.
'Tis not their Cause, their Courage or their Might,
That keepes them now from pale distrust and Flight.
Hedges and Hills defend them yet; which, oh,
Prove now that Walls and Mountaines would not doe.
Their helpes are yours, and will your Conquest grace;
Since 'tis the Place guards them, not They the Place.
Alas they'le quit it soone, when once they know,
And feele that you're resolv'd to have it soe.
For none can use advantages aright,
But those who dare sometimes without them fight.
Thinke your Forefathers all before yow stand,
And humbly beg that noe Mechanick Hand
May match those glories their high labours bought,
Or those for which your selves have nobly fought.
Thinke on your Fortunes, Honours, Lives, and all
Which they Malignant meane, whilst yow they call.
Behold yon Hill where those proud Troopes appeare;
My Crowne and all your Liberties are there.
Both call your Swords; and if both move not, see
The thing more deare then Crowne or Libertie,
See where the Church, our sacred Mother stands,
And with much Faith implores your Christian Hands.

293 dreames: *inserted in margin in* c1
307 them: *inserted above the line in* c1 317 those c2] thoise c1

Soe much this Cause your Valour does invite;
In this one Feild for Earth and Heav'en yee fight.
  On th'other side th'Essexian Rebell strove,
His fainting Troopes with powrelesse words to move;
His Speech was dull and tædious; for him made
By some great Deacon of the Preaching Trade.
Of Tyr'anny and Pop'ery much hee told;
An hundred Declaration Lies of old;
Unhappy Man; even their ill Phrase hee tooke,
And helpt it nether with his Toung nor Looke.
But with long stops the livelesse sentence broke;
Noe Muse nor Grace was neere him when hee spoke.
  The Canon next their Message 'gan to say;
On came the dreadfull bus'ines of the Day.
Here with sharp neighs the spritefull horses sound,
And with proud Tramplings beat the putrid ground.
The Drummes grave voice, and sullen noyse of Gunnes,
With the shrill Trumpets brighter accent runnes,
(A dismall Consort!) through the trembling aire;
Whilst groanes of wounded men the Burthen beare.
Through dust and Smoake (that Dayes untimely Night)
The Powders nimble Flames, and restlesse light
Of glitt'ering Swords, amaze and fright the Eyes;
Soe through black Stormes the winged Lightning flies.
Death in all shapes, and in all habits drest
(Such was his sportfull rage) the feild possest.
Could nought on earth at once affoord the sight,
Variety soe great without Delight.
Noe place but saw some unexpected wound,
Noe part of Man but some wild bullet found,
Uncertaine Fate o're all the feild did range;
Heere strange Deaths seene, and there Eschapes as strange.
More æqually noe fight did ere dispence,
The acts of Fortune, and of Providence.
At last bright Vict'ory over Charles his head
Thrust forth some beames; the clowdes before it fled.
Wee forc'ed th'Enclosures, and the Hill wee wonne;
Ah, how much Sweat and Blood did downe it runne!

344 With the shrill: *written in* c1 *above* (A dismall Consort) *deleted*

When, loe, t'assist their Freinds the Furies rose;
'Twas strange; but yet just Heav'en did soe dispose.
Some with false Objects stopt their feare and flight,
And some lasht on the horses of the Night.
Some brought the Nation's Sinnes forth into veiw,
Black Sinnes, and black the aire around them grew.
Some from all parts drove thether clowds apace;
With them they hid the Sunns and Vict'rys Face.
Some from the Lakes and Seas moist Vapours brought;
And some with nimble art those vapours wrought
Into darke vailes of clowds; faire Vespers Light
Admir'ed to see it selfe behind the Night.
Thus God some Conquest to his Host did send;
But not enough this fatall strife to end.
Hee mixt at once his Justice and his Love,
Punisht our Sinnes, yet did our Cause approve.
For thowsands then, thowsands of Rebells fell,
And sacrific'ed their Soules to greedy Hell.
What should I here their Great ones Names reherse?
Low, wretched Names, unfit for noble Verse?
There Swart, a drunken, banisht Dutchman fell;
At home a Sailour, here a Colonel.
In his bold draughts the Villaine slew his freind;
And fled from Justice there, worse here t'offend.
Noe part of him was left to curse the place;
His very Death the Canon did deface.
A swift and easy death the Villaine gaines;
Easy the death, but, oh, it led to paines.
Neere whom another Col'onel bleeding lay;
An high-land Scotchman; who disdain'd to stay
Till his expecting Countrymen came in;
Delay was dull; hee hasted to the Sinne.
There Stane a Col'onel and a Butcher fell;
A mighty Man esteem'd in Isráell.
A Carriar and his Man hee robd and beat,
Since that bold act they calld him Stane the Great.
High were his boasts; yet at first charge hee fled;
In a thick bush hid his unworthy head.

369 Nation's: *possibly should read* Nat'ions

In vaine; the Poleaxe came, and cleft it wide;
The parted head hung downe on ether side.
Josiah was next to him in Command;
A tunefull Weaver once; who left the Land
In hate to Bishops and long Haire; hee caught
The Spirit abroad, and oft six howres hee taught.
Twise was the wretch baptiz'd, and back was sent,
To preach Damnation and the Parlament.
For all his heat, oft had hee runne; which now
The just and hasty Sword would not allow.
'T oretooke his back, and forc'ed the body stay,
Whilst his curst Soule made greater speed away.
But Towse the sturdy Dyer scornd to fly,
Though his fond men did round him slaughterd ly.
An æger, leading Brownist, who could call
His hundreds downe to the great busy Hall.
Through both his Temples the hot Bullet prest,
The Sword at the same Instant ript his brest.
Too much of Death did make his end more slow,
The Spirit awhile doubted which way to goe.
Ket too th'Embroad'erer, and th'Atturney Prinne,
(One to th'unweari'ed Scribler neere of Kinne)
Both Captaines, and both men whose furious zeale,
The Crosses and Church windowes oft did feele.
Both fell, and both at once Heavens Justice tride;
The one blaspheming, th'other weeping dide.
A worse mischance Frith the big Tanner slew;
The stolne Malignant Mare her Rider threw,
Shee fell, and crusht his Life into the ground;
The Fates noe signe of Newb'erry on him found.
But none soe much did the lewd Saints deplore,
None sigh'd, none wept soe much as Simon Blore.
A woemans Taylour once, and high in prize,
For cheateing with good words and turnd-up eyes,
Shrill was his voyce at Psalmes, and swift his Quill
At Sermon-notes more lying then his Bill.
Thus practis'd long, hee scorn'd the Yard and Sheares;
Turnd lowd Devine, and taught the naked Eares.

413 'T oretooke] T'oretooke c1
422 Spirit: *written in margin in* c1 *as a substitute for* Soule, *which is not deleted*

At last grew Prophet; did strang sights behold;
And much of Beasts, of Hornes, and Weekes hee told.
Till now his zeale to Plunder and the Cause,
Forth to curst warres this various Monster drawes.
A Major there; and none more richly bright,
In silver lace, or better horst for flight.
Ah foole! thow'dst better still have preacht and praid!
Much better practiz'd still thine ancient Trade!
Through his false mouth the vengefull bullet fled;
It sing'd the Braine and peirc'ed his seely head.
Fifty more such, men whom they Worthies call,
In that black feild did ripe for vengeance fall,
But with them let their Names forever dy;
Too vile, and base for well-writ Infamy.
Good God! what other kind of men were those,
Heaven for it selfe from out our Army chose?
Plac'ed above theise by Virtue higher farre,
Then they above the Beasts by Nature are.
Feilding and Morgan! theise were Men indeed!
Yee earthlesse Spirits, who for your Country bleede,
This small reward of your vast merits take;
And would my Verse were nobler for your sake!
Nor did the rash and heedlesse Canon there,
Thy Youth, birth, fortune, and much Virtue spare,
Excellent Spencer! in thy bloome of day,
From all the joyes of Life thow'rt snatcht away;
Noe more must thow behold the Sunns deare light,
Noe more thy brighter Wife must blesse thy sight,
Noe more must Mankind thine high Virtues see;
Thy very Tombe is robd of part of Thee.
Soe a young beawteous Palme or Cedar lies,
Struck by bruit Thunder from the parted skies;
With one lowd blow by Heav'ens artill'ery given,
The root's pluckt up and Trunck deformdly riven.
Much to bee wept by all the Nymphs around,
Blasted it lies and torne on Mother ground.
The great Carnarvan too, that Soule of Might,
(See how around the Souldiers weepe and fight)

451 call,] call c1
464 spare,] spare c1
472 skies;] skies, c1
475 around,] around c1

Mortally wounded on the plaine does ly;
His freinds stand weeping, and Death smiling by.
Whilst from their Hill hee forc'ed them to retire,
[(High were their Bodies, but his Spirit was high'er)]
Where they soe strong were plac'ed, that one would say,
The Hill might bee remoov'd as soone as They.
A namelesse Wretches unregarded blade,
Through's back a base and theevish passage made.
What mean'st thow, Death? must this great Hero dy,
This dauntlesse fighting Man, like those that fly?
'Twas poorly donne! art thow that mighty Power,
Which Kings and swelling Kingdomes doest devour?
How vile and low this treacherous act appeares,
Midst thy proud Triumphs of six thowsand yeares?
Thow should'st have met him face to face, as hee
Has often nobly met and challengd Thee;
Hadst thow donne thus, feirce though thow art and grimme,
Thow wouldst have started and fled back from him.
Hee would have forc'ed thee back uppon his foes,
And glutted thy dry thirst with blood of those;
Thow worst of Names! Coward and Foolish! who
Neglect'st thine Honour and thy Profit too!
Each Sword, each Bullet which did t'owards him fly,
Thow should'st have bid passe tame and guiltlesse by;
How would this Providence have encreast thy store?
Thow'dst had at least ten thowsand Rebells more;
Hast thow forgot how much above the rest
Hee sent thee in at thy great Keinton Feast?
Hast thow forgot with what full plenty hee
At Lansdowne and at Roundway treated Thee?
Where ere the noble Earle advanc'ed his head,
Hundreds before him fell, and thowsands fled;
Resistlesse was his Sword, like that that's given
To some destroying Spirit by angry Heaven.
Noe wound hee gave, but Death did on it waite,
Ev'en his owne Wound became the Strikers Fate.
With vengefull hast the Wretch that slew him fell,
Ere hee could beare that boastfull newes to Hell.

482 *The line is deleted in* c1, *and omitted without any indication in* c2.
487 thow,] thow c1
494 Thee;] Thee, c1

Nor was his death in those black Countries knowne,
Till they saw Rebell Soules come slowlier downe.
Meane while his Murd'erer did mild Justice beare,
And saw some Ghosts in worser torments there,
But when they knew for what high Sinne hee came,
They plung'd him deepe into th'æternall Flame.
Deeper then any, till a Soule all red
In Falklands blood, was thether Pris'oner lead.
Ah Godlike Falkland! Thee each Hill and Vale,
Thee all the Trees, and Feilds, and Floods bewayle,
Thee all the Graces wept, and Muses all;
Amoung the rest thus mine bemoan'd thy Fall.
  I saw, meethoughts, the Conquering Angell fly
From Newb'ury Feilds towards Oxford through the Sky;
Hee flew not where the aire was cleare and gay,
But cut through Clowds his melancholly way,
His eyes noe joyfull beames before them sent,
His blood-staind Wings hee clapt not as hee went.
Hee made dull speed to tell the battaile past,
Like wounded Birds that fly with broken hast.
Such I beleive, such was his mournfull Flight
Ore the pale Baltick from sad Lutzens fight.
Some mighty man is slaine there, and (ah mee!)
Something within will needes say Falkland's Hee.
An æsterne wind from Newb'ury rushing came,
It sigh'd, meethoughts, it sigh'd out Falklands Name.
Falkland, meethoughts, the Hills all Eccho'ed round,
Falkland, meethoughts, each Bird did sadly sound.
A Muse stood by mee, and just then I writ
My Kings great acts in Verses not unfit.
The trowbled Muse fell shapelesse into aire,
Instead of Inck dropt from my Pen a Teare.
O 'tis a deadly Truth! Falkland is slaine;
His noble blood all dyes th'accursed plaine.
Had Essex and his whole ungodly Host,
Had all the Puritan Name that day binne lost,
Yet would our losse too, rightly understood,
Cost us as much in Teares as them in Blood.

538 fight.] fight, c1
544 sound.] sound, c1
548 Teare.] Teare, c1
553 too,] too c1

Men of all vices, all mixt Sinns wee slew,
But they the Man in whom all Virtues grew.
They're gainers then; for in theise frantick dayes,
They may with ease Armies as wicked raise,
But something like a Mir'acle must bee showne,
If ever wee recruit his losse alone.
Wee slew a rout which nature fram'd soe ill,
That they had nothing of a Soule but Will.
They killd a Man, whose Knowledge did containe,
All that the Apple promis'd us in vaine.
The farthest lands of Art did hee invade,
And widestretcht Nature was his Triumph made,
What unjust weights into this Scale were hurl'd?
Wee gain'd a Feild, and lost in him a World.
Whether are all those thowsand Notions fled,
Whether, alas? for sure they are not dead.
I see, I see each Virtue and each Art,
Crowd through the gapeing Wound from out his Heart.
In a long row through the glad aire they runne,
Like Swarmes of guilded Atomes from the Sunne.
There flew the happy Soule, and with it they;
A track of heav'enly Light still signes the Way.
There all things naked at one glance appeare,
That cost his Soule discoursive Journeys here.
Like a full Vict'ory in an open Plane;
Where all mens glorious hopes at once they gaine.
Whilst here wee beat up Ign'orance by degrees
From Trenches, Hedges, Works, and Fastnesses,
There all the Spires of lofty Science show
As plaine as their first Principles below.
Wee therefore must confesse (if wee devest
Our publick greife of private Interest)
That 'twere great Pitty such a Wit as his,
Should bee in any place but where it is.
Others wee justly now admire and love,
With their Lives course if one bright Virtue move.
Even soe heavens lower Orbes affect the sight
With but one planets unattended Light.

571 Art: *preceded in* c1 *by a deleted word, probably* Grace
582 Fastnesses,] Fastnesses. c1
584 below.] below, c1

His Soule was high like the eight glorious Sphære,
Numberlesse were the Starres that glisterd there.
Bounteous and free, without deseigne to Give,
Humble as if hee alwayes did Receive.
More civill, then Romance ere fancied yet;
Above the noblest draughts of Sidneys Wit.
How good a Father, Husband, Master, Freind!
Love in all shapes did his kind wayes attend.
How Just in all thinges! alwayes strangely just,
Till into too much danger now hee thrust
His owne great head; himselfe hee us'd not then
With the same rules hee us'ed towards other men.
How dearely did hee love his Countrys peace!
Scarse heaven it selfe can now that love encrease.
All men, all sure, doe theise sad dayes bemoane,
But their Greifes Cause as well as Greife's their owne,
Some their lost Friends, more their lost Wealth lament:
Their Sorrowes, and Estates of one Extent.
His greife was publick, and hee waild noe lesse
His Enemies Sinne, then his good Kings distresse.
His Sighs were common as the aire to all;
Large as theise Stormes which our just sorrowes call.
Soe wide a Charity in each Teare was found,
Each like a Sea compasst our Island round.
Soe when he sees Gods arm'd and stretcht-out hand,
Soe greives the Guardian Angell of a Land.
But when hee found all sober hopes were past,
Look'ed farre, and nought but ruin saw at last,
Their madnes thus farre pleas'd him, that thereby
H'ad got a just and handsome Cause to Dy.
  Wretches, your losse will now triumphant bee,
You'le Falkland name when wee name Victorie.
Yee ment to root out Learning, Reason, Wit,
And thinke by this yee'have halfe effected it.
Yee ment all good and virtuous men should dy;
Beleive mee and this losse has strucken high;
Boast not for this; for though't bee sadly true
That Falklands dead, hee's yet not dead to yow,
His blood amidst yow in your fights will bee,
As feirce and powerfull as before was hee.

617 he: *written in margin in* C1 *as a substitute for* it, *which is not deleted*

The place around with slaughter it will fill
As if the conqu'ering Spirit were in it still.
Since such short time was given his Life by Fate,
'Twas fit his Cowrage should have longer date.
The deaths of our slaine Heroes doe not boast;
Their Lives, but not their Victories are lost.
  Yet rather, gracious God, stop here thine hand,
And let this losse excuse our perishing Land,
Let moist repentance his black Murd'erers save;
Such milde revenge his peacefull Ghost would have.
If this red warre last still, it will not leave,
Enough behind great Falklands death to greive;
Wee have offended much, but there has binne
Whole Hecatombs oft slaughterd for our Sinne.
Thinke on our sufferings, and sheath then againe;
Our Sinnes are great, but Falkland too is slaine.

NOTES

Book I

The Civill Warre. The title seems to be written in the first hand of c1 (which is scribal) but the spelling may well be Cowley's own, for 'civill' and 'warre' occur in the part of c1 that is probably in his hand, and he writes 'Civill Warre' in holograph letters (for example, that of 23 April 1660, in *RES*, n.s. XVIII [1967] 258). In his printed works, however, these words were usually given modern spellings, as in his only printed reference to this poem, in the preface of the *Poems* (1656): '*three Books of the Civil War*'; and the title would probably have been 'The Civil War' if the poem had been published in his lifetime. I have taken the liberty of modernizing the title in my own references to the poem and in the general title of this edition.

10 Cf. *Davideis* IV (*Poems*, p.391): 'doubly dyde/ In *Blood* and *Blushes*'; and Crashaw, 'A Hymn to the Name and Honor of the Admirable Sainte Teresa' (*Poems* ed. L.C. Martin), ll.25-6:

> Scarse has she Blood enough to make
> A guilty sword blush for her sake.

11-12 Cf. Cowley's 'On his Majesties Return out of Scotland' (*Poems*, p.23):

> The gain of *Civil Wars* will not allow
> *Bay* to the *Conquerors* Brow.

13-20 Henry II received the submission of Roderick (Rory O'Connor), King of Connaught and High King of Ireland, in 1175. Cowley may have been familiar with Thomas May's description of this event in his *The Reigne of King Henry the Second* (1633), Book IV. The current Irish rebellion had broken out in the middle of October 1641. Royalists charged that Parliament exploited the rebellion to increase its own power, rather than allowing the King the means of restoring order. Cf. *The Puritan and the Papist*, ll.209-12.

21-6 In 1191 Richard Cœur de Lion conquered Cyprus, which in classical legend was the home of Venus, and then proceeded to Palestine, where he won several victories, although he did not succeed in his object of capturing the Holy Sepulchre.

23-4 The crescent moon was the ensign of the Islamic powers, as the cross of St George was of the English.

29-30 Cf. Cowley's 'Prologue' to the *Guardian* (*Poems*, p.31). Among the numerous crosses destroyed by Puritans as idolatrous objects were the famous monumental crosses of Charing and Cheapside, demolished in May 1643. *Mercurius Aulicus* (5 May 1643, pp.230-1) reported that the Puritans pulled down the latter to the sound of trumpets 'as if they had obtained some remarkable victory upon the greatest enemies of the *Christian* faith.'

31-2 See 1 Corinthians 1:23: 'But we preach Christ crucified, unto the Jews a stumblingblock, and unto the Greeks foolishness.'

33-6 The restatement of a central theme of *The Puritan and the Papist*.

37-40 At the opening of the Hundred Years War, Edward III's claim to the French throne, derived from his mother, was opposed by the French supporters of Philip VI, with the argument that the so-called Salic Law, attributed to the legendary King Pharmond, excluded females and their heirs from rights of succession. See Holinshed, *Chronicles* (London 1807-8), III 65; and Shakespeare, *Henry V*, I ii 33-95.

41-6 Under Edward III the English defeated a much superior French fleet in the naval battle of Sluys (1340), initiating the series of great victories which included Crecy (1346) and Poitiers (1356). Cf. the description of Sluys in the anonymous play, *The Raigne of King Edward the Third* (1596) (in *The Shakespeare Apocrypha* ed. C. Tucker Brooke [Oxford 1908]), III i 161-2: 'Purple the Sea, whose channel fild .../ With streaming gore'; and see also Thomas May's *The Victorious Reigne of King Edward the Third* (1635), sig. E2.

47 *Two Kings*. David II of Scotland was captured at Neville's Cross in 1346 and remained an English prisoner until 1357. John II of France was captured at Poitiers and taken to England in 1356. The fact that in this last year both kings were in English hands is proudly recorded by Holinshed (v 387) and other chroniclers. Cf. Shakespeare, *Henry V*, I ii 161-2. If Cowley means that the captivity in England of the two kings began at the same time, he may have been misled by the unhistorical conflation of the two events in the anonymous *The Raigne of King Edward the Third*, Act v.

51-2 Henry v's archers were aided in their great victory at Agincourt (1415) by the heavy rains preceding the battle, which caused the French cavalry to bog down in the soft ground, and by the sun, which during the crucial period of combat shone in the faces of the French, dazzling them. See J.W. Fortescue, *A History of the British Army* (London 1899), I 60.

53 *fight*. Possibly an error for 'sight', but all texts have this reading.

54 See Joshua 10: 12-13.

58, 67 *Cæsar*. Allusions to Julius Caesar's conquest of Gaul in 58-52 BC and to his expeditions to Britain in 55 and 54 BC. In comparing the English military achievements in the Hundred Years War with the great Roman triumphs in arms Cowley follows the precedent of Thomas May in *King Edward the Third*, sig. L6^{v}, etc.

59-62 The Battle of the Armada (1588), the victory of Elizabeth, the Virgin Queen, and defeat of Philip II of Spain, head of the Habsburg house of Austria and champion of Roman Catholicism.

69 *ofspring sure, our Heralds*. I have here retained the punctuation of C1, but P has 'off-spring, sure our Heralds', which provides a somewhat different meaning.

72 *Cadmus*: in Greek legend, the founder of Thebes. On the instructions of Athena, he sowed in the ground the teeth of a dragon, from which sprang a fierce race of armed men, who killed each other. See Ovid, *Metamorphoses*, III 95-130, and cf. Lucan, *Pharsalia*, IV 549-51.

74 *Rhene and Sennen*: Rhine and Seine ('Sequan' in P, A, and D, from 'Sequana', the Roman name for the Seine). English Protestants had long urged military intervention on behalf of Charles' brother-in-law, Prince Frederick of the Rhine, King of Bohemia, who had been driven from his possessions by Roman Catholic powers in 1620; and there was similar agitation for a renewal of the attempt to aid the French Huguenots which had been made unsuccessfully in 1627-8. Cf. 'On his Majesties Return out of Scotland' (*Poems*, p.24), where Cowley expresses the hope that Charles may become a 'new *Gustavus*.'

76 *As fitt for both*. Cf. the description of Jonathan in *Davideis* IV (*Poems*, p.377). In truth, Charles' military record before the Civil War consisted of a series of humiliating failures: the Cadiz and Isle of Rhé expeditions, disastrously mismanaged by Buckingham in 1625 and 1627, and the unsuccessful attempt to suppress the Scottish rebellion in 1639-40.

78 *Lambent*. The earliest examples of the word given in the *OED* are from Cowley, and they are later (1647 and 1656) than the date of this poem. See Cowley's note on 'Lambent fire,' *Davideis*, III n.40.

79 *those happy Yeares*. Cf. Cowley's ode, 'In commendation of the time we live under the Reign of our gracious K. Charles'; and Clarendon's well-known description of the happy condition of England in the years 1629-40: 'all his majesty's dominions ... enjoyed the greatest calm and the fullest measure of felicity that any people in any age for so long time together have been blessed with; to the wonder and envy of all the parts of Christendom' (*History*, I 159).

92 *Sixteene Yeeres*. In a declaration issued on 21 October 1642, the King pro-

claimed his desire for peace, referring to the bloodlessness of 'Our former sixteene yeares reigne.' See *His Maiesties Declaration and Manifestation to all his Souldiers, by Himselfe declared in the Head of his Army* (n.p. 1642) (Bodleian, 4° L72 Art. 3), p.3.

94 *Tempest.* The image of the violent northern storm which disrupts the calm golden age occurs in other Royalist writings of the period, and it is particularly prominent in the anonymous *The True Informer* (referred to in the Introduction, p.23, above).

96 *Peace maker.* James VI of Scotland, who succeeded to the English throne as James I in 1603, prided himself on his policy of peace, adopting as his motto *Beati Pacifici.*

97-102 In the First Bishops' War the Scottish and English armies were camped within sight of each other, separated only by the Tweed, during May and June 1639. In the Second Bishops' War the Scots crossed the Tweed in pursuit of the English army in August 1640, but the second war was almost as bloodless as the first. Cf. Cowley's 'On his Majesties Return out of Scotland' (*Poems*, p.22): 'this happy *Concord* in no *Blood* is writ.'

97-100 Cf. Drayton's description of an earlier conflict between the English and the Scots, *Poly-Olbion* (*Works* ed. J.W. Hebel *et al.*, IV [Oxford 1933]), Song XVIII, l.196: 'When *Tweed* hath sunk down flat, within her Banks for feare'.

103-4 Jove, taking the form of a golden shower, visited the imprisoned Danaë. By the Treaty of Ripon, October 1640, Charles made a truce with the Scots, agreeing to pay them £850 a day until the conclusion of peace.

109-12 The Grand Remonstrance, passed by the House of Commons on 22 November 1641, charged Charles with a long series of offences, extending to the earliest years of his reign. Cf. Clarendon's criticism: 'In a word, they left not any error or misfortune in government, or any passionate exercise of power, unmentioned and unpressed; with the sharpest and most pathetical expressions to affect the people, that the general observation of the wisest, or the particular animosity of the most disobliged or ill-affected, person could suggest, to the disadvantage of the King, from the death of his father to the unhappy beginning of the present Parliament' (*History*, IV 67).

112 *Empirickes*: empirics, i.e., quack physicians

115-16 Cf. Cowley's 'Upon the happie Birth of the Duke' (1640) (*Essays*, p.484):

> That dreadful plague, which, wheresoe're't abide,
> Devours both man and each disease beside.

118 *strang.* C1 has 'strong', but this is probably a scribal error for 'strang' or 'strange', the reading of P, A, and D, which gives a more strongly pointed couplet. The spelling 'strang' occurs in Cowley's holograph writing.

124 *Arons Sonnes.* See Numbers 10:8: 'And the sons of Aaron, the priests, shall

blow with the trumpets.' Such Puritan preachers as Calybute Downing and Stephen Marshall were frequently condemned by *Mercurius Aulicus* and the Royalist pamphleteers, for inciting men to rebellion and bloodshed. Cf. Lionell Gatford, *An Exhortation to Peace* (1643); and Clarendon, *History*, VI 42: 'no good Christian can without horror think of those ministers of the church, who, by their function being messengers of peace, are the only trumpets of war and incendiaries towards rebellion.'

125 *that.* C1 has 'yet', probably a corruption resulting from a misreading of the contraction 'y[t]', which is retained in D.

129-30 Although the witty development is Cowley's own, the image may embody an echo of Virgil, *Georgics*, I 480: 'et maestum inlacrimat templis ebur aeraque sudant.' Cf. Milton, 'On the Morning of Christs Nativity,' l.195.

133 *Petitions.* In late 1640 and early 1641 a series of petitions calling for root-and-branch reformation of the church were presented to Parliament as from the inhabitants of London and various countries. They were similar in phrasing, as appears in printed copies (for example those in the Thomason Tracts volume, E.135), and Cowley implies that they were actually drafted by the Puritan party in Parliament. Cf. Clarendon, *History*, III 66-7; and Butler, *Hudibras*, I ii 609-10:

> The Parliament drew up *Petitions*
> To't self ....

136-8 Cf. Sir John Denham's ironic contrast between the standard form of the petitions and the Puritans' dislike of fixed forms (as opposed to spontaneity) in prayer, 'To the Five Members of the Honourable House of Commons. The Humble Petition of the Poets' (*Poetical Works* ed. T. Banks), ll.5-6:

> Though set form of *Prayer* be an *Abomination*,
> Set forms of *Petitions* find great Approbation.

139-42 During the debate on the Bill of Attainder of the Earl of Strafford, between 3 and 9 May 1641, great crowds gathered at Westminster, taking up the cry 'Justice,' as they called for Strafford's execution (Clarendon, *History*, III 196-7). The execution took place on 12 May.

141-2 An interesting, perhaps intentional, contrast with the 'Epitaph on the Earl of Strafford' attributed to Cleveland, a poem which had not been published but which appears to have circulated widely in manuscript (*The Poems of John Cleveland* ed. B. Morris and E. Withington [Oxford 1967]), ll.13-14:

> Here lies Blood; and let it lie
> Speechlesse still, and never crie.

145-8 Orpheus of Thrace was the inventor of the lyre and had the power through his song and music to move even the stones. He was stoned to death by the frenzied Bistonian (or Thracian) women when he resisted their advances. (Ovid, *Metamorphoses*, XI 1-43)

149 *Miter.* Archbishop Laud was impeached on 18 December 1640, and the Root

and Branch Petition was presented in the same month. In May 1641 the first bill for the abolition of the episcopacy was introduced in the House of Commons, and in December of that year crowds gathered at Westminster, crying 'No Bishops,' just as they had earlier cried for justice against Strafford (Clarendon, *History*, IV 111).

153 *Mary*. Queen Henrietta Maria sailed for Holland on 23 February 1642, seeking financial support and arms for her husband's cause. Cowley's phrasing in ll.153-4 is similar to William Cartwright's in 'On the Queens Return from the Low Countries,' first printed in *Musarum Oxoniensium* Επιβατηρια (Oxford, July 1643), sig. D1^{v}:

> *When greater Tempests, then on Sea before,*
> *Receav'd Her on the shore ....*

155 *Charles*. Following the popular demonstrations prompted by his unsuccessful attempt to arrest the Five Members of the House of Commons, the King left London for Hampton Court on 10 January 1642, and then moved to the north, establishing himself at York on 19 March. In his repeated use of the verb 'drove,' 'driven,' Cowley seems to echo the King's emphatic statement that he was driven to the north by the Parliamentary party, rather than drawn there by a 'malignant' party (*His Majesties Answer to ... The Declaration, or Remonstrance of the Lords and Commons, of the 19th of May, 1642* [1642], p.5).

157 *tumults*. Charles refused appeals from Parliament that he return to London; he declared that the 'barbarous and seditious tumults at *Westminster* and *Whitehall*' had made his residence there unsafe, and he indignantly repudiated the assertions of his opponents that they 'knew no tumults' (*His Majesties Answer*, pp.18-19).

159-60 For this meaning of 'large' see the *OED*, A.III.11. Parliament took steps to secure to itself fortresses and militarily important towns in January 1642, with such effect that the gates of Hull were shut against the King when he approached that town on 23 April. Cf. Dudley Digges, *The Unlawfulnesse of Subjects taking up Armes* ([Oxford] 1643), p.156: 'by the same justice He [Charles] was kept out of *Hull*, they might have kept him in what Village, what House, what Prison they pleased.'

161 In a message to Parliament on 8 April 1642, Charles declared his intention of leading an army in his own person to Ireland in order to suppress the rebellion there. Parliament, mistrustful and alarmed, sent a strongly unfavourable reply, effectively prohibiting the project. (Clarendon, *History*, V 58-66)

162 Cf. Dudley Digges' comment on the King's opponents: 'These politique phisitians ... will be sure so to manage the disease, that they will be paied as much as they please to demand' (*The Unlawfulnesse*, p.144).

165 *The Sea.* The navy was secured to Parliament and placed under the command of the Earl of Warwick on 2 July 1642.

169-73 Charles raised his standard at Nottingham on 22 August 1642, an event which is usually taken to mark the outbreak of the Civil War, and forces soon rallied around him in a manner which Clarendon, like Cowley, regards as almost miraculous: 'There cannot be too often mention of the wonderful providence of God, that, from that low despised condition the King was in at Nottingham after the setting up his standard, he should be able to get men, money, or arms ...' (*History*, VI 71).

174 *Lord of Hosts.* See Psalm 24:10, and Revelation 17:14. Cowley's lines may be read as a reply to Jeremiah Burroughes' *The Glorious Name of God, The Lord of Hosts. Opened in two Sermons ... Vindicating the Commission from this Lord of Hosts, to Subjects, in some case, to take up Arms* (1643). Burroughes' argument that the Lord of Hosts supported the Parliamentary cause and his statement that God had made the Earl of Essex 'the Lord of his Hosts' (sig. A2) were much resented and ridiculed by Royalists. See *Mercurius Aulicus*, 27 July 1643, pp.401-2.

176 *Assyrian Host.* See 2 Kings 19:35: 'And it came to pass that night that the Angel of the Lord went out and smote in the camp of the Assyrians an hundred fourscore and five thousand: and when they arose early in the morning, behold, they were all dead corpses.'

178 *your.* This reading of P, A, and D seems preferable to the 'their' of C1, as making it immediately clear that the reference is to the 'Vaine Men' or the rebels, rather than to the angels.

181 *Worc'ester.* In the first serious skirmish of the Civil War at Powick Bridge near Worcester on 23 September 1642, the Royalists led by Prince Rupert routed their opponents.

183 *Twise.* Holinshed mentions several occasions on which Worcester was damaged in civil war, including two when parts of the city were burned, in the reigns of William Rufus (1088) and Stephen (1150) (*Chronicles*, II 28, 100).

189 *two great Bretheren*: the Princes Rupert and Maurice, youthful nephews of Charles, who quickly became prominent in the war as Royalist cavalry leaders. They are compared to Castor and Pollux, the twin sons born to Leda after her rape by Jove. These twins were often represented as horsemen; they were believed to have power to grant victory in battle and to calm stormy seas.

195-6 Cf. Clarendon's comment on the terror which Rupert's victory at Powick Bridge caused among the Parliamentary forces: 'it ... rendered the name of prince Rupert very terrible, and exceedingly appalled the adversary; insomuch as they had not in a long time after any confidence in their horse, and their very numbers were much lessened by it' (*History*, VI 46).

203 *Sands.* Edwin Sandys (b 1613?) of Northbourne Court, Kent, a colonel in the Parliamentary army, was mortally wounded at Powick Bridge; he was the first officer to fall in the war. He was viewed with particular bitterness by Royalists because, although he was the son of a prominent courtier and statesman, and the grandson of an Archbishop of York, he had plundered Royalist gentry in Kent and defaced Canterbury Cathedral. See [Bruno Ryves], *Mercurius Rusticus* (Oxford 1646), pp.6-11, 68-70, 182-96. Before his death Sandys published a *Vindication* and a *Declaration* repudiating Royalist claims that at the end of his life he repented his support of the Parliamentary cause.

207 *On two faire Hills.* Cowley describes the positions of the opposing armies on the morning of the Battle of Edgehill, the first major fight of the Civil War, 23 October 1642. Charles' army occupied the height of Edgehill; the Parliamentary army commanded by the Earl of Essex did not in actuality occupy a corresponding height but drew up on the plain to the east on a 'little rising ground' (Nathaniel Fiennes, *A Most True and Exact Relation* [1642], p.5). See A.H. Burne, *The Battlefields of England* (second edition, London [1951]), pp.190-2. Essex refused to charge the hill; the royal army came down, and the battle was fought on the plain near the village of Kineton.

207-8 Cf. *Davideis* III (*Poems*, p.333):

> On two near *Hills* the two proud *Armies* stood.
> Between a fatal Valley stretcht out wide.

217 *rags.* Anglicans frequently charged the Puritan sectaries both with tearing the seamless garment of Christ's church and with staining its white purity. Cf. III, 84 and note.

218 *torne Liturgies.* Cowley's image gains special meaning from episodes such as the one described in *Mercurius Aulicus*, 13 June 1643 (p.312): Parliamentary soldiers are alleged to have marched through the streets of London, 'first 4 in Buffe-coates, next 4 in *Surplices* with the Book of *Common Prayer* in their hands, singing in derision thereof, and tearing it leafe by leafe, and putting every leafe to their *Posteriours*, with great scorne and laughter.'

234 *knew not why.* Cf. Digges: 'What fury hath robb'd men of their understandings ... that they should hate, and teare, and kill one another they know not why!' (*The Unlawfulnesse*, p.161); and Butler, *Hudibras*, I i 1–2.

240 *Justice pluckes downe Justice.* The repetition of '*Justice*' in C1 may be a scribal error, for P, A, and D read '*Justice* pulls down *Vengeance*', but cf. the preceding lines, in which Mercy cries for mercy.

244 *the Ghost of mighty Strafford.* Cf. *The Puritan and the Papist*, l.298, where the bloodshed of the war is termed 'That fatall debt paid to great *Straffords* Ghost.'

245-50 During the fighting at Edgehill a cannon ball fell near the King (Burne, *The Battlefields of England*, p.189). Cowley satirizes the profession of the Parliamentary forces that they are fighting for the King while actually fighting against him. Cf. *The Puritan and the Papist*, l.202: 'you dare *shoot* at th' *King*, to *save* his *life*'; and the anonymous *The True Informer* (1643; British Museum, E.96.10), p.41 (misnumbered as p.35): 'but these men [the rebels] by a new kind of *Metaphysick* have found out a way to abstract the *Person* of the King from his Office, to make his Soveraigntie a kind of *Platonick Idea* hovering in the aire, while they visibly attempt to assaile and destroy his Person (and *Progeny*) by small and great shot, and seek him out amongst his Life-Gard with fire, and sword; yet they give out, they fight not only not *against* him, but for him ....' See also Butler, *Hudibras*, I ii 513-14.

259ff In the central action of the Battle of Edgehill, Prince Rupert, commanding the right wing of the Royalist cavalry, and Henry Wilmot, commanding the left wing, put the Parliamentary cavalry to flight. Rupert, either through error or circumstances beyond his control, pursued the flying troops far from the field (ll.271-2); meanwhile the Parliamentary infantry inflicted heavy damage upon the Royalist foot. The battle broke off at the fall of night, with a result so indecisive that both sides were able to claim victory. See Peter Young, *Edgehill 1642: The Campaign and the Battle* (Kineton 1967). Cowley's account of the battle seems generally accurate, although he exaggerates the degree of Royalist success.

260 *White-feather'd*. Emblematic of good. Cf. *Libri Plantarum* VI (*Poemata Latina*, p.358): '*Pax longa* revertitur Exul,/*Albionemque* albis plaudens amplectitur alis'; and Jonson, *The Masque of Queenes* (*Ben Jonson* ed. C.H. Herford and P. and E. Simpson, VII 305): '*Fama bona*, as she is describ'd, in Iconolog. di Cesare Ripa. attir'd in white, w[t]h white Wings.'

265 *Rebells*. Consideration should be given to the reading 'Miscreants,' which occurs in P, A, and D. It avoids an awkward repetition in C1, but it creates a metrical problem unless the word is taken as a disyllable.

268 *Organs*. Cf. Cowley's satire on the Puritan objection to church music in *The Puritan and the Papist*, ll.155-8. The Puritan destruction of the organs of the Cambridge chapels familiar to Cowley was reported by *Mercurius Aulicus*, 10 March 1643, p.127.

276 In stating that ten Parliamentary soldiers fell for every Royalist Cowley seems to be trying to match the enemy propaganda which claimed exactly the opposite ratio of casualties. One of Essex's officers, Lord Wharton, declared that 3000 Royalists were killed and fewer than 300 Parliamentary soldiers (*Eight Speeches Spoken in Guild-Hall* [1642], p.9). Clarendon, more moderate than Cowley, estimates that the Parliamentary casualties were twice those of the Royalists (*History*, VI 89). One of the best comments

on the subject is Thomas May's: 'there is no consent at all concerning the number of men slain, but so great a discrepancy, as it is almost a shame to insert it into an History' (*The History of the Parliament of England* [1647], III 23).

277-80 Cf. *Davideis* IV (*Poems*, p.375):

> Drops of that *Royal Moisture* which does know
> No Mixture, and disdains the place below.

281 *Lindsey ... Aubigny*. Among the Royalists killed at Edgehill were Robert Bertie, Earl of Lindsey (b 1582), who had resigned the command of the King's army on the eve of the battle, and George Stuart, Seigneur d'Aubigny (b 1618), who was related to the royal house.

290 *Stephen*: St Stephen, the first martyr.

291 *Wharton*. Philip, Lord Wharton (1613-96), commanded a regiment under Essex at Edgehill. Royalists asserted that when his men took flight he saved himself by hiding in a sawpit. Cf. *The Puritan and the Papist*, l.34: 'the *Baron* of the *Saw-pit*'; and *Mercurius Aulicus*, 23 September 1643, pp.533-4. Probably the real reason why Wharton became a special butt of Royalist satire is the fact that he carried the first official news of Edgehill to London, claiming a great Parliamentary victory. See John Taylor (alias Thorny Ailo), *A Letter Sent to London From a Spie at Oxford* ([Oxford] 1643): 'You [the rebel leaders] mocked God in your publique Thankesgivings, for Your invisible Victories, when you were publiquely beaten, as at *Edge-hill*, when You and the Sawpit-Lord, with some others did make the People believe lies ...' (p.12).

306 *Sisera's*. See Judges 5:20: '... the stars in their courses fought against Sisera.' Cf. Charles Mason's 'To his Majestie upon the peace concluded with Scotland,' published in a volume to which Cowley contributed two poems, *Irenodia Cantabrigiensis* (Cambridge 1641), sig. K3:

> Such fight against heav'ns cause, whose unjust warres,
> Like Sisera's, are check'd by th'host of starres.

308 *Lucifer*. On the connection between Lucifer and the stars see II, 387-90 and note.

309-20 The Puritan preacher Thomas Case gave thanks for Edgehill as a Parliamentary victory in a sermon preached before the House of Commons on 26 October, *Gods Rising, His Enemies Scattering* (published belatedly, London 1644). Since the Royalists also celebrated Edgehill as a victory, they were offended by the celebrations of the Parliamentary party. *Mercurius Aulicus* repeatedly satirized Parliamentary celebration of defeats as victories. Cf. *The Puritan and the Papist*, ll.21-8, 77-8, 302: 'when you thank't *God* for being *beat*'; and Butler, *Hudibras*, III iii 281-8:

> *Disperse the News, the Pulpit tells,*
> *Confirm'd with Fire-works, and with Bells,*

And though reduc'd to that extream,
They have been forc'd to sing Te Deum,
Yet with Religious Blasphemy
By flattering Heaven, with a Lie,
And for their Beating, giving thanks,
Th' have rais'd recruits, and fill'd their Banks.

321 *Brainford*: Brentford. In his advance to the environs of London after Edgehill, Rupert sacked Brentford on 12 November, inflicting heavy losses on the Parliamentary troops who attempted to defend it.

323 *Red Coates.* The Parliamentary regiment which suffered the heaviest casualties at Brentford was the one, commanded by Denzil Holles, 'called the Red Coates' (*A Continuation of Certaine speciall and remarkable Passages*, 12-18 November, sig. A^v).

325-32 In the aftermath of the Battle of Brentford, Royalist artillery opened fire on Parliamentary craft on the Thames, blowing up an ammunition barge or two near Sion House. Cowley follows Royalist news reports in much exaggerating the scale and significance of the action. Anthony Wood states that news was received in Oxford on 14 November that 'fifteene hundred of the parliament side were blowen up &c' (*Life and Times*, I 71). The Parliamentary newspapers ridiculed such reports, declaring that only one life was lost in this supposed engagement. See *Englands Memorable Accidents*, 25 November, p.95, and *A Continuation of Certaine speciall and remarkable Passages*, 12-18 November, sig. B3^v.

333-44 Cf. Denham, *Coopers Hill* (London 1642), pp.10-11:

Thames the most loud [lov'd] of all the Oceans sonnes,
By his old sire to his imbraces runnes,
Hasting to pay his tribute to the Sea,
...
... behold his shore;
O're which he kindly spreads his spacious wing,
And hatches plenty for th'ensuing Spring.

337 *white-nam'd pallace*: the royal palace of Whitehall, deserted since the King's abandonment of London. Cf. the opening of the anonymous pamphlet, *A Deep Sigh Breath'd Through the Lodgings at White-Hall, Deploring the absence of the Court, and the Miseries of the Pallace* (1642): 'A Pallace without a Presence! A *White-Hall* clad in sable vestments!'

345 *Oxford.* On 29 November Charles returned to Oxford where he had first established himself a month earlier, and which henceforth he made his headquarters. The fact that he had been obliged to abandon his advance on London was hidden in the enthusiasm of his welcome into Oxford, just as it is concealed in Cowley's lines. See Wood, *Life and Times*, I 67-8.

349-52 During their temporary occupation of Oxford in September 1642, the

Puritan troops commanded by Lord Saye and Sele searched through the books in the Schools, and burned 'Popish' books and manuscripts which they found in the colleges; and a trooper fired at images on the porch of St Mary's, the university church. See Wood, *Life and Times*, I 60–7; and W.D. Macray, *Annals of the Bodleian Library* (second edition, Oxford 1890), p.96.

352 *Malignants*: Royalists. As Clarendon complains, the Royalists were commonly termed by their opponents '*evil counsellors, malignants, delinquents*, and *cavaliers*' (*History*, VI 31).

358 *glorious*. The King protested against Parliament's hypocrisy 'in telling Us, *That they will make Us a Great and Glorious King*, in their Petitions and Remonstrances' (*His Majesties Answer*, p.7).

364 *thy Sister*. Cambridge suffered, in December-January 1642-3, from the notorious Puritan iconoclasm that is recorded in William Dowsing's diary. See J.B. Mullinger, *The University of Cambridge*, III (Cambridge 1911), 266-72.

368 Marlborough and Cirencester were captured and sacked by Royalist forces, the former on 5 December 1642, the latter on 2 February 1643.

369 *for Peace*. Peace negotiations took place in the 'Treaty of Oxford,' February-April 1643, without any success. The King was in truth no more willing than his opponents to accept any compromise. See Gardiner, I 78-126.

372 *Brookes and Hambdens blood*. Robert Greville, Lord Brooke (b 1608), and John Hampden (b *c*1594) are linked not only as prominent leaders of the Parliamentary party who died in the earlier part of 1643, but also because the circumstances of their deaths, for reasons explained below, were taken by Royalists to exemplify the workings of providence. Cf. *Mercurius Aulicus*, 24 June 1643, p.330: 'But whether the life and death of Lord *Brooks* or Master *Hampden* be the better lesson against Treason and Rebellion, let posterity judge.'

373-6 Brooke, commander of the Parliamentary forces in the counties of Warwick and Stafford, was killed in an attack on the fortified cathedral close of Lichfield, on 2 March 1643, the day of the festival of St Chad, to whom the cathedral was dedicated. *Mercurius Aulicus* (10 March 1643, p.127) states that he died 'in his assaulting the Church *Close*, by a shot in the forehead neare the eye, on S. *Chads* day, (the first Bishop of that Church) and by the hands of a Clergy-mans sonne,' and Clarendon (*History*, VI 277) states that many discourses were made upon the circumstances of his death. Cowley satirizes Brooke's religious views in *The Puritan and the Papist*, ll.91-6.

374 *Red*. The mark of a saint's day in the calendar. Cf. Cowley's 'On his Majesties Return out of Scotland' (*Poems*, p.22):

No drop of *Blood* is spilt which might be said
To mark our joyful *Holiday* with *Red.*

376 I have here adopted two readings of A, D, and P, 'Nought was' and 'thy', as giving more sense to this obscure line than those of C1, 'Was nought' and 'his'. The '*Booke*' is presumably Brooke's attack on the episcopacy, *A Discourse Opening the Nature of that Episcopacie, which is Exercised in England* (1641, enlarged 1642). It is just possible, however, that the allusion may not be to Brooke's book but to St Chad's. The famous and venerated manuscript known as St Chad's Gospel was hidden during the Civil War to save it from Puritans intent on destroying Popish objects and is still possessed by Lichfield Cathedral.

377-80 Hampden succumbed on 24 June 1643 to wounds that he had received six days earlier at Chalgrove, in the area where he had first raised troops for Parliament. Cf. *Mercurius Aulicus,* 24 June 1643, p.330: '... *Shawgrave* field (where he now received this mortall wound) was the selfe same place where he first muster'd and drew up men in armes to rebell against the *King*.'

381-92 Cf. Clarendon's character of Hampden, *History*, III 31; and VII 83: 'For the first year of the Parliament he seemed rather to moderate and soften the violent and distempered humours than to inflame them. But wise and dispassioned men plainly discerned that that moderation proceeded [rather] from prudence, and observation that the season was not ripe, than that he approved of the moderation; and that he begat many opinions and motions, the education whereof he committed to other men, so far disguising his own designs that he seemed seldom to wish more than was concluded ....' The Royalist Sir Philip Warwick similarly emphasizes Hampden's ability and his subtlety, and the Puritan Sir Simonds D'Ewes regards him as the framer of many plots executed by Pym. See J.H. Hexter, *The Reign of King Pym* (Cambridge, Mass. 1941), p.93.

381-2 Cowley applies ironically to Hampden's work the description of the Creation in Genesis 1:2.

385 *Ætnas Shop*. The forge of Vulcan and the Cyclops, who made thunderbolts, was under Mount Aetna. See Virgil, *Aeneid,* VIII 416-23. Cf. Cowley's 'The Monopoly' (*Poems*, p.120): '*Ætna* .../The sounding shop of *Vulcans* smoaky art.'

387 *Martin*: Henry (Harry) Marten (1602-80), a leader of the extreme anti-Royalist group in the House of Commons.

388 *Pym*. John Pym (1583-1643) shared with Hampden the effective leadership of the House of Commons during the early part of the Civil War.

394 *Cornish might*. Cornwall declared for the King at the outbreak of the Civil War, and Royalist forces gained complete control over the county in

October-November 1642. The Cornish subsequently fought with such distinction in the royal cause that the King issued a special proclamation of thanks on 10 September 1643: *His Maiesties Declaration to all his Loving Subiects in the County of Cornwall* (Oxford 1643).

395-8 The Cornish, descendants of the ancient Britons, the race founded, according to Geoffrey of Monmouth, by Brute, Prince of Troy, were driven by the Saxon invaders to the west country. Cf. Cowley's account of the legend of Brute in *Libri Plantarum*, VI (*Poemata Latina* [1668], pp.340-1), and see also Drayton, *Poly-Olbion*, Song I, ll.547-51:

... where
Great *Brute* first disembarqu't his wandring Trojans, there
His ofspring (after long expulst the Inner land,
When they the *Saxon* power no longer could withstand)
Found refuge in their flight.

Roberta F. Brinkley points out that the struggle between King and Parliament was naturally associated with that between Briton and Saxon, since the Stuarts emphasized their British descent, while Parliament based its claim to power partly on Saxon precedent. See her *Arthurian Legend in the Seventeenth Century* (Baltimore [1932]), pp.102-3.

402 *Tamars Flood.* The river Tamar, the boundary between Cornwall and Devon, separated Briton from Saxon, and, during the winter of 1642-3, territory held by the King from that held by Parliament.

403-6 The authenticity of the legends of King Arthur (son of Uther Pendragon) was much debated in the seventeenth century. See Brinkley, *Arthurian Legend*, pp.26-88.

409-14 Contrast Drayton's emphasis on the Tamar's 'equall sides' in his description of a peaceful England in *Poly-Olbion*, Song I, ll.205-8:

Proude *Tamer* swoopes along, with such a lustie traine
As fits so brave a flood two Countries that divides:
So, to increase her strength, shee from her equall sides
Receives their severall rills. ...

415-18 Cowley glosses over the fact that the Cornish trained bands refused to cross the Tamar and insisted that they were raised to serve only in their own county. See Gardiner, I 81. Hopton subsequently raised a special Cornish force to carry the war into Devonshire and beyond.

419 *that Fate.* The reading 'the fates' in C1 is clearly erroneous, since agreement is required with 'she' in the following line.

420 *Hopton.* Sir Ralph Hopton, later Baron Hopton of Stratton (1596-1652), benefiting from military experience on the continent, brilliantly organized the Cornish forces in the autumn of 1642, and in the earlier part of 1643 led

them in an impressive series of victories over the Parliamentary army in the west, including Braddock Down, Stratton, and Lansdown. See F.T.R. Edgar, *Sir Ralph Hopton, The King's Man in the West (1642-1652)* (Oxford 1968).

428 *Barkley, Slaning, Digby*: Sir John Berkeley, later Baron Berkeley of Stratton (1607-78), Sir Nicholas Slanning (1613-43), and either Colonel John Digby, a son of the Earl of Bristol, or Sir John Digby, brother of the well-known Sir Kenelm. All four men served with distinction in the battles of the western campaign.

429 *Godolphin*. Sidney Godolphin (b 1610), the poet, was killed while serving in the royal army at Chagford, Devonshire, 9 February 1643; his death was lamented by his friends, Clarendon (*History*, VI 251), and Hobbes (*Leviathan* ed. M. Oakeshott [Oxford 1960], pp.2, 461).

429 *Greenvill*: the heroic and much loved Cornish leader, Sir Bevil Grenville (b 1596), whose death at Lansdown on 5 July 1643 is described below.

431 *Stamford*: Henry Grey, Earl of Stamford (*c*1600-73), commander of the Parliamentary army which was signally defeated by Hopton at Stratton on 16 May 1643. He was alleged (probably unjustly) by Royalists to have deserted his army during a crucial period of the battle. Cf. Clarendon, *History*, VII 89, and Denham, 'The Western Wonder.'

433-56 Cf. the Royalist account of the battle of Stratton, *The Round-Heads Remembrancer* ([Oxford] 1643, received by Thomason 7 June), pp.3-4: '... *Sir Ralph Hopton* was never so low as now, his whole body of foot being not full 3000, and his Ammunition not sufficient for those men hee had, as appeared in the event. Yet Sir *Ralph* and those other noble Gentlemen, did not only prepare to meet the Rebells in the field, but (to the perpetuall honour of the County of *Cornwall*) assaulted this great Rebellious body in their strong workes and trenches, fighting bravely with them for full 10 houres, and when these loyall gentlemen had spent their Ammunition, and had not powder left for one houre longer, they then (with unexpressible valour) fell upon the Rebels with their swords and pikes, and fought it out so manfully, that at last they wholly routed the Rebels Army, killed many hundreds of them dead in the place, wounded many more; tooke 1700 prisoners ... They tooke likewise all the Rebels Canon ... and betwixt 2 and 3000 armes ....' See also Mary Coate, *Cornwall in the Great Civil War and Interregnum 1642-60* (Oxford 1933), pp.66-70.

439 *Germany*. The Thirty Years War had raged since 1618.

442 *Hundred-handed Gyants*: the Hecatoncheires or Uranids, sons of heaven and earth, who won Zeus' war with the Titans, by each hurling a hundred stones at a time. See Homer, *Iliad*, I 401-4, and Hesiod, *Theogony*, l.714ff.

457-9 After his victory at Stratton, Hopton marched north, and on 4 June near

Chard, Somerset, joined his forces with the large Royalist army commanded by the Marquis of Hertford and Prince Maurice.

460 *Belgian Trophies*. Maurice had fought in the Lowlands and Hopton in Germany.

461-4 In April Prince Maurice had prevented the Parliamentary army of Sir William Waller from advancing into Wales, but Waller preserved his forces intact (Gardiner, I 121). The fact that Waller had been nicknamed 'William the Conqueror' by his supporters became the subject of Royalist irony, especially after the general's defeat at Roundway, described below.

466-70 Grenville fell at the moment of victory, in his third heroic charge up a hill held by Waller's army, during the battle of Lansdown, near Bath, on 5 July. See Coate, *Cornwall*, pp.79-89. Cowley had no doubt seen the Oxford collection of elegies, *Verses on the Death of the Right Valiant Sr Bevill Grenvill* ([Oxford] 1643, received by Thomason 12 August), including William Cartwright's poem (pp.8-11), which concludes with the exhortation to Grenville's spirit:

> Look downe, and say: I have my share in All,
> Much Good grew from my Life, Much from my Fall.

467 *Decius*. Decius Mus Publius, in Roman legend, sacrificed himself in a charge on the enemy to secure victory. Cf. the poem by I.M. in the *Verses on the Death of ... Grenvill* (p.7):

> ... whom Death
> Snatcht like a *Decius* hence; whose hallowed breath
> Flew from Thee like an Offering; who dyed'st twice,
> Our Souldier once, and once our Sacrifice.

471-82 At the Battle of Roundway Down, on 13 July, Waller's army was virtually destroyed by the forces led by Hopton and Wilmot. According to the Royalist account, *Sir John Byrons Relation* (York 1643), the main body of the King's horse numbered only 1200, as opposed to Waller's far more numerous forces. The charge of cowardice against Waller is not entirely just, but Byron and *Mercurius Aulicus* (14 July 1643, p.371) both state that he and the remnant of his forces fled the field in great haste, and that they left cannon, munitions, and many prisoners in the hands of the Royalists. The latter took every opportunity thereafter to remind Waller of 'Run-away Down.' Cf. Denham, 'A Second Western Wonder' (*Poetical Works* ed. T. Banks, p.134):

> But now without lying, you may paint him flying,
> At *Bristol* they say you may find him
> Great *William* the *Con* so fast he did run,
> That he left half his name behind him.

477 *Iron Regiments*: a single London regiment, commanded by Sir Arthur

Hesilrige, the men of which were encased in complete armour, and often referred to as 'Lobsters.' At Roundway the weight of the armour handicapped the regiment and caused its defeat. See Coate, *Cornwall*, pp.92-3. Cf. the poem by 'I.M.' in the *Verses on the Death of ... Grenvill* (p.6): 'their Iron Men, and men of Steele.'

485 *Luds proud Towne*. London, according to legend, was rebuilt by King Lud, who named it after himself '*Caire-Lud*, as *Luds* towne' (John Stowe, *A Survey of London* ed. C.L. Kingsford [Oxford 1908], I 1). After the Battle of Roundway, Waller hastened to London, where he complained that his defeat had been caused by the Earl of Essex's failure to send him reinforcements. See Hexter, *The Reign of King Pym*, p.124.

491-508 After fifteen months absence in Holland, where she procured arms and munitions, and in the north of England, where she joined in military activity, Queen Henrietta Maria was reunited with Charles at Kineton, the site of the Battle of Edgehill, on 13 July 1643, the day of the great Royalist victory at Roundway Down. It is Cowley's fiction that the couple knew of this victory at the time of their reunion, but the coincidence was subsequently much commented upon. See Clarendon, *History*, VII 121. Cowley's lines have much in common with some of the verse in *Musarum Oxoniensium* Επιβατηρια (Oxford 1643), the volume which members of the university produced to mark the royal reunion and re-entry into Oxford. See, for example, John Berkenhead's poem (sig. Aa):

Thou Honourd Mount, She grac'd thee more
Then all thy Blood and Spoyle before!
'Twas Conquest then, 'tis Triumph now,
...
Angells look'd downe and lik'd it well,
All but the Lower House *and* Hell.

See also the anonymous contemporary verses preserved in manuscript by Sir William Dugdale, *Two Copies of Verses, on the Meeting of King Charles the First and his Queen Henrietta-Maria, in the Valley of Kineton* (Birmingham 1822), for example (p.10):

Yee both joyn'd hands, and strait the Rebells fled,
Soe Moses' hands at distance conquered.

499 *lowd*. P, A, and D have 'lewd', but 'lowd' seems appropriate where the reference is to gunpowder. Cf. Donne, 'The Perfume,' ll.41-4.

502 *travaild*: 'travelled', as well as 'travailed' (the two spellings not being clearly distinguished in the seventeenth century). P, A, and D have 'Travel'd'.

509-22 William Cavendish, Earl (later Marquis and Duke) of Newcastle 1593-1672), was the Royalist commander in the north of England. 'He was a very fine gentleman, active and full of courage, and most accomplished in those qualities of horsemanship, dancing, and fencing, which accompany a good breeding; in which his delight was. Besides that, he was amorous in poetry and music, to which he indulged the greatest part of his time ....' (Clarendon, *History*, VIII 82) Abandoning these private pursuits when the King called him to arms, he raised an army through his own resources and influence, secured Newcastle and the four northern counties, then moved into Yorkshire in late September 1642, where he suffered some reverses before achieving the victory which is celebrated in the lines below. See Margaret, Duchess of Newcastle, *The Life of William Cavendish, Duke of Newcastle* ed. C.H. Firth (second edition, London [1906]), pp.13-26; and A.S. Turberville, *A History of Welbeck Abbey and its Owners* (London [1938]), I 66-89.

511 *state*. Lines 511-12 in C1 are in a hand which may be Cowley's own, but this reading of P, A, and D suits the context better than the 'fate' of that manuscript. Newcastle was well known for his love of courtly splendour and chivalric ceremonial.

523 *Bradford and Leeds*. Both towns were strongly Puritan, and they successfully resisted attacks by Newcastle in the winter of 1642-3, surrendering to him only after his victory at Adwalton Moor. The capture of the two cities is described in *An Expresse Relation of the Passages and Proceedings of his Majesties Armie, Under ... the Earle of Newcastle* ([Oxford] 1643).

524 *Fairfax*. Ferdinando, second Lord Fairfax (1584-1648), and his son, Sir Thomas, later third Lord Fairfax (1612-71), commanders of the Parliamentary forces in Yorkshire, were Newcastle's chief opponents.

525 See the textual notes. This line is obscure in C1 because Fairfax's name is not given in the possessive form, and the reference of the pronoun 'his' is not immediately clear. A and D provide the right form of the name, but P, A, and D are probably wrong in giving 'their' for 'his'. The reference is to Newcastle and his capture of Bradford and Leeds and a large part of Fairfax's army following the Battle of Adwalton Moor. In the preceding and following lines 'they' refers to the rebels.

527 *Boötes*: the constellation of the Great Bear, sometimes called Charles' Wain, and frequently associated with the King. Cf. Cowley's 'Verses uppon my Lady Elisabeth birth on Christmass even, 1635' (*Essays*, p.483).

529-40 Newcastle gained a great victory over the Fairfaxes at Adwalton Moor, near Bradford, on 30 June 1643, forcing the Parliamentary armies to withdraw from the whole of Yorkshire except Hull. Cowley's description of the battle is probably based on the account in *Mercurius Aulicus* (3 July 1643, p.350): '... His Majesties Forces were fain to give ground untill they came within the reach of their owne Canon, which the Earle of *New Castle* perceiving, he presently alighted from his Horse, went himselfe to his Foot, and taking a Pike into his hand, bid them *follow him*, assuring them, *not a man should goe further then he himselfe would lead them* ... whereby the Noble Earle so animated the whole Army that they charged with unexpressible courage, and so amazed the Rebels with the bravery of their coming on, that the Rebels soon fell into confusion, and were not brought againe into rank and order, till the Earle made himselfe master of the Rebels Canon, which he presently turned against the Rebels; The sight whereof wrought such astonishment amongst them, that they fled disorderly towards Leedes ....'

535 *Capaneus*. In an attack upon Thebes, Capaneus climbed the walls of the city, declaring, to the astonishment of both friend and foe, that not even Jove should stop him, upon which he was killed by a thunderbolt. See Statius, *Thebaid*, x 827-939. Cf. *Davideis*, III n.53.

541-2 Royalists alleged that Parliamentary gunners deliberately directed fire on the King during the Battle of Edgehill (cf. ll.246-8, above) and that Parliamentary ships fired intentionally on the Queen after her landing at Burlington (Bridlington) Bay in Yorkshire, on 23 February 1643. On the latter incident see *Mercurius Aulicus*, 27 February 1643, p.109; and [Peter Heylin], *A Briefe Relation of the Remarkeable Occurrences in the Northerne Parts* ([Oxford] 1642[-3]). The two events are linked by Heylin, and by John Fell in the poem which he contributed to *Musarum Oxoniensium* Επιβατηρια (sig. A4^{v}):

> *Nor staies Rebellion there, but on does goe,*
> *It has His* [the King's] *Goods, whose Blood it would have too,*
> *Let* Edge-hill *witnesse that, and alwayes be*
> *Next to Your* Burlington, *in history*
> *Delivered unto each succeeding age,*
> *A Monument o'th Rebells bloody rage.*

544 *Papists*. Following the King's instructions, Newcastle had admitted Roman Catholics as officers in his army. Charges by his opponents that he was engaged in a Catholic design to suppress Protestantism were embodied in *A Declaration of the Lords and Commons Assembled in Parliament: For the Vindication of Ferdinando Lord Fairefax, and others imployed in their service against the Earle of New-Castle, and his Army of Papsts* [sic], *which threatens ruine and Desolation of our Religion*[,] *Lawes and Liberties* (3 February 1643). Newcastle replied with his own *Declaration*, which in turn prompted a *Confutation*.

549-58 Parliament's claim to defend the liberty and property of the subject was repeatedly attacked in *Mercurius Aulicus* and in official Royalist statements, with vigorous protests against the heavy extraordinary taxes imposed by Parliament to maintain its army, against the confiscation of Royalists' estates, and against the imprisonment of the King's supporters and Anglican clergy. See, for example, the King's Declaration of 8 December 1642, in Clarendon's *History*, VI 197-8; and Digges, *The Unlawfulnesse*, pp.160-1.

551-2 Cf. *The Puritan and the Papist*, l.262: 'New *Prisons* made to defend *Libertie*,' and the anonymous *The True Informer* (1643), p.21: 'Many hundreds more of the best sort of Subjects have been suddenly clapt up, and no cause at all mentioned in many of their commitments, and new Prisons made of purpose for them, where they may be said to be buried alive.' The new prisons included ships on the Thames in which a number of Anglican clergy were confined.

554 *stiffe decree*: the Calvinistic interpretation of the doctrine of predestination, with its corollary of eternal reprobation. In repudiating it Cowley places himself in the company of many Anglicans of his period, both in Laudian or Arminian and in liberal or latitudinarian circles, as well as in that of John Milton. Cf. Falkland's statement that the Calvinistic denial of free will 'wholly overthrowes His [God's] justice' (*Sir Lucius Cary, Late Lord Viscount of Falkland, His Discourse of Infallibility, with an Answer to it: And his Lordships Reply* [1651], p.126).

555-6 Cf. *The Puritan and the Papist*, l.265: 'Our *Goods forc'd* from us for *Propriety's* sake.'

557-8 Parliament issued, on 27 March 1643, 'An Ordinance for sequestring notorious Delinquents Estates' (*Acts and Ordinances of the Interregnum* ed. C.H. Firth and R.S. Rait, I 106). It adopted a system of rewarding the 'discoverers' of Royalist estates with a proportion of the value, which was exploited by the unscrupulous. Cf. [Peter Heylin], *Theeves, Theeves* ([Oxford] 1643): 'who sees not, how easily that man may be called *malignant*, or Voted up for a *delinquent*, whose large *revenues* may invite them so to stile the owner, in hope to benefit themselves by the confiscation' (p.7).

560 *Yeomans ... Bourchier*. Robert Yeomans and George Bourchier (or Boucher) were leaders of a plot in March 1643 to deliver Bristol to the Royalist forces besieging the city. Their plot was discovered, they were tried by court martial, although they were civilians, and they were executed. See *The Two State Martyrs, or, the Murther of Master Robert Yeomans, and Master George Bowcher Citizens of Bristoll* ([Oxford] 1643); and *Mercurius Aulicus*, 4 June 1643 (p.294), which refers to the King's statement that he regarded their execution as 'the most barbarous Act which the impudence and cruelty of this Rebellion had produced against Him.'

561 *Coward*: Nathaniel Fiennes, the Parliamentary governor of Bristol. He was held responsible for the execution of Yeomans and Bourchier, and he was

charged with cowardice after his surrender of the city on 26 July 1643. See below, II 264-74, and II 526.

565 Cf. *The Puritan and the Papist*, ll.275-6:

'Twas fear'd a *New Religion* would begin;
All new Religions now are entred in.

568 *mild Lamb, and gaullesse Dove.* Cf. *Davideis* II (*Poems*, p.286): 'a gall-less *Dove* .../ A gentle *Lamb*.'

571-2 Plague, famine, and the sword are traditionally the three great instruments of divine punishment. See Jeremiah 24:10. Cowley terms them '*God's* great *Triumvirate* of *Desolation*' in his 'Ode. Upon his Majesties Restoration and Return' (*Poems*, p.423).

571 *restlesse Sword.* Cf. *Davideis* IV (*Poems*, p.388): '*Abdons* restless Sword.'

574 *Earth-workes.* In the attempt to fortify London against Royalist attack, great numbers of citizens joined in the building of earth-works in the spring and summer of 1643. See *A Perfect Diurnall of the Passages in Parliament*, 3 May 1643; and Thomas May, *The History of the Parliament of England* (1647), III 91.

Book II

4 *Albions.* In the *Davideis* II, n.98, Cowley denies that 'Albion' is derived '*Ab Albis Rupibus*,' but he plays upon the word as meaning 'white,' just as he does here, in 'To Dr. Scarborough' and in 'Upon his Majesties Restoration and Return' (*Poems*, pp.197, 422).

5 *Alecto.* One of the Furies, she is represented by Virgil as spreading the seeds of discord and war. See the *Aeneid*, VII 323ff.

9 *Triptol'emus.* In classical myth, the inventor of agriculture and the resulting civilization, Triptolemus drove a chariot drawn through the air by winged dragons, and sowed seeds of wheat or barley.

10 *fertill glebe.* Cf. *Davideis* IV (*Poems*, p.389), where an angel of destruction sows 'all th' *Ingredients* that swift ruine make':

> The fertile glebe requires no time to breed;
> It quickens and receives at once the *Seed*.

19-68 The indecisive Battle of Hopton Heath was fought near Stafford on 19 March 1643. The Royalist army led by the Earl of Northampton for a time gained the upper hand over the Parliamentary army led by Sir John Gell, but it lost its advantage when enemy reinforcements were brought up by Sir William Brereton; and Northampton was killed. See Gardiner, I 123.

19-20 In the *Aeneid* Alecto is termed 'virgo sata Nocte' (VII 331); and she is represented as blowing a horn, which sounds the outbreak of war between the Latins and the followers of Aeneas (VII 511-15).

22-8 Cf. *The Battaile on Hopton-Heath* ([Oxford] 1643, received by Thomason 25 April), the Royalist account that seems to be Cowley's principal source for the action of the battle: '... *Sir* William Brereton *and Sir* John Gell, *two that (one would think) have conspired together to be beaten as often as they unite their mutuall forces. Witnesse* Ashby de-la-zouch *and other places where they shamefully have beene worsted by that noble couragious Colonell* Hastings' (p.1). Gell (1593-1671) and Brereton (1604-61), after achieving local successes in their own counties, Derbyshire and Cheshire, had been obliged in January 1643 to abandon a siege of Ashby-de-la-Zouch, which was held against them by Colonel Henry Hastings, later Lord Loughborough (*c*1609-67), and in February their armies, then in retreat, were further harassed by Hastings. See *Mercurius Aulicus*, 21 and 23 January and 27 February 1643, pp.33, 45, 110.

28 *In a blind Clowd.* Cf. Homer, *Iliad*, III 380-4, the episode in which Aphrodite saves Paris from Menelaus in battle, by snatching him away in a cloud.

31 *drad.* Perhaps an error for 'dread' or 'dred' (the reading of c2), but this form, although archaic by Cowley's time, was still in use.

33-42 According to *The Battaile on Hopton-Heath* (p.2), the Parliamentary forces numbered 3000 and the Royalists only 900. The Royalist horse drove the Parliamentary cavalry to flight and captured enemy cannon, but 'following the Execution beyond command' (as Rupert's cavalry had done at Edgehill), they lost their temporary advantage. The battle, again like Edgehill, broke off inconclusively at nightfall.

43-56 Cf. the account of the death of Spencer Compton, Earl of Northampton (b 1601), in *The Battaile on Hopton-Heath* (pp.3-4): '... upon the first charge with our horse, being engaged upon Execution neare their foot, his horse was shot, so that he was constrained to alight, and being encompassed with enemies he fought on foot a long time, killing (as they themselves confesse) a Colonel of foot, and striking another Captain into the brest with his Poleax, besides other common souldiers whom he wounded and slew, untill such time as he was overborne by multitudes, and then being knockt downe with a musket and grievously wounded, and his head-peece taken off, was offered quarter (as they say) but he answered that he scorned to take quarter from such base rogues & Rebels as they were; and so fought it out a long while after, till such time as he was slaine by a blow with a halbert, on the hinder part of his head, receiving at the same time another deep wound in his face.' See also Clarendon, *History*, VI 279-80.

52 Cf. the anonymous poem, *An Elegy on the Death of the Right Honourable Spencer, Earle of Northampton* [Oxford 1643] (received by Thomason 24 May), pp.3-4:

> So in faire *Beaumont* I have seen an *Oake*,
> When mercenary hands by many a stroak
> Have made him nod, all tottering as he stood,
> Threaten a ruine to the underwood.

59-64 James, Lord Compton, Northampton's eldest son and heir, served under his father at Hopton Heath and was wounded in the leg. Cf. *The Battaile on Hopton-Heath* (p.5) : '... we have such excellent Copies of him [the dead earl] in his rare sonnes, and chiefly in the gallant young Earle himselfe, who hath so much of the father in him, that he only wants time and opportunity to make him more like him.' In the anonymous *Elegy* (p.6) the writer addresses Northampton's spirit which takes its flight to heaven while the souls of the enemy dead descend cursing to hell, and declares that his widow

Beholds thy picture in her noble Sonne,
Who after thee, being dead, made hast to runne,
But that *Bellona* in love with him assay'd
To wound his foot, and so his journey stay'd.

65-6 *Planet*: Mars, which is red in appearance.

67-8 Cf. *The Battaile on Hopton-Heath* (p.3). Fighting was suspended 'by reason of the night and our Horses being weary .... The next morning by breake of day we made ready to fall on againe, but finding no Enemy, we then understood that they had marched away in the night.'

69-94 Prince Rupert captured Birmingham on 3 April 1643, after overcoming the determined resistance of its inhabitants and garrison, and his army subsequently burned many of its buildings. Royalists regarded the town with bitter dislike, *Mercurius Aulicus* (5 April 1643, p.176) terming it 'pestilent and seditious,' because it was strongly Puritan and had supplied Essex's army with swords and other weapons, for the manufacture of which it was famous, while denying them to the King's forces. See the Royalist *A Letter Written from Walshall, By a Worthy Gentleman to his Friend in Oxford, Concerning Burmingham* (n.p. 1643, received by Thomason 14 April).

69 *Cornavian*. Some writers (following Ptolemy) state that the Cornavii were a Caledonian tribe, while the Cornovii were the tribe which in Roman times occupied the area of modern Warwickshire and adjacent counties, but the name of the Midlands tribe (to which Cowley obviously refers) is spelled 'Cornavii' by William Camden (*Britannia* ed. R. Gough [London 1806], II 443).

75 *Pyracmon ... Brontes*: two of the Cyclops, assistants of Vulcan, who in their forge under Aetna made thunderbolts and other weapons. Cf. I 385 and note, above.

77 *Welch*. Welsh troops in Rupert's army led the attack on Birmingham (*Mercurius Aulicus*, 5 April 1643, p.176).

77 *stop*. This may be an error for 'shop'. Cf. 1.88.

81 *Denby*. William Feilding, first Earl of Denbigh, serving in Rupert's army, was mortally wounded in the attack on Birmingham and died five days later on 8 April. Born about 1582, he was already in advanced years when he took up arms for the King. See Clarendon, *History*, VII 33.

85-94 The burning of Birmingham added to Rupert's already bad reputation for plunder and destruction, and it was bitterly protested in such Parliamentary pamphlets as *Prince Ruperts Burning Love to England: Discovered in Birminghams Flames* (1643). In contrast to Cowley, other Royalist writers emphasized that the town was fired after Rupert's own departure and contrary to his orders. See, for example, *Mercurius Aulicus* (5 April 1643, p.176), and *A Letter Written from Walshall.*

93 *Rea*: a stream which flows through Birmingham.

95-136 The fortified cathedral close of Lichfield, which had been captured by Parliamentary forces on 4 March 1643 (following the assault mentioned above, I 373-6), was recaptured in April for the King by Rupert, after a fiercely resisted siege. Rupert summoned the town on 6 April, then surrounded and laid battery to it. After the failure of an attempt to scale the walls on 15 April, he undermined parts of them and sprang mines, blowing up a tower and breaching the wall on 20 April. A force which entered this breach was beaten back with heavy losses, but the defenders surrendered the next day on honourable terms. See *Valour Crowned. or A Relation of the Valiant Proceedings of the Parliament Forces in the Closse at Lichfield, against Prince Ruperts* (1643); and Captain John Randolph, *Honour Advanced: Or, A briefe account of the long keeping, and late leaving of the Close at Liechfield* (1643, received by Thomason 27 April). These are Parliamentary accounts, but Cowley's description of the action agrees substantially with them, although his emphasis is naturally different.

97-100 Oswi, King of Northumberland, is reputed to have built a church at Lichfield in 656, after he had defeated the pagan Mercians in battle, and to have appointed Duina there as first bishop of Mercia. See Camden, *Britannia* ed. Gough, II 497.

102 *Ced.* Cowley seems to confuse St Ced (Cedda) (d 664) with his brother St Chad (Ceadda) (d 672). The former has no connection with Lichfield; the latter as Bishop of the Mercians was often regarded as the founder of Lichfield Cathedral, which contains his tomb. Cowley makes the right association above, I 373; but, as Thomas Fuller comments, St Ced and St Chad are 'so like in name, they are oft mistaken in authors one for another' (*The Church History of Britain* ed. J.S. Brewer [Oxford 1845], I 213).

109-10 Cf. the description of Cain's killing of Abel in *Davideis* I (*Poems*, p.247); and see the Introduction, p.53, above.

115-21 This is said to be the first occasion on which a land mine was used in England. See C.V. Wedgwood, *The King's War*, p.193. The contemporary accounts indicate that Cowley does not exaggerate its effect.

122 *Korahs Sinne.* Korah led a rebellion against Moses (Numbers 16). Cf. *Davideis* I (*Poems*, p.247).

125-6 In the unsuccessful Royalist attempt to storm the breach in the wall of Lichfield Close on 20 April, George, Lord Digby, later second Earl of Bristol, was wounded in the knee, and Colonel James Usher was killed. The Parliamentary *Valour Crowned* (pp.3-4) states that 100 Royalist soldiers were killed and 120 taken prisoner.

129-33 According to the Parliamentary accounts, the real reason for the surrender was that the defenders had exhausted their powder and other munitions. See, for example, *Valour Crowned*, p.4.

135-6 Rupert paid tribute to the courage of the defenders of Lichfield after their surrender to him (Clarendon, *History*, VII 34).

139 *noble Youth*: Charles Cavendish (b 1620), second son of the Earl of Devonshire. Royalist commander-in-chief in Nottingham and Lincolnshire, he captured Grantham in March 1643, and achieved other successes, but he was killed on 28 July 1643, in an attempt to prevent Parliamentary forces from raising the siege of Gainsborough.

140 *Hector in his Hands*. A godson of the King, Cavendish was trained in arms under the Prince of Orange, and he displayed great courage at Edgehill, as well as in his subsequent actions in Lincolnshire.

140 *Paris in his Face*. White Kennett cites a contemporary description of Cavendish: 'the Sun behelt not a Youth of a more manly Figure, and more winning Presence' (*Memoirs of the Family of Cavendish* [1708], p.8). Cf. Edmund Waller, 'Epitaph on Colonel Charles Cavendish.'

141 *Parham*. Francis, Lord Willoughby of Parham (1613?-66), Parliamentary commander-in-chief in Lincolnshire, was Cavendish's opponent at Gainsborough and in other actions. The Royalist *A Relation of a Fight in the County of Lincolne* ([Oxford] 1643) states that in an engagement near Ancaster on 11 April Cavendish defeated Parham, who was heard to demand quarter before he made his escape.

144 *Trents*. The River Trent flows by Gainsborough. According to David Lloyd, Cavendish fell to the enemy when his horse became bogged in the river's muddy shore (*Memoires* [1668], p.673). On the thirty tributary rivers and the fish of the Trent, cf. Spenser, *Faerie Queene*, IV xi 35; and Drayton, *Poly-Olbion*, Song XXVI, ll.164-274.

145-56 Cavendish's death caused extraordinary displays of grief. See [Thomas Pomfret], *The Life of the Right Honourable and Religious Lady Christian Late Countess Dowager of Devonshire* (1685), pp.53-4: '... when his Body was brought to *Newark* to be interred, the whole Town was so fond of it, (even dead) that they would not suffer it, for some days to be laid into the Ground, but wept over it, and admired it, and not without the greatest Reluctancy, at last committed him to his Dormitory; covering his Hears with Tears and Laurels.'

150-4 Cf. Virgil, on the death of Pallas, *Aeneid*, XI 67-70:

hic iuvenem agresti sublimem stramine ponunt,
qualem virgineo demessum pollice florem

seu mollis violae seu languentis hyacinthi,
cui neque fulgor adhuc nec dum sua forma recessit.

157-8 Essex had captured Reading (*'Redding Blaze'*) on 26 April, and then begun an advance toward Oxford. A part of his force was routed by Prince Rupert at Chalgrove Field on 18 June. Cf. I 377, above.

159-91 Essex's army was much weakened by sickness in the later part of June when it was camped around Thame, Oxfordshire, and the advance on Oxford had to be abandoned. See the Parliamentary account, *A Remonstrance to Vindicate His Excellence Robert Earle of Essex From some false Aspersions cast upon his Proceedings. To the 17. of August. 1643* (n.p. 1643, received by Thomason 16 October): 'At *Thame* the hand of God in an extreme increase of sicknes (hundreds in a day falling desperately il) and by strong unseasonablenesse of weather, and great raine continuing 14. dayes, the place being upon a flat, clayie, and moist ground, made it impossible to advance from that quarter' (p.7).

179 *from such a curse defend.* As Cowley must have known, the Royalist forces in Oxford suffered numerous fatalities in the summer and autumn of 1643 from an epidemic of the disease which was termed *morbus campestris.* See Frederick J. Varley, *The Siege of Oxford* (Oxford 1932), pp.96-7.

193 *tawny Host.* Orange-tawny was the colour of the uniforms of the Earl of Essex's regiment, and it was adopted by Parliamentary officers generally. See Peter Young, *Edgehill 1642*, p.30.

195 *Keinton*: Kineton, site of the Battle of Edgehill.

197-200 After Essex's abandonment of his advance on Oxford, and Waller's defeat at Roundway Down, the two generals and parties of their supporters engaged in mutual recriminations in London. Cf. I 485, above, and see Gardiner, I 182-3, 212-13, etc.

201-2 Rupert and Maurice laid siege to Bristol on 23 July 1643, capturing it on 26 July.

202 *Crosses.* Royalist colours usually displayed the cross of St George. See Peter Young, *Edgehill 1642*, p.35 and plate 3.

203-4 The River Frome flows into the Avon at Bristol. Cf. Drayton, *Poly-Olbion*, Song III, ll.227-8:

Then came the lustie *Froome*, the first of floods that met
Faire *Avon* entring in to fruitfull *Somerset.*

206 Bristol, on the borders of Somerset and Gloucestershire, was itself constituted a county by a charter of 1373.

209-15 Bristol, from which John Cabot sailed in 1497, had long been famous for its activities in commerce, shipping, and exploration.

210 *Magellanick.* The word may refer either to the Straits of Magellan or to the South Pacific (*OED*).

211 *Thetis*: a Nereid, or sea goddess. Sea deities are traditionally represented as

having blue or green hair. See, for example, Homer, *Iliad*, XIII 563; Jonson, *The Masque of Blacknesse* (*Ben Jonson* ed. Herford and Simpson, VII 170); and Milton, *Comus*, l.29.

216-18 Charles had alienated commercial interests in Bristol by attempting to procure a forced loan in 1626 and by the assessment of Ship Money in 1634. The city refused admission to a Royalist force in July 1642, but in the following December admitted the Parliamentary troops which held it until its capture by Rupert. See [Richard Robinson], *The Sieges of Bristol During the Civil War* (Bristol 1868), pp.5-12.

222 *Say*. The Parliamentary governor of Bristol, Nathaniel Fiennes (or 'Fines'), was the second son of Viscount Saye and Sele, one of the leaders of the Parliamentary party.

225 *strong-built Castle*. Bristol Castle formed part of the city's extensive fortifications. After their capture of Bristol the Royalists tended to emphasize the strength of the castle as evidence of the greatness of their achievement. See, for example, Clarendon, *History*, VII 125. Fiennes, however, declared that the castle was so weak as to be indefensible. See *Colonell Fiennes Letter to My Lord General, Concerning Bristol* (1643), p.3.

226 *King*. In 1327 the deposed Edward II was imprisoned in Bristol Castle before his removal to Berkeley.

227 *workes*. Adding to Bristol's ancient fortifications, Fiennes built a system of earthwork defences. See [Robinson], *The Sieges of Bristol*, p.18.

229 *Briareus*: one of the hundred-handed giants. See above, I, 442 and note.

230-2 See Homer's account of the giants who threatened to war against the gods by piling mount Ossa on Olympus, and Pelion on Ossa, *Odyssey*, XI 305-20.

235-64 On 26 July Maurice attacked Bristol from the south-west, while Rupert attacked from the north. Maurice's forces, 'strong-limm'd *Westerne* Youth,' were the Cornish regiments which had earlier triumphed at Lansdown and Stratton. On this day they suffered terrible losses, leaving the ditch below the city's ramparts filled with their dead, and they were beaten off by the defenders. Rupert, however, forced his way through a weak point in the defences, upon which Fiennes surrendered the city. See Clarendon, *History*, VII 123-34; [Robinson], *Sieges of Bristol*, pp.21-35; and A.H. Burne and Peter Young, *The Great Civil War* (London [1959]), pp.92-6.

247 Cf. *Davideis* I (*Poems*, p.255):

An *Angell* whose unseen and easie might
Put by the *weapon*, and *misled* it *right*.

249 *Slaning, and Trevanion*. The two distinguished Cornish commanders, Sir Nicholas Slanning (cf. above, I 428), and Colonel John Trevanion (b 1613) fell in the costly assault led by Maurice. Clarendon (*History*, VII 132) describes the two men as 'the life and soul of the Cornish regiments,' and as being 'of entire friendship to one another'; and he gives this account of their

deaths: 'they were both hurt almost in the same minute and in the same place; both shot in the thigh with a musket bullet, their bones broken, the one dying presently, the other some few days after; and both had the royal sacrifice of their sovereign's very particular sorrow.'

259 *Lunsford.* Colonel Henry Lunsford (b 1611), who is described by Clarendon (*History*, VII 133) as 'an officer of extraordinary sobriety, industry, and courage,' was shot through the heart, as he served in Rupert's force, just before the moment of victory.

264-6 According to the terms of surrender, Fiennes and his men were to march out of the city unmolested, foot soldiers only being disarmed, but these terms were violated by Royalist soldiers (Clarendon, *History*, VII 129-30). Fiennes was later tried by court martial for improperly surrendering Bristol and was condemned to death, although the sentence was not carried out.

272 *Bourchier ... Yeomans.* Cf. above, I, 560-2 and note. Fiennes was charged by members of his own party at his trial with having improperly resorted to court martial in the case of these two Royalist martyrs, although the death sentences had been confirmed by Parliament.

277-352 Exeter, which had been held by Parliament from the beginning of the Civil War, fell to Prince Maurice on 4 September after a siege (conducted by others before the Prince took command) lasting eight months and nineteen days. *Mercurius Aulicus* (8 September 1643, p.497) celebrated the capture of 'that factious Citty,' 'which had so long bid defiance to their native and gratious Soveraigne.'

278 *Isca's.* Isca Damnoniorum was the Roman name for Exeter.

281 *Saxon.* At an unknown date, perhaps in the seventh century, the Saxons conquered Exeter and drove its British inhabitants across the Tamar, which henceforth marked the western limit of Saxon territory. Cf. I 395-410.

282 *Troyes fatall seed.* According to legend, Exeter was founded by the followers of Brute, Prince of Troy. See John Vowell (alias Hooker), 'The description of the citie of Excester,' in Holinshed, *Chronicles* (London 1807-8), III 926-7.

283-4 The Danes temporarily occupied Exeter in 875, and they unsuccessfully besieged it in 893 and 1001. In 1003 the city fell to the Danish king Sweyn Forkbeard, who burned it and slaughtered its citizens.

285-7 Exeter at first refused to acknowledge William the Conqueror, who laid siege to it in 1068, but, as Camden states, 'on the falling down of part of the wall, which the historians of that age ascribe to the hand of heaven, it presently surrendered' (*Britannia* ed. Gough, I 36).

292 *Courtneys wrath.* In 1470 the Yorkist Sir Hugh Courtenay of Haccombe laid siege to Exeter, then held by the Earl of Warwick, but he abandoned his attempt after twelve days (Vowell, in Holinshed, III 937).

293 *Warbecks tragick Pageant.* Perkin Warbeck, the pretender, laid siege to

Exeter in 1497, but the city refused to surrender, and it was relieved by a force sent by Henry VII.

295 *Painted Rose*. Perhaps 'painted' as being feigned or pretended. Perkin Warbeck professed to be the son of Edward IV, and thus head of the House of York, the emblem of which was the white rose.

298 *Henries Sword*. See Francis Bacon, *The Historie of the Raigne of King Henry the Seventh* (1622): after the defeat of Perkin Warbeck, 'The King ... made a Ioyfull entrance into *Excester*, where hee gaue the *Citizens* great commendations and thankes; and taking the *Sword* hee wore, from his side, hee gaue it to the Maior, and commanded it should bee euer after carried before him' (p.184).

300 *Sonne*. Charles was the direct descendant of Henry VII, the Stuart title to the English throne deriving from that king's daughter, Margaret.

303-6 In 1549, during the reign of Edward VI, Roman Catholic rebels of Cornwall and Devon laid siege to Exeter, which was relieved by a royal army. See Vowell, in Holinshed, III 939-61. In 1643, however, Cornish troops provided much of the strength of the army which captured Exeter for the King.

307 *Warwick, the Publick Pyrat*. On 21 July the admiral of the Parliamentary fleet, Robert Rich, Earl of Warwick (1587-1658), attempted unsuccessfully to relieve the besieged city by forcing a passage up the river Exe. Warwick was from the Royalist viewpoint a pirate in that his naval activities had been outlawed and declared treasonous by the King. His public 'piracy' was preceded by twenty-five years of involvement in privateering activities against the Spaniards. See F.W. Craven, 'The Earl of Warwick, A Speculator in Piracy,' *The Hispanic American Historical Review*, x (1930) 457-79.

311 *Jonas*. See Jonah 1:5: 'But Jonah was gone down into the sides of the ship; and he lay, and was fast asleep.'

317-48 Warwick was forced to withdraw by the fire of Royalist cannon from the shore, and by the falling tide, which put his ships in danger of stranding. *Mercurius Aulicus* (25 July 1643, p.398) claims that three of his ships were set afire, that two of his lighters, attempting to land men, were sunk, and that three of his ships were captured.

320 *canoas*. In seventeenth-century usage 'canoa' (or 'canoe') may mean any small boat or skiff propelled by paddling or rowing (*OED*).

327-8 Cf. Virgil, *Aeneid*, x 559-60: 'aut gurgite mersum/ unda feret piscesque impasti volnera lambent.'

333-6 Cowley adapts these lines for his ode, 'To Mr. Hobs.' See the Introduction, p.54, above. He states in a note on the ode: 'The Description of the Neighbourhood of *Fire* and *Snow* upon *Ætna* (but not the application of it) is imitated out of *Claud*[*ian*] *L.* 1. *de Raptu Pros*[*erpinae*],' quoting from the latter, I 166-70 (*Poems*, p.191).

349-52 After the failure of Warwick's attempt at relief, and renewed assaults by Maurice, Exeter was surrendered by the Parliamentary general, the Earl of Stamford, on 4 September. The terms were the same as those on which Nathaniel Fiennes had surrendered Bristol. *Mercurius Aulicus* (8 September 1643, p.497) reports that Stamford 'crept out of *Exeter* after he had begged his life.'

353 *Plymmouth.* After the fall of Exeter great alarm existed among the Parliamentarians for the fate of Plymouth, one of their few remaining strongholds in the west. A plot to deliver the city was thwarted in August, but the Royalists conducted a close siege in September-December. Their strongest effort to capture the city began in the later part of November, reaching its crisis in an unsuccessful attack led by Maurice on 3 December. See Robert Burnard, 'News from the West, 1643-1646,' *Reports and Transactions of the Devonshire Association*, XXI (1889) 218-20.

354 *prophesing.* The word is evidently intended as an elided form of 'prophesying' with two pronounced syllables, but no simple emendation conveys at once the sense and the sound. c2 reads 'prophesying', an emendation that converts the line into a hexameter.

357 *Gloc'ester.* The Royalist siege of Gloucester began on 10 August 1643. On the city's successful resistance and its relief in September by Essex, see below, III, 46 and note.

359-64 The entire fate of the Parliamentary cause seemed in doubt after the loss of Bristol, the other reverses which have been described above, and the opening of the siege of Gloucester.

365-96 This entire passage, except ll.385-6, is incorporated in the *Davideis* I (*Poems*, p.244). See the Introduction, p.52, above. The following are the only substantive variants: l.378 which] that (*Davideis*); l.383 drops] *Gems*; l.390 on] forth; l.395 then] when. I have retained the punctuation of c1 throughout this passage, although it is a little less satisfactory than that of the *Davideis*.

369 *unflecht.* This word is transcribed in c2 as 'unflesht', but the *Davideis* has 'unfletched', i.e., unfledged. Cowley defends his use of the epithet in the *Davideis*, I n.9.

372 In the *Davideis*, I n.10, Cowley argues, rejecting Aristotle's opinion and citing biblical authority: 'To give a probable reason of the perpetual supply of waters to *Fountains* and *Rivers*, it is necessary to establish an *Abyss* or deep gulph of waters, into which the *Sea* discharges it self, as Rivers do into the Sea; all which maintain a perpetual *Circulation* of water, like that of *Blood* in mans body.'

374 *undisturb'd by Moones.* See the *Davideis*, I n.10: 'For I suppose the *Moon* to be the principal, if not sole cause of the *Ebbing and Flowing* of the Sea,

but to have no effect upon the waters that are beneath the Sea it self.'

377 *Noe bound controules.* See the *Davideis,* I n.11: 'This must be taken in a Poetical sense; for else, making *Hell* to be in the *Center* of the Earth, it is far from infinitely large, or deep ....' The note concludes with a discussion, not wholly serious, of the locations and dimensions of hell given by Bellarmine, Lessius, Ribera, Virgil, Hesiod, Statius, and Aeschylus.

387-90 Lucifer (light-bringer) is both the name given to Satan before his downfall (Isaiah 14) and that of the planet Venus as the morning star. As the evening star Venus is known as Hesper.

391 *like Lightning.* See Luke 10:18: '... I beheld Satan as lightning fall from heaven.'

401-2 Cf. 'An Homily Against Disobedience, and wilfull Rebellion' (*c*1571), in which Lucifer is described as 'the first authour, and founder of rebellion,' and rebellion is termed 'the first, and the greatest, and the very roote of all other sinnes' (*Certaine Sermons or Homilies* [1635], p.276).

420 *Earth-quakes.* Cf. *Davideis* IV (*Poems,* p.367), where civil war is termed 'this general *Earthquake* of the *Land.*'

423 *Korah.* Cf. II 122, above. Korah and his followers were swallowed up by the earth, as a result of their rebellion against Moses (Numbers 16).

427-32 Rebels and complainers against Moses during the journey through the desert were punished by plague and the visitation of the fiery serpents (Numbers 16 and 21).

433 *Davids proud Sonne.* Absalom, who rebelled against his father, was slain by Joab and ten young men, when caught by his hair in an oak (2 Samuel 18).

437 *Pol'itick wretch.* Ahitophel, the counsellor who encouraged Absalom in his rebellion, hanged himself when his advice was rejected (2 Samuel 17:23).

439 *Shimei.* He cursed David and threw stones at him, later being executed by command of Solomon (2 Samuel 16:5-13; 1 Kings 2:36-46).

441 *Sheba.* He led a rebellion against David. See 2 Samuel 20:1: '... he blew a trumpet and said, We have no part in David.'

443 *those, who cut old Jacobs Stemme.* Under the leadership of Jeroboam, northern Israel revolted against the tyranny of King Rehoboam of the house of Jacob and Jesse. Rehoboam, forbidden by God to fight the rebels, retained the throne of Judah, while Israel became a separate monarchy under Jeroboam. (1 Kings 12)

444 *Jess'ian.* This adjective form of 'Jesse' (perhaps coined by Sylvester) occurs in the *Davideis* II (*Poems,* p.297).

449 *Baâshas head.* Baasha, King of Israel, deposed his predecessor Nadab, and caused him to be murdered (1 Kings 15:27-8).

450 *Zimri.* This king of Israel murdered his predecessor Elah. Evading capture

by his enemies, he burned his palace and died in the flames (1 Kings 16: 9-18).

451-2 Cf. *Davideis* I (*Poems*, p.263), concerning the destruction of Sodom: '*Alive* they felt those *Flames* they fry in *Dead.*'

457 *Barons.* The barons, who in 1215 forced King John to sign Magna Carta, formed an alliance in 1216 with Prince Louis (later King Louis VIII) of France.

463 *their Sonnes.* Under Simon de Montfort, the barons revolted against Henry III, forcing upon him the Provisions of Oxford (1258), and limiting his power further after their victory at Lewes (1264). The king's power was so weakened that he was obliged to abandon plans for continental military ventures.

468 The penultimate word has been heavily inked over in C1, but the first letter appears to be 'H', and the name 'Hambden' (as 'Hampden' is elsewhere spelled in C1) would exactly fit the space. The fact that Hampden was already dead when Cowley wrote does not rule out the possibility of his name here; it may provide a motive for the subsequent deletion.

469 *Edward.* Edward II was overpowered in 1326 by his queen, Isabella of France, and her lover, Roger Mortimer. In the next year he was deposed and put to death.

475 *Th'unchristian Bishop.* Adam of Orlton (d 1345), successively bishop of Hereford, Worcester, and Winchester, supported the party of Isabella and Mortimer; he preached against Edward II in 1326 and subsequently advised the deposition and imprisonment of the king. Holinshed states (probably inaccurately) that he gave the order for Edward's murder (*Chronicles*, II 582-7). Cf. Drayton, *The Barons' Wars*, Canto III, stanzas 69-70, and V 6-9.

480 *Matrevers ... Gourneys.* Sir John Maltravers (later Baron Maltravers) (d 1365) and Thomas Gourney (d 1333) are reputed to have murdered Edward II at Berkeley Castle. See Holinshed, II 586-7; and Marlowe, *Edward the Second*, V V.

483 *Richards dolefull end.* Richard II, deposed by Henry IV, died a prisoner at Pontefract in 1400. According to some chroniclers, followed by Shakespeare, he was murdered. His imprisonment was ordered by Parliament.

486 *Priveledge.* Reference is to the claims of Parliamentary privilege advanced by the party of rebellion. Cf. Clarendon (*History*, IV 233): 'It is not to be believed how many sober, well-minded men ... were imposed upon, and had their understandings confounded, and so their wills perverted, by the mere mention of *privilege of Parliament.*'

487 *Warwick.* Richard Neville, Earl of Warwick (1428-71), the 'king-maker,' helped establish Edward IV on the throne, then led forces against him, and deposed him in favour of Henry VI.

489 *Gloc'ester*. Richard, Duke of Gloucester, in 1483 usurped the throne as Richard III. According to the Tudor historians and to Shakespeare, he was responsible for the deaths of Henry VI, Edward V, and many other persons; and by them he is represented as hunchbacked and otherwise deformed.

494 *Kets, and Cades, and Tylers*. Robert and William Ket (or Kett) led a popular uprising in Norfolk in 1549. John Cade was leader of the Kentish rebellion in 1450, and Wat Tyler of the Peasants' Revolt in 1381. Cf. the Royalist pamphlet, *The iust reward of Rebels, or The Life and Death of Iack Straw, and Wat Tyler, who for their Rebellion and disobedience to their King and Country, were suddenly slaine, and all their tumultuous Rout overcome and put to flight* (1642).

497 *powder-traitours*: Guy Fawkes and his fellow conspirators in the Gunpowder Plot of 1605.

501 *Threshing-floore*. Cf. *Davideis* IV (*Poems*, p.369); '*Ophras Threshing Floore*'; and Jeremiah 51:33.

507 *Bel-zebubs*. See Cowley's note on Belzebub, *Davideis*, I n.18: 'That one evil *Spirit* presided over the others, was not only the received opinion of the Ancients, both *Jews* and *Gentiles*; but appears out of the *Scriptures* ....' See also 'The Plagues of Egypt,' stanza 8, n.2.

517-18 Cf. *Davideis* I (*Poems*, p.247): 'Great *Belzebub* starts from his burning Throne.'

526 *Fines*. See II 264-74, above.

530 *peace*. Proposals for peace were debated in Parliament in August 1643. See III, 32 and note, below.

533 *sixteene hundred yeares*. Cf. Joseph Hall, *An Humble Remonstrance to the High Court of Parliament*: *By a Dutiful Son of the Church* (1640-1) (*Works* ed. Philip Wynter [Oxford 1863], IX 287): Episcopacy is 'exceeding ancient, of more than fifteen hundred years standing.' The Anglican argument that episcopacy as understood by the Church of England was a Primitive or Apostolic institution was vigorously attacked by Puritans, including the Smectymnuus writers and Milton in 1640-1.

537 *Say, or Pym*: William Fiennes, Viscount Saye and Sele, and John Pym, the Parliamentary leaders.

538 *Luds seditious Towne*. The view that London was the seed bed of the rebellion, which was generally held by Royalists, was developed in detail in two pamphlets published in Oxford in 1643, *Lord Have Mercie Upon Us*, attributed to Peter Heylin, and *A Letter from Mercurius Civicus to Mercurius Rusticus*, attributed to John Berkenhead.

543 *Jerus'alem*. Possibly an allusion to Ezekiel 10-11.

545 *Saint-Johns, the Vanes, Kimbolton, Pym, and Say*: Oliver St John, Earl of Bolingbroke (1580?-1646), his relative, Oliver St John (1598?-1673), Sir

Henry Vane the Elder (1589-1655), his son, Sir Henry Vane the Younger 1613–62), Edward Montague, Lord Kimbolton and Viscount Mandeville, from 1642 Earl of Manchester (1602-71), John Pym, and Viscount Saye and Sele. They are probably linked here not merely as prominent Parliamentarians but as leaders of the 'war party,' which in August 1643 resisted proposals of peace amounting virtually to surrender.

559 *Catiline*: leader in 63-2 BC of a conspiracy and uprising against the Roman republic.

561 *Cic'ero*. Cicero, who was consul at the time, exposed the danger from Catiline and attacked him in a famous series of orations.

573 *The Crowne cast downe to Earth, the King more low*. At the time Cowley wrote, the leaders of the Parliamentary party were far from advocating either the abolition of the monarchy or regicide, but a few Parliamentarians seemed already to consider these possibilities. On 16 August 1643 Henry Marten was expelled from the House of Commons for suggesting such a course (Gardiner, I 238).

574 *The Churches Lands*. Parliament voted on 9 July 1641 that bishops' lands should be sequestered, and on 27 March 1643 it confiscated the lands of a number of the higher clergy, although the more general confiscation and sale of ecclesiastical lands was not ordered until 1646. See *Acts and Ordinances of the Interregnum* ed. Firth and Rait, I 106; and Christopher Hill, *Puritanism and Revolution* (London 1956), p.170. Cf. the satire on the Puritan greed for church lands in *The Puritan and the Papist*, ll.245-50, and in Butler's *Hudibras*, III ii 31ff.

577 *borr'owing, plunder, stealth*. Parliament raised money at first by voluntary loans 'on the public faith,' but it soon had to resort to compulsory loans and assessments. On 18 August 1643 a heavy forced loan was assessed against the inhabitants of London, and other large taxes were levied during this summer and autumn. See Clarendon, *History*, VI 187-207; and Gardiner, I 237. Charges of plunder were repeatedly made by and against both parties from the opening of the war.

580-1 Cf. I, 557-8 and note.

583 *Marius ... Sylla*. Gaius Marius (155-86 BC), Roman soldier and consul, massacred his enemies, the followers of Lucius Cornelius Sulla (138-78). When he gained power as dictator, Sulla took revenge by carrying out a notorious proscription of his own enemies. See Plutarch's life of Sulla. Cf. Cowley's *A Discourse By way of Vision, Concerning the Government of Oliver Cromwell* (*Essays*, pp.351, 367).

591 *Large feasts*. Gluttony is one of the stock charges against the Puritans, from Ben Jonson (*The Alchemist*, III ii 74-5, 90) to Samuel Butler (*Hudibras*, I i 223-8, 293-302; II ii 793-8).

593 *Ilands.* A Puritan settlement had been established on Providence Island in the Caribbean, which was captured by the Spaniards in 1641. The Providence Company responsible for the colony included the Earl of Warwick, Lords Saye and Brooke, John Pym, and other leaders of the Parliamentary party, a number of whom were also active in the settlement of New England. See Arthur P. Newton, *The Colonizing Activities of the English Puritans* (New Haven 1914).

594 *knock the pulpit.* Cf. Butler, *Hudibras,* I i 11-12:

> And Pulpit, Drum Ecclesiastick,
> Was beat with fist, instead of a stick.

597 *Texts of wicked Princes.* See the Introduction, p.30, above.

598 *mouth-Granadoes.* Cleveland employs this compound word in 'The Rebell Scot,' l.24. The word 'granado' is a seventeenth-century variant of 'grenado,' i.e., grenade.

601 *Plagues.* See Exodus 7-12, and cf. Cowley's 'The Plagues of Egypt.'

608 *Paul.* See 1 Corinthians 9:22: 'To the weak became I as weak, that I might gain the weak: I am made all things to all men, that I might by all means save some.' Cf. Cowley's 'Of Liberty' (*Essays,* p.380): 'the Character of an *Anti-Paul,* who became all things to all men, that he might destroy all.'

Book III

28 *long watchings*. Royalists charged that their opponents forced extreme measures through the House of Commons during late night sittings, when moderate members had retired. The Grand Remonstrance was passed on 22 November 1641, during a sitting of the House that lasted until 2 a.m.

32 *T'avert the dangers of sweet Peaces name*. The party in Parliament that favoured making peace with the King had grown in strength with the Royalist victories in the west and north. On 4 August 1643 the House of Lords adopted propositions for peace which amounted virtually to capitulation, and the Commons began on the next day to consider the proposals, despite opposition from the 'war party' led by Pym, and from the city. On 10 August the Commons rejected the propositions. See Gardiner, I 214-20. Cowley may have derived his information about these and related events in London from *Mercurius Aulicus*, 10-14 August 1643, pp.431-42.

34 *cov'enant*. The word may bear special weight, since the Solemn League and Covenant with the Scots was a major subject of Parliamentary debate during the summer of 1643. After amendment, the Covenant was taken by the Commons on 25 September.

37 *Preists*. On Sunday, 6 August, many of the Puritan preachers of London attacked from the pulpit the proposals for peace which were currently being debated. See Gardiner, I 217.

37 *viperous*. See Sir Thomas Browne's discussion of the ancient belief that vipers tear their mother apart on their birth, *Pseudodoxia Epidemica*, Book III, Chapter xvi.

38 *beawteous Mother*. Cf. George Herbert, 'The British Church,' and 'Church-Rents and Schismes.'

41 *Mechanicks*. *Mercurius Aulicus* (Saturday, 12 August 1643, p.434) states that on the previous Wednesday there came down to Westminster 'some 5 or 6000 of the usuall *hacksters*, which had beene alwayes ready for such purposes at a minutes warning; and they cryed *No Peace*.'

44 *The same noyse*. See I, 149 and note, above.

46 *Gloc'ester*. Gloucester, under its Parliamentary governor, Colonel Edward Massey, stubbornly resisted the Royalist siege, after refusing Charles' summons on 10 August. In London the saving of Gloucester was recognized as crucial to the Parliamentary cause, and great efforts were hastily made to fit out an expedition under the Earl of Essex for the city's relief. Both funds and men were quickly raised, including six regiments of the London trained bands and auxiliary London troops. See Gardiner, I 237-8.

47-50 Cowley's comment on the zeal of the women of London in contributing their men to the Parliamentary cause is similar to Peter Heylin's description of their response to Parliament's appeal for plate and other valuables, in *Lord Have Mercie Upon Us* ([Oxford] 1643): 'How did the *Widows* presse to cast in their *Mites*, the married *Wives* their *wedding-rings*, the zealous *Virgins* their whole stocke, to their *Silver bodkins*?' (p.11). Cf. Butler, *Hudibras*, II ii 769-814.

51-2 On 21 August the Committee for the Militia of the City of London ordered the closing of all shops to release men for the expedition for the relief of Gloucester. The order was published as a broadsheet, at least one copy of which survives (British Museum, 669.f.7.33).

53 *Gownemen*: aldermen. Six aldermen were colonels of the regiments of London militia. See *A List of the Names of the several Colonells ... appointed by the Committee, for the Ordering of the Militia of this Honourable City of London* (1642; British Museum, 669.f.6.8).

56 *Finsburies Drumme*. Finsbury Fields, on the northern outskirts of the city, was the exercise ground of the London trained bands, and of the Honourable Artillery Company, to which many merchants and tradesmen belonged.

59 *Calvinists*. The Presbyterians were the largest of the religious sects in London, holding a position of dominant power in city and Parliament in 1643.

60-6 Calvin cautiously maintained the right of the public representatives of the people to resist an ungodly monarch, in his *Institutes* (IV XX 31). The Calvinistic theory of political resistance was further developed by John Knox in his *The Appellation of John Knoxe* (Geneva 1558) and by Christopher Goodman in his *How Superior Powers Oght to be Obeyd* (Geneva 1558). The arguments of Knox and Goodman were frequently cited by Puritan writers, including Milton in *The Tenure of Kings and Magistrates* (1649) (*Complete Prose Works*, III 248-51).

64 *Ravillacs*. François Ravaillac, who in 1610 assassinated Henry IV of France,

was usually associated by Protestant writers with bloody and unscrupulous Catholic and Jesuit policy. His introduction here is in keeping with Cowley's argument in *The Puritan and the Papist* that Catholicism and Puritanism, although they appear opposites, really meet on a common ground of false extremes.

67-70 Cf. I, 553-4 and note, above.

73-6 Cowley's image (although not his argument) has some affinity with George Herbert's in 'The Church Triumphant' (*Works* ed. F.E. Hutchinson [Oxford 1945]), ll.241-2:

> When *Sein* shall swallow *Tiber*, and the *Thames*
> By letting in them both pollutes her streams ....

73 *fam'd Lake*: Lake Geneva, representing Calvinism. Cf. John Donne, *Sermons* ed. G.R. Potter and Evelyn Simpson, V (Berkeley 1959), 251: 'a Church in the lake.'

74 *Tybers Flood*: Roman Catholicism.

83 *Independents*: the Puritans who insisted upon the autonomy of each congregation, as independent from any central church body, in contrast to the Anglican and Presbyterian forms of church government. Their numbers were scarcely so great in 1643 as Cowley suggests. According to one contemporary estimate, there were only a thousand Independents in London in 1645. See George Yule, *The Independents in the English Civil War* (Cambridge and Melbourne 1958), p.21.

84 *seamelesse Vesture*. See John 19: 23-4; and cf. Henry Vaughan, 'The Brittish Church,' and 'L'Envoy,' l.30: 'Thy seamless coat is grown a rag.'

86 *More Popes*. This criticism seems to have been made indiscriminately of both Presbyterian and Independent systems of church government. See Joseph Hall, *Episcopacy by Divine Right* (1640), *Works* ed. Wynter, IX 270: 'And what do you think of this lawless Polycoyrany; that every parish minister and his eldership should be a bishop and his consistory; yea, a pope and his conclave of cardinals within his own parish'; George, Lord Digby, *Third Speach* (1640-1), quoted by William Haller, *Liberty and Reformation in the Puritan Revolution* (New York 1955), p.22: 'insteed of every Bishop wee put down in a Diocese, we shall set up a Pope in every Parish'; and Milton, *Of Reformation, Complete Prose Works*, I 605. Cf. *The Puritan and the Papist*, l.195, and Butler, *Hudibras*, I iii 1201-05.

87 *Muncers crew*: Anabaptists. Thomas Münzer (*c*1489-1525) led a German Anabaptist movement which advocated common ownership of property, until his execution upon the defeat of his followers in the Peasants' War. The English Anabaptists of the Civil War period were commonly, if inaccurately, associated by their opponents with the excesses of the German Anabaptists of the previous century, and extreme religious enthusiasts of many kinds

were loosely termed Anabaptists. See, for example, *A Warning for England Especially for London in the Famous History of the Frantick Anabaptists Their wild Preachings & Practises in Germany* (n.p. 1642).

89 *Monsters.* A pun on Münster (cf. I.110). In 1532-5 a group of Anabaptists led by John of Leiden gained power in Münster, where their regime became notorious for anarchy and profligacy, before its brutal suppression.

94 *Philos'opher*: Plato, in *The Republic.*

95-6 Cowley may intend an allusion to John Milton's *The Doctrine and Discipline of Divorce*, with its argument in terms of Christian liberty, which was published anonymously about 1 August 1643. No reference to this pamphlet in the months immediately following its publication has previously been known, but in the second edition (before 2 February 1644), and in *The Judgment of Martin Bucer Concerning Divorce* (July or August 1644) Milton writes of the hostile reception that was given to it. See Ernest Sirluck, Introduction, *Complete Prose Works of John Milton*, II (New Haven 1959), 138-42. In the controversy stirred by the divorce tracts in the second half of 1644 and in 1645-6 Milton was frequently associated by his opponents with the Anabaptists and attacked in words similar to Cowley's. See W.R. Parker, *Milton's Contemporary Reputation* (Columbus 1940), pp. 17-22, 73-6; and *The Life Records of John Milton* ed. J. Milton French, II (Rutgers 1950), 91-144.

95 *Wives.* John of Leiden legalized polygamy (the 'Turkish Lawe'), and took four wives.

97 *th'Easterne Moone*: the crescent symbol of Turkey and the Moslem religion. Cf. I 23, above.

101-10 Cf. Hooker's condemnation of the Anabaptists' denial of the validity of infant baptism, of their repudiation of secular authority, and of the claims of prophetic and visionary powers made by such leaders as John of Leiden (*Of the Laws of Ecclesiastical Polity*, Preface, par. 8).

109 *bring in the Scot.* Parliamentary commissioners opened negotiations with the Scots in Edinburgh on 8 August 1643, with the object of securing the aid of the Scottish army, but the Scots refused to move until their conditions had been met, and their army did not cross the Tweed until 19 January 1644.

111 *Brownists*: properly the separatist Puritan sect established about 1579 by Robert Browne and his associates. During the early 1640s the term was used very loosely, as Milton protests in *The Reason of Church-Government* (*Complete Prose Works*, I 784).

117 *Antinomians*: those who hold that Christians are freed by the Gospel from the moral law of the Old Testament. A modern Antinomian sect was founded in Germany in the earlier sixteenth century by John Agricola, and during the Civil War period a number of Puritan groups, especially in the army, displayed strong Antinomian tendencies.

120 *Moses Zeale.* See Exodus 32:19.

123 *Novatus*: either Novatianus, the Roman presbyter born near the beginning of the third century, or his lesser known contemporary, Novatus the Carthaginian, who held views similar to his and is sometimes confused with him. Novatianus was excommunicated by the Roman synod for excluding from communion those who after baptism had relapsed and sacrificed to idols. His followers called themselves *Cathari* or 'Puritans.' See Cyprian, *Epistles.*

129 *beastly Monsters.* The Adamites attempted to imitate the innocence of Adam and Eve. According to their opponents they practised nudity and were sexually licentious. Appearing first as a second-century sect of Gnostics, they were taken in the seventeenth century to be represented by such groups as the Family of Love, founded by Henry Nicholas (Niclaes) (*c*1502-80) of Amsterdam, and they were alleged to be active in London. See *A Nest of Serpents Discovered. Or a knot of old Heretiques revived, Called the Adamites* (n.p. 1641).

137 *Pelagius*: (*fl*382), the famous heretic who denied original sin and hence the necessity of divine grace for salvation.

139 *Resist.* Two special meanings of this word were in the forefront of controversy at the time Cowley wrote, and both are involved here. Calvinists held but Arminians rejected the theological doctrine that divine grace is irresistible. The political doctrine of non-resistance, which had scriptural foundation and which denied the right to use force against constituted authority, was advocated by Royalists but challenged or given a different interpretation by Parliamentarians.

143 *Arian Unbeleife*: the denial of the divinity of Christ, promulgated by Arius about 290.

145 *Bishop*: St Augustine, Bishop of Hippo, the chief opponent of Arius.

147 *In a more dang'erous shape reveiv'd anew.* The Socinians, followers of Lelio Sozini (1525-62) and Faustus Sozini (1539-1604), denied the orthodox view of the Trinity, emphasizing the unipersonality of God and, as a corollary, the humanity of Christ. No organized group of Socinians existed in England in the 1640s, but various persons and groups had come under their influence, and they had been attacked in such works as George Walker's *Socinianisme in the Fundamentall Point of Justification Discovered, and Confuted* (1641). See H. John McLachlan, *Socinianism in Seventeenth-Century England* (Oxford 1951).

157 *Sect of Freedome.* Some contemporary writers describe a Puritan sect called 'Libertines,' which held that Christians are exempt from the moral law, although it is not clear how this group is to be distinguished from other Antinomians. See, for example, *A Relation of Severall Heresies* (1646), pp. 7-8.

162 *the ancient Rest.* The most prominent of the Sabbatarian groups, which

argued for the observance of the Jewish Sabbath rather than the Christian Sunday, were the Traskites, followers of John Traske (*fl*1617-18). See Thomas Fuller, *The Church History of Britain* ed. Brewer, v 459-60.

163 *Circumcis'ed.* A sect known as the Pasagians or Circumcisi, which observed the law of Moses and practised circumcision, existed in Lombardy in the late twelfth and early thirteenth centuries, but it seems doubtful that there was any such group in England during the 1640s.

165 *Chiliasts.* Millenarianism flourished in the 1640s among members of left-wing Puritan groups, who regarded the religious reformation begun by the Long Parliament as direct preparation for the reign on earth of Christ and his saints. See P.G. Rogers, *The Fifth Monarchy Men* (London 1966).

170 *Antichrist.* See 2 Thessalonians 2.

172-8 *Marcion ... Nicolaitans*: heretics and heresies of the first to the fifth centuries, both well-known and obscure, in an order which seems determined by metrics and sound, rather than by chronology or logic. Cowley's list derives directly or indirectly from such Patristic catalogues of heresies as Augustine's *Liber de Hæresibus* and Epiphanius' *Panarion* or *Adversus Octoginta Hæreses.* Concise modern accounts of these heresies will be found in John H. Blunt's *Dictionary of Sects, Heresies, Ecclesiastical Parties, and Schools of Religious Thought* (London 1874).

179 *Wicleffians, Hussites, and the Zwinglian crew*: followers of John Wyclif (*c*1320-84), and the continental reformers, John Hus (1369-1415) and Ulrich Zwingli (1484-1531). See the Introduction, p.34, above.

180 *Hemerobaptists*: practitioners of daily baptism. Found first as a Jewish sect before the rise of Christianity, they were reported to have reappeared as an Anabaptist group in the seventeenth century, and they came under attack by Daniel Featley in his *The Dippers dipt. Or, the Anabaptists Duck'd and Plung'd over Head and Eares, at a Disputation in Southwark* (1646).

180 *Sebaptists*: a small sect which developed in the earlier seventeenth century, receiving its name from the action of its leader, John Smith, in baptising himself. See Richard Bernard, *Plaine Evidences: The Church of England is Apostolicall, the seperation Schismaticall. Directed Against Mr. Ainsworth the Separtist, and Mr. Smith the Se-baptist* (1610).

181 *Weigelians*: followers of Valentine Weigel (1533-88), the German mystic, whose writings gave him some influence in England, although the first English publication of his work did not occur until 1648. See Rufus M. Jones, *Spiritual Reformers of the 16th and 17th Centuries* (London 1914), pp.133-50.

181 *Vorstians*: followers of Conrad Vorstius (1569-1619), the Dutch divine, who was attacked by James I of England and condemned in 1619 by the Synod of Dort for heresies including Socinianism.

181 *Suencfeldians*: Schwenckfeldians, followers of Caspar Schwenckfeld (1489-1561), the Silesian reformer, whose extreme emphasis upon the inward nature of religion and strong anti-sacramentalism caused him to be repudiated and condemned by Luther.

183-6 *Mercurius Aulicus* reported on 3 March 1643 (p.115) the capture at Newark of 'some *French* Papists, who served under the command, and for the pay of the two Houses of Parliament,' and subsequently it frequently repeated the charge that Catholic mercenaries served in the Parliamentary army (23 July, 12, 19, 26, 28 August; pp. 394, 438, 454, 470, 474). The Parliamentary *Mercurius Britanicus* (5-12 September 1643, pp.17-18) satirized these claims as absurd.

187-8 Cf. Andrew Marvell's comment on the religious fanatics of the Commonwealth period, some eleven years later, in his 'The First Anniversary of the Government under O. C.' (*Poems and Letters* ed. H.M. Margoliouth), ll.299-300:

> Whose frantique Army should they want for Men
> Might muster Heresies, so one were ten.

189 *Synod*. Cowley probably refers here to the heterogeneous sectarian composition not only of the Parliamentary army but also of the Westminster Assembly. Cf. Cleveland's 'The Mixt Assembly.' Established by Parliament to advise on the reformation of the church, the Assembly met first on 1 July 1643 and continued its debates through the summer and autumn.

194 *Arke*. Cf. Cowley's 'Ode. Of Wit,' stanza 8, where a similar image is given a very different application. See also D.C. Allen's discussion of images related to Noah's ark in his *The Legend of Noah* (Urbana 1949), p.148.

199 *King*. On 5 September 1643, Charles withdrew his forces from the siege of Gloucester as Essex's army advanced to relieve the city. Cowley attempts to conceal the fact that the relief of Gloucester was a remarkable achievement by Essex, and a major triumph and turning point for the Parliamentary cause, but he is accurate in indicating that Charles' intention in abandoning the siege was not to evade Essex but to fight him on other ground and to block his return to London. The withdrawal appeared to make sense strategically. See Gardiner, I 242-3.

207 *rugged Beare*. Cf. *Davideis* III (*Poems*, p.336).

211 *homewards drew*. Essex occupied Gloucester on 8 September, and then moved back with his army in the direction of London. Through a series of Royalist blunders, which Cowley passes over silently, he was able almost to reach Newbury before he was intercepted in the action described below.

215 *Auburne*: Aldbourne Chase, where in a skirmish on 18 September Rupert surprised Essex's army and inflicted considerable damage upon it. See Clarendon, *History*, VII 207-8.

216 *Jermin*: Henry, Lord Jermyn (*c*1604-84), later Cowley's employer and patron, created on the Restoration Earl of St Albans. According to the Royalist account attributed to Lord Digby, *A True and Impartiall Relation of the Battaile ... neare Newbery* (Oxford 1643), Jermyn in command of the Queen's Regiment at Aldbourne Chase behaved 'with much Gallantry, being received very steadily, by a strong body of the Enemies Horse.' Advancing 'with the Marquesse *de la Vieuville* on the one hand, and the Lord *Digby* on the other,' he passed through the enemy's volley, striking an enemy officer who had fired point-blank (although without much harm) at Digby. 'Immediately upon this shocke, the Queens Regiment was so charged in the Reare by a fresh body of theirs, that the greatest part of it, shifting for themselves, the Lord *Iermyn*, accompanied with the French Marquesse, and the Officers onely of his Regiment, thought it as safe a way as well as the most honourable, to venture forwards through their whole Army, rather than to charge back through those that had invironed him, and so with admirable successe (the unhappy losse of that gallant Marquesse excepted) he brought 4 Colours and all his Officers off safe, having made their way round through the grosse of the enemies Foot.' (Sig. A2^{v})

217-18 Cf. *Davideis* IV (*Poems*, p.377):

That *Jonathan* in whom does mixt remain
All that kind *Mothers* wishes can contain.

225 *their hate*. Jermyn was regarded with great suspicion and hostility by the Parliamentary party even before the outbreak of the war, and he was forced into a period of exile in France in March 1641 for his part in the Army Plot. See the Introduction, p.14, above.

227 *Digby*. Lord Digby had previously fought at Edgehill, and he had been wounded in the capture of Lichfield (see above, II 126). He had displayed his skill with his pen in his *Apologie* (1642), and probably in verse which circulated in manuscript. Anthony Wood states that he is the Digby who is given a place by Sir John Suckling in 'The Sessions of the Poets' (written *c*1637) (*Athenae Oxonienses* ed. Bliss, III, col. 1104).

228 *Vivevile*. Vincent, Marquis de la Vieuville, son and heir apparent of Charles, Duc de la Vieuville, Grand Fauconnier de France, had come to England on a diplomatic mission, subsequently joining the Royalist army. According to *Mercurius Aulicus* (19 September 1643, p.526) in the fight at Aldbourne he 'was first taken Prisoner, and afterward inhumanely slaine in cold bloud.' *Mercurius Britanicus* (19-26 September 1643, p.38) states, however, that he was killed by an officer whom he wounded during an attempt at escape.

231 *Gorgons pow'er*. Pallas Athena bore on her shield the head of the Gorgon, Medusa, which had the power to terrify or paralyse enemies.

239 *Canniballs*. Montaigne describes the fondness of the cannibals for dancing,

their musical instruments ('great Canes open at one end'), and their practice of taunting their enemies, although he does not consider them so barbarous as Cowley's description suggests ('Of the Caniballes,' *Essayes* tr. John Florio [1632], pp. 100-7). Cf. Spenser, *Faerie Queene*, VI viii 35-46.

251-3 According to *A True and Impartiall Relation* (sig. A3), Essex's forces, upon catching sight of the King's army on the evening of 19 September, 'retreated into certain hedges & Fastnesses, a mile and a halfe distant from *Newbury* westward.' *Mercurius Aulicus* (20 September 1643, p.527) also claims that the Parliamentary forces entrenched themselves in strong positions before the Battle of Newbury, but Parliamentary accounts claim that, on the contrary, the King's forces had all the advantage of the ground.

255 *Ruthen.* The Scottish soldier, Patrick, Lord Ruthven, Earl of Forth and Brentford (*c*1573-1651), was General-in-Chief of the King's army. He had earlier won honours as a general in the army of Gustavus Adolphus.

256 *Oake.* The image is suggested by the Roman custom of erecting as the trophy of victory the trunk of an oak bearing the arms of the defeated enemy. Cf. Virgil, *Aeneid*, XI 5-11, 83-4, 173-5; Lucan, *Pharsalia*, I 135-43; and Statius, *Thebaid*, II 707-12.

260 *Prince*: Rupert, the commander of the Royalist cavalry.

261 *Charles.* Contemporary accounts of the King's part in the Battle of Newbury are varied and mutually inconsistent. See Burne and Young, *The Great Civil War*, p.105. According to the Parliamentary Sergeant Henry Foster, Charles led two regiments into the field, and fired some pieces of ordnance, 'riding up and down all that day in a souldiers gray coat' (*A True and Exact Relation* [1643], sig. B4).

267-70 Saturn, when in love with Philyra, tried to elude his jealous wife Ops by changing himself into a horse. Cowley follows Virgil, *Georgics*, III 75-94, where the qualities of the ideal horse are described: his high and light step, his best physical conformation, and colour (bay or grey):

talis et ipse iubam cervice effundit equina
coniugis adventu pernix Saturnus, et altum
Pelion hinnitu fugiens implevit acuto. (92-4)

271-4 Poseidon (Neptune) created the horse, and Athena created the olive tree, in a competition to give man the most useful gift. Athena was judged the winner and awarded the honour of giving her name to the capital of Attica. Cf. Virgil, *Georgics*, I 12-14:

tuque o, cui prima frementem
fundit equum magno tellus percussa tridenti,
Neptune.

277-328 In giving the King a formal speech before the battle, Cowley follows epic precedent rather than historical fact, for there is no record that on this occasion Charles delivered any address to his army or his officers. Some of the arguments may be adapted from Caesar's and Pompey's speeches before the battle of Pharsalia in Lucan (VII 250-382), but most are the commonplaces of contemporary Royalist belief and propaganda. Some occur in speeches by Charles that were in print at the time Cowley wrote, but on occasions when the King addressed his army before battle, as he did at Edgehill, he seems to have delivered brief and dignified exhortations to courage and loyalty, and to have engaged neither in lengthy argument nor in the expression of contempt for the rebel soldiery. See, for example, *Three Speeches Made by the Kings most Excellent Maiesty ... immediately before the late Battell at Keinton neer Banbury* (1642).

286 *base Sonnes of earth.* Cf. II, 231-3 and note. In Hesiod the giants are the sons of Earth (Gaia), sprung from the blood of the mutilated Uranus (*Theogony*, ll.184-5).

289 *formall Tumults.* In a proclamation dated 20 June 1643, Charles set out the illegalities committed by the Lords and Commons sitting in London, declaring that they no longer had the authority or freedom of a Parliament. See Gardiner, I 181.

290 *Clubs.* Local Parliamentary volunteers, lacking proper weapons, armed themselves with clubs and scythes on a number of occasions. Hence they were known as 'club men,' and this term was applied also by *Mercurius Aulicus* (10, 14 August 1643, pp.431, 441) to the city mobs who demonstrated against peace at Westminster.

291-6 Cf. *His Majesties Speech and Protestation, Made in the Head of His Army, between Stafford and Wellington, the 19. of September, 1642* (1642), in which Charles commends his troops that their conscience has brought them to fight for their religion, their king, and the law of the land, and assures them: 'you shall meet with no Enemies but Traitours, most of them Brownists, Anabaptists, and Athiests.'

299 *way.* This may be an error for 'war', but it may be accurate, having reference to l.297.

303 *Finsb'ury.* Cf. III 56, above. Cowley's ridicule of the London trained bands is badly misplaced here, since even their enemies were obliged to concede that the bands fought with great courage at Newbury. Clarendon comments that 'men had till then too cheap an estimation' of them: they 'behaved to wonder and were in truth the preservation of that army that day' (*History*, VII 211).

329-38 There is no historical evidence that Essex, any more than Charles, made such a formal or lengthy speech before the battle as Cowley suggests. According to *Mercurius Britanicus* (19-26 September, p.38) early on the morning of the battle 'to try his Souldiers mindes, he went from Regiment to Regiment, and put the question of a battell unto them, telling them the enemy had all the advantages, as the hill, the Towne, the hedges, the lanes and the river,' to which the troops responded: 'let us fall on, we will beat them from them all.' Another Parliamentary newspaper, *Mercurius Civicus* (21-8 September, p.139) states that Essex during one period of the battle addressed 'many excellent encouragements' to the trained bands, with good result: 'the souldiers were so animated, that they charged upon the enemy with more resolution then ever.'

334 *Declaration Lies of old.* Among the Parliamentary declarations most offensive to the Royalists was that of 9 March 1642, which formulated in detail the charge that Charles or his evil counsellors and courtiers had the design of establishing popery and crushing Parliament. See Clarendon, *History*, IV 331-7.

339-78 The first Battle of Newbury, 20 September 1643, is, as C.V. Wedgwood remarks, 'the most confused and controversial battle of the entire Civil War' (*The King's War*, p.653, n.150). The action seems to have commenced in the early morning when Parliamentary cannon opened fire on the King's forces. Confused, bloody, and inconclusive fighting occurred over a large area, among hedges which enclosed low ground on the northern part of the battlefield, and on hills and a plateau on the southern part. It continued until late at night, and both sides subsequently claimed the victory. See Burne and Young, *The Great Civil War*, pp.99-107. Cowley's description of the action is generally consistent with such Royalist accounts as *A True and Impartiall Relation* and *Mercurius Aulicus* (20, 21 September, 14 October, pp.527-31, 581-2).

341-2 Cf. *Davideis* IV (*Poems*, pp.382-3):

Here with sharp neighs the warlike *Horses* sound;
And with proud prancings beat the putrid ground.

See also Cowley's note on the latter line: 'In emulation of the *Virgilian* Verse, *Quadrupedante putrem sonitu quatit ungula campum*' (*Aeneid*, VIII 596).

358 *Eschapes*: escapes. Here, as in some other instances, Cowley revives a form which was already distinctly archaic in his day.

363 *th'Enclosures, and the Hill. A True and Impartiall Relation* and *Mercurius Aulicus* (20 September, p.527) emphasize the success achieved by the Royalist cavalry, including the capture of a 'round hill' from which Essex's forces had directed devastating cannon fire.

377-80 Cf. *Davideis* II (*Poems*, p.298):

Yet could not this the fatal strife decide;
God *punisht one*, but *blest not* th'other side.

381 *thowsands of Rebells fell.* The usual disputes regarding the numbers of

casualties developed after Newbury. *Mercurius Britanicus* (26 September-3 October 1643, p.46) declared upon the return of Essex's army to London: 'Not a hundred men of the Trained Bands are missing (whatever the reports at Oxford be) upon this expedition.' No reliable estimates have ever been established, but some authorities give support to Cowley's statement and hold that the Parliamentary forces lost between two and four thousand men. See Walter Money, *The First and Second Battles of Newbury* (second edition, London 1884), p.60.

383-4 Cf. Dryden, *Absalom and Achitophel*, Part I, ll.569-70:

Titles and Names 'twere tedious to Reherse
Of Lords, below the Dignity of Verse.

384 *Low, wretched Names.* The Parliamentary forces at Newbury, consisting largely of the London trained bands, had among their officers a high proportion of City tradesmen and merchants, rather than gentry or aristocrats. Cf. *Mercurius Aulicus* (20 September, p.529): 'Now if you will shew me what Lords & Gentlemen were in the Rebels Army, I shall tell you how many of them are slain'; and *A True and Impartiall Relation* (sig. A4): 'Your Lordship doth not expect that I should tell you of noble men killed on the other side, nor much of Gentry, but of such things as they cal Officers ... the most and principall of them are slaine.'

385-454 The names, Swart, Stane, Towse, Ket, Prinne, Frith, and Simon Blore do not occur in the lists of Parliamentary casualties published following the battle or in those compiled in later times; neither does it seem possible to identify the 'high-land Scotchman' (l.394) or Josiah, the weaver (l.405). Most, if not all, of the names and characters are probably fictitious, intended as types; but see the notes below on Towse (l.415) and Prinne (l.423). Details broadly similar to those that appear here are given in some Royalist accounts of the rebel casualties. For example, *Mercurius Aulicus* (5 October, p.560) describes Captain Hunt, who perished in the battle, as a 'Confect-maker' of London, and states that he was the first who committed sacrilege upon his parish church after Pym's orders for defacing churches.

404 Cf. Cowley's description of Jonathan's slaying of Elcanor in the *Davideis* IV (*Poems*, p.387): 'The parted Scull hung down on either side.'

415 *Towse.* Alderman John Towse was colonel of the Orange Regiment of the London trained bands, but there seems to be little if any connection between him and the figure described by Cowley. Alderman Towse was a grocer, not a dyer; he appears to have suffered no harm at Newbury; and he lived until 1645. See Valerie Pearl, *London and the Outbreak of the Puritan Revolution* (London 1961), p.325.

423 *Atturney Prinne.* No record seems to exist concerning this relative of 'th'unweari'ed Scribler,' i.e., William Prynne (1600-69), the prolific Puritan

writer. It is possible, although not very likely, that Cowley has confused Prynne with Pym. Captain Charles Pym, son of the Parliamentary leader, was wounded at Newbury. See Money, *Newbury*, p.63.

430 *Malignant*: Royalist. Cf. I 352.

440 *Eares*. Cf. Butler, *Hudibras*, I i 10.

442 *of Beasts, of Hornes, and Weekes*. See Daniel 7-9, and Revelation 13. Among the fantastic millenarian interpretations of these passages attracting attention at the time Cowley wrote were Henry Archer's *The Personall Reign of Christ upon Earth* (1642), and Robert Maton's *Israel's Redemption* (1642). See Rogers, *The Fifth Monarchy Men*, pp.1-13.

455 *what other kind of men*. Cf. Clarendon, *History*, VII 214: 'On which side soever the marks and public ensigns of victory appeared most conspicuous, certain it is, that ... the loss on the King's side was in weight much more considerable and penetrating; for whilst some obscure, unheard of, colonel or officer was missing on the enemy's side, as some citizen's wife bewailed the loss of her husband, there were above twenty officers of the field and persons of honour and public name slain upon the place, and more of the same quality hurt.'

459 *Feilding and Morgan*. Colonel Edward Fielding was fatally wounded, and Colonel Thomas Morgan was killed at Newbury (Money, *Newbury*, pp.vii, 61).

465 *Spencer*: Henry Spencer, Earl of Sunderland (b 1620). See Clarendon, *History*, VII 215: 'Here fell the earl of Sunderland, a lord of great fortune, tender years, (being not above three and twenty years of age,) and an early judgment; who, having no command in the army, attended upon the King's person under the obligation of honour; and putting himself that day into the King's troop a volunteer, before they came to charge was taken away by a cannon bullet.'

468 *thy brighter Wife*. Sunderland's wife was the Dorothy Sidney whom Edmund Waller had celebrated as 'Sacharissa' in poems which were already well known through their circulation in manuscript, although they were not published until 1645.

470 Sunderland was buried on the battlefield, perhaps because of the mangled condition of his body, although his heart was removed and taken to a family vault near Althorp. See J.P. Kenyon, *Robert Spencer, Earl of Sunderland 1641-1702* (London [1958]), p.3.

471 *Palme or Cedar*. Cf. Psalm 92:12.

477 *Carnarvan*: Robert Dormer, Earl of Carnarvon (born c1610). He had fought with both courage and skill at Edgehill (or 'Keinton,' I.506) and in the battles of the western campaign. Clarendon, who pays high tribute to his character, describes his death at Newbury: 'after he had charged and

routed a body of the enemy's horse, coming carelessly back by some of the scattered troopers, [he] was by one of them, who knew him, run through the body with a sword, of which he died within an hour' (*History*, VII 216). Other accounts of his death are discussed by Money (*Newbury*, pp.89-91).

483-4 Cf. *Davideis* IV (*Poems*, p.386):

Which lies so strongly ['e]ncampt, that one would say
The *Hill* might be remov'd as soon as *they*.

492 *six thousand yeares*. Cowley presumably follows one of those systems of biblical chronology which, like the famous one published a few years later by James Ussher in his *Annales* (1650-4), gives a date of about 4000 BC for the Creation. Cowley states in a note to the *Davideis* (I n.23) that he gives whole (or round) numbers because '*Poetry* will not admit of *broken ones*.'

510 This line is incorporated verbatim in the *Davideis* IV (*Poems*, p.388).

514-16 Cf. *Mercurius Aulicus* (20 September 1643, p.528): 'the armed Rebels shall hereafter feele they have murthered the *Earle* of CARNARVON, and so he that killed him did in another world within a minute afterwards.'

524 *Falklands blood*. Lucius Cary, Viscount Falkland (b 1610?), the Secretary of State, acting with reckless courage, was instantly killed by a bullet early in the battle. Cowley, who had personal as well as public reasons for mourning, concurs with much contemporary opinion in regarding his death as the most terrible of the losses of Newbury. In his great prose elegy, Clarendon describes his death as 'a loss which no time will suffer to be forgotten, and no success or good fortune could repair' (*History*, VII 217).

529 *meethoughts*. Cowley has the custom of using this word to mark flights of fiction or hyperbole. Cf. *Davideis*, III n.46: 'This perhaps will be accused by some severe men for too swelling an *Hyperbole*; and I should not have endured it my self, if it had not been mitigated with the word *Methought*.'

530 *Oxford*. Clarendon states that the news of Falkland's death reached Oxford on the day after the event (*Life*, I 201).

538 *Lutzens fight*. Gustavus Adolphus of Sweden was killed at the battle of Lützen, 6 November 1632.

548 A more extravagant version of this conceit had appeared in one of the elegies published in *Justa Edouardo King* at Cambridge in 1638, early in Cowley's period of residence at the university, Cleveland's poem, titled later 'Upon the death of M. King drowned in the Irish Seas,' ll.5-6:

my penne's the spout
Where the rain-water of my eyes run out.

563 *Knowledge*. Cf. Cowley's earlier praise of Falkland's learning and wit in his 'To the Lord Falkland. For his safe Return from the Northern Expedition against the Scots.' Clarendon describes the qualities Oxford men found in Falkland: 'such an immenseness of wit and such a solidity of judgment ... so

infinite a fancy, bound in by a most logical ratiocination, such a vast knowledge that he was not ignorant in any thing, yet such an excessive humility as if he had known nothing' (*History*, VII 220).

568 *Wee gain'd a Feild.* The phrase bears some special weight, since Royalists in claiming Newbury as a victory used the argument that they were left in possession of the battlefield when Essex's army marched back to London (although this point, like everything else relating to the battle, was heatedly disputed).

593 *eight glorious Sphære.* The spelling 'eight' is not necessarily an error, since this form was still in use as a variant of 'eighth' (*OED*), although the usage does not seem to occur in Cowley's printed works. The eighth sphere was that which contained the fixed stars. Cf. Chaucer's description of the flight of Troilus' spirit in *Troilus and Criseyde*, V 1808-9; and Cowley's 'Reason. The use of it in Divine Matters' (*Poems*, p.47):

> The *Holy Book*, like the eighth *Sphere*, does shine
> With thousand Lights of *Truth Divine*.
> So numberless the *Stars* ....

598 *Sidneys Wit.* Cf. Cowley's reference to the idealized characters of the *Arcadia* in 'The dangers of an Honest man in much Company' (*Essays*, pp.446-7).

599 *How good a Father, Husband, Master, Freind!* Cf. the description of Jonathan in the *Davideis* IV (*Poems*, p.377): 'The tendrest *Husband, Master, Father, Son.*' If there is any significance in the omission of reference to Falkland's role as a son, it may be in the fact that his relations with both his father and mother had been troubled, although few would judge the fault to be his. See J.A.R. Marriott, *The Life and Times of Lucius Cary, Viscount Falkland* (London [1907]), pp.60, 67, 71. Falkland's fine qualities as husband and father are attested by Clarendon (*Life*, I 203). Contemporary tributes to his remarkable talent for friendship, from which Cowley himself benefited, include Ben Jonson's ode, 'To the Immortall Memorie, and Friendship of that Noble Paire, Sir Lucius Cary, and Sir H. Morison.'

602-3 Clarendon comments similarly upon the combination in Falkland of aversion to bloodshed and personal carelessness of danger. Of his action at Edgehill he writes: 'a man might think he came into the field only out of curiosity to see the face of danger, and charity to prevent the shedding of blood' (*History*, VII 230). According to Sir John Byron, who witnessed his death, he fell at Newbury when 'more gallantly than advisedly' he spurred his horse through a gap in a hedge which was under heavy enemy fire. See Money, *Newbury*, p.52.

605-16 Cf. Clarendon, *History*, VII 233: 'When there was any overture or hope of peace he would be more erect and vigorous, and exceedingly solicitous to press any thing which he thought might promote it; and sitting amongst his friends, often, after a deep silence and frequent sighs, would, with a shrill and sad accent, ingeminate the word *Peace*, *Peace*, and would passionately profess that the very agony of the war, and the view of the calamities and desolation the kingdom did and must endure, took his sleep from him, and would shortly break his heart.'

615-16 Cf. Marvell, 'A Poem upon the Death of O. C.', ll. 169-70:

We demand not your supplies
To compass in our *Isle*; our Tears suffice.

621-2 Clarendon writes that Falkland 'died as much of the time as of the bullet: for, from the very beginning of the war, he contracted so deep a sadness and melancholy, that his life was not pleasant to him; and sure he was too weary of it' (*Life*, I 202). According to Bulstrode Whitelocke, when friends tried to dissuade Falkland from going into the battle at Newbury, 'he said *he was weary of the times, and foresaw much Misery to his own Country, and did believe he should be out of it ere night*, and could not be persuaded to the contrary, but would enter into the Battle, and was their slain' (*Memorials of the English Affairs* [1732], pp.73-4). See Marriott's discussion and criticism of the story that Falkland deliberately sought death, *Falkland*, pp.316-23.

647 *sheath*. Cf. Cowley's earlier allusions to the sword of divine justice, I 571, and III 617.

APPENDIXES AND INDEX

A: Textual Variants in Book I

The following list includes all substantive variants from C1 in *A Poem on the Late Civil War* (1679) that have not been incorporated in the present text and recorded in the textual notes. Substantive variants in the Additional and Douce MSS are included when they seem to have any possible interest or value, but a number of patently erroneous readings in these two manuscripts are omitted. Variants in C2 are not listed, since it seems clear that this manuscript has no authority independent of C1. Such variants as 'does' and 'doth', and 'yee' and 'you' have been excluded, and no attempt has been made to list the very numerous variants in spelling and punctuation. Accidentals are those of the text that is listed first following the variant. In instances where one or more of the sigla, P, A, and D, are omitted, the agreement of the text or texts which they represent with C1 is to be understood.

2 Seas doe] the Seas PAD
3 *Canon*] Cannons PAD
6 and] but AD
7 some] the PAD
8 And] Tho' PAD
9 *Triumph*] Triumphs PAD
15 conquests] conquest AD
16 glories] Glory PAD
17 holds] Hold P
29 dead] dread AD
40 *woemans*] Womens PAD
41 affrighted] afflicted P
42 drove] drave AD
sad] Said DA
43 at] with PAD
55 *Death*, old] Death's old P
56 hit] shoot PAD
57 Stories] story PAD
59 the] that PAD
60 ore the injur'd] on the *English* PAD
67 as] that PAD

68 they did once] once they did PAD
69 not: *omitted in* A *and* D
our] or AD
74 *Sennen*] *Sequan* PAD
75 that] War PAD
79 we] you P; yee AD
80 who] that PAD
81 renu'ed] Return'd PAD
84 measur'd] Measures PAD
89 might] should PAD
90 that] the PAD
93 from] in PAD
95 So] As P
97 rest] Peace PAD
100 sunke] sank PA
101 flow] grow PAD
102 that] but AD
105 conquest] Conquer PAD
106 *Thrifty*] thirsty AD
112 *Malady*] Remedye AD
115 This] The PAD
ills] ill PAD
116 will drive all lesse] we know, drives all PAD
119 part] place P
126 to] for PAD
127 murd'erous] Murdring AD
132 crowd] shroud PAD
133 for] from PAD
134 those] them PAD
136 *formes*] forme AD
137 nether *men* would] Men would neither PAD
138 *formes*] Form P
140 many-mouthed *Rout*] many headed Rout ADP
142 them] they PAD
149 lowd] great AD
153 rude] great PAD
154 noe] not PAD
tempest] Tempests PAD
155 drove] drave AD
156 rudelier] Readilier P
157 and] of PAD
158 him] them P
160 ore] in PAD
162 made] make PAD
165 Commands] command PAD
166 *Lands*] Land PAD
169 meete] mett D
171 his] this PAD
173 swift] first P
176 *Assyrian Host*] Assyrian PA; Assirians D
182 she] they AD
186 Broke] Brake PAD
those] the PAD
187 shores] shore PAD
188 this] that P
191 of] from PAD
199 *lawrell*] Lawrels PAD
200 they'le] they D
202 not *he* will] he will not PAD
203 *Sands*] – – P
fields] Field PAD
204 and *Kents*] and's Countreys P; and Countrys AD
211 hungry] hunger P
215 but] tho' PAD
216 skin] skins PAD
218 hands] hand PAD
219 Here] There AD
221 crimson] silver AD
224 all her *Serpents*] every Serpent P
227 *Canon* roar'd] Cannons roar PAD
232 Acts] Arts AD
234 knew] know P
236 for th'old *Monks*] the *Monks* dull P; the dull Monkes AD
240 pluckes downe *Justice*] pulls down *Vengeance* PAD
249 shot] sent PAD

254 *Peoples*] Countries PAD
256 *Triumph*] *Triumphs* PA
258 their] did P
259 brave] great P
264 swiftly as] swift as strait PAD
265 *Rebells*] Miscreants PAD
266 fram'd] had fram'd AD
269 did new by-wayes] new by-ways do PAD
276 slaves] Knaves PAD
280 th'ignobler] the nobler P
Moistures] moisture PAD
283 honour'ably] honourable AD
Essex] – – P
284 Traytors] Creatures D
285 to your valiant Soules] valiant Souls in peace PAD
286 deaths] death AD
289 they] thus AD
in] with PAD
291 *Wharton*] – – P
292 these] those PAD
294 thought] thought'st PA
296 that] which AD
blacke] dark P
302 strong] strange P
given their rayes by Fame] and so vail their shame PAD
303 they] thus P
304 err'd] Err PAD
306 they] had PAD
307 Rebellions] rebellious AD
end] ends PAD
308 that] their PAD
311 brightnes] Lightness PAD
313 *vex*] tire PAD
319 is] was AD
320 for't] since PAD
325 those] their PAD
blowne high] blowed up P; blown up AD
326 ruin] Ruins P
329 who] thou PAD
330 their lives] themselves PAD
334 *floods*] Blood P
335 thy faire] do thy PAD
336 Move] Are PAD
339 who] which PAD
340 thine owne] thy kind AD
canst] can P
342 from] at PAD
343 Murmur] murmuring PAD
344 *Tributes*] Tribute PAD
345 triumphant] in Triumph P
350 gott but] once got PAD
352 All] For PAD
354 times] Time PAD
356 that] this PAD
this] that PAD
357 they'd] they D
359 to whom] that to PAD
360 these] those PA
gives] givest PAD
361 Thee] The PAD
with] which PAD
362 this] thy AD
363 kind] which PAD
364 shed then] then shed PAD
365 bad] sad PAD
367 farr-lost] far tost AD
368 fate: *omitted in* PAD
369 Still, still] Yet still PAD
371 Not] Nor PAD
that] the P
372 *Brookes*] *B* – P
Hambdens] *H*'s – P
374 Holiday] Holy day PAD
375 man] Men P
378 *Hambden*] – – P
381 *Hambden*] – – P
the goodly] this mighty P; his mighty AD

382 *world*] Isle PAD
383 *Hambden*] – – P
a] The PAD
Confusion] Confusions PAD
384 This] His PD
385 *Hambden* whose] His Active PAD
Shop] Top PAD
386 *Thunder's*] Treason's PAD
sound outwards] noise outward PAD
387 contriv'd] continued P
Martin] *M* – P
388 *Pym*] *P* – P
has] had AD
389 to rise] how to rise D
391 great] Black PAD
392 by] bee D
397 long] great AD
404 And] Or PAD
405 now] then PAD
410 of] the PAD
411 Hee] It PAD
415 Acts] Arts A; art D
420 Coast] Coasts P
423 both those two, his tryd] his so often tryed P; his too oft try'd AD
427 to *thee*] thee AD
428 *Slaning*] *Stanning* PAD
430 *teares*] Fears AD
431 backwards] backward PAD
434 where] when P
443 *Campe*] *Arms* P
444 *Armes* nor *men*] Men nor Armes AD
445 breake] breaks PD
447 doubt] doubts P
strengths] strength PAD
448 *Campes*] *Arms* PAD
Magazeens] *Magazine* P
449 *Sword*] Swords PAD
their] the PAD
451 their] the AD
452 *Canon*] Cannons AD
453 *Tumult*] *Tumults* PAD
454 bit] bite PAD
455 *Wealth*] were *Wealth* P; – wealth AD
456 could] can PAD
459 Joyn'd] joyns P
461 That] The PAD
Wallers] *W* – P
463 Still] Till P
this] that PAD
466 fury] power AD
470 remembred] remember P
471 On] At PAD
Downe] *Heath* PAD
for] at PAD
476 as] us PAD
477 helpt] meant PAD
these] those PAD
481 fight] sight P
482 *flight*] fight P
490 walkt] walks PAD
fields] Field AD
493 In] On AD
meete] met P
495 *Keinton*] Keynton's AD
499 lowd] lewd PAD
504 that crownes] which Crowns P
506 *Gods*] *God* PAD
508 so much] such a PAD
511 issu'ed] led them PAD
512 *Tempests*] tempest P
519 forc'd Hee] he forc'd PAD
522 wilde] a P
523 sickly] sinking PAD
528 *Victories*] Victory P
529 his] the PAD
532 *God*] *Heaven* PAD
Ah] Oh PAD
533 *Canon*] Cannons P

535 *Capaneus*] *Capaneu's* P
537 pale] with PAD
538 *they* all, not *He*] not he, but they PAD
543 your] their D
547 would] will PAD
548 deare] fond PAD
550 *Line omitted in* PAD
551 *Prisons*] *Prison* PA
553 thus: *omitted in* AD
557 *Estates*] 'states A; States D
561 alwayes us'd] used alwayes us'd AD
564 *Sacriledge*] Sacriledges P
566 *Final line of* P
567 thow] the AD
Powers] Power AD
568 and gaullesse *Dove*] Eternall love AD
Final line of A *and* D

B: The Cowper Version of Cowley's 'To the Duke of Buckingham'

Among the verse transcribed by Sarah Cowper in the commonplace book titled 'Paper Booke' or 'The Medley' (Panshanger MS D/EP/F.37) is a copy of Cowley's poem 'To the Duke of Buckingham' (pp.221-3) which has a number of variants from the only text previously known. The initials 'M C' appear in the margin beside the title, probably as an indication that Lady Cowper's source for the poem was Martin Clifford. She chose to include the poem in her collection no doubt for the reason that when she copied it sometime in the later seventeenth century it was, like *The Civil War*, an unpublished work, for it remained unprinted until 1700.

The Cowper copy of 'To the Duke of Buckingham' gains interest from the fact that Cowley seems to have suppressed this poem, just as he suppressed *The Civil War*, from motives that were in part at least political. He wrote it to commemorate the Duke's marriage in 1657 with the daughter of Thomas, Lord Fairfax, Mary (who is best remembered as the Maria of Marvell's 'Appleton House').[1] The Restoration occurred before he published his next collection of poetry, *Verses Lately Written upon Several*

1 Information concerning the extensive and well established but still rather mysterious connections between Cowley and Buckingham will be found in all detailed biographies of the two men. Some first-hand evidence of the closeness of their friendship is provided by Brian Fairfax, Buckingham's kinsman by marriage and sometime agent, in his 'Memoirs of the Life of George Villiers, Duke of Buckingham,' first published in *A Catalogue of the Curious Collection of Pictures of George Villiers, Duke of Buckingham* (1758), pp.24-39. Fairfax's narrative has been used by Buckingham's modern biographers, but it has not received so much attention as it deserves from Cowley's.

Occasions (1663). If he had been moved purely by literary considerations he would surely have given the poem a place in this volume, for in its artistry it is by no means the least impressive of his occasional poems. He excluded it presumably because it contained complimentary allusion to Lord Fairfax's great military achievements as a Parliamentary general. Publication would have added to Cowley's difficulties in answering the charge that during the later 1650s he had been disloyal to the Royalist cause, and it might not have been pleasing to Buckingham, who faced similar criticism. For the Duke the marriage had been a means of regaining estates confiscated by Parliament and granted to Fairfax.[2] Although his alliance with the Fairfax family was disliked by Cromwell, it inevitably created the suspicion among Royalists that he had made some compromise with the Commonwealth regime. After the Restoration Buckingham can have had little desire that public reminders of the circumstances of his marriage should be published.[3]

Since Sprat, the editor of Cowley's posthumously published *Works* (1668), was very much concerned to refute the charge of disloyalty against the poet and had special reasons also for desiring to protect the reputation of Buckingham, who was his patron, it is not surprising that the poem remained unpublished for many years after Cowley's death. It was printed for the first time in the ninth edition of the *Works* (pp.135-6), published by Henry Herringman in 1700. Herringman advertised the inclusion of the poem by a statement (following other items) on his title-page: 'To which are added, some Verses by the AUTHOR, Never before Printed,' and he placed the last three words also after the title of the poem itself, which was in fact the only new work to appear in this edition, but he gave no indication of the source of his copy. Herringman's text has inevitably been reprinted in all subsequent editions of Cowley which have included the poem, since no other text has been known. There is good reason, however, to suppose that Sarah Cowper's text possesses at least as much authority as his, since his has an uncertain origin, while hers appears to derive from Martin Clifford. Clifford was not only the close friend of Cowley but also the secretary of Buckingham, to whom the poet is likely to have presented a carefully made copy.

In order to list the variants, I have numbered the lines of Herringman's

2 See Winifred Gardner, Lady Burghclere, *George Villiers, Second Duke of Buckingham* (London 1903), pp.79-103; and John H. Wilson, *A Rake and his Times, George Villiers, 2nd Duke of Buckingham* (London [1954]), pp.7-8.

3 There was also another, although probably less decisive, reason against publication. After the Restoration the Duke so quickly became notorious as a rake and spendthrift that Cowley's emphasis upon his virtue and judgment might have invited some ridicule, although the poet's praise of his wit proved to be better justified.

text (which is easily available, for example, in A.R. Waller's edition, *Essays, Plays and Sundry Verses*, pp.462-4). All substantive variants are listed, but not accidentals. In each instance the reading of the Herringman text (H) is given first, followed by that of the Cowper (Panshanger) manuscript (c3).

TITLE *To the Duke of* Buckingham, *upon his Marriage/ with the Lord* Fairfax *his Daughter.*] A pindarick Ode, to the Duke/ of Buckingham

TEXT 1 Beauty and strength together came,] Beauty and strength, and Witt, togather came 2 Birth] womb *The first stanza ends in* H *with l.14, in* c3 *with l.21.* 23 dist] didst 25 a great] thy Ladyships 26 here] there did] didst 28 power] Votes 29 routed] routing 32 And] Yet 43 thy] that 48 who] that c3 *omits ll.49-50.* 54 its] her 56 layd] lain a hundred] an hundred 59 art born of] beest born from 60 Victorie] Victory's 65 overcome] orecome 70 Three] two *Following l.70,* c3 *has the additional line*: One Conquerd England, the other Conquerd you. 73 shown] shewd 81 turnings] turning 82 c3 *omits* Alas! 85 of] to *Beneath the last line of the poem* c3 *has*: On the Dukes marriage

Comparison of the two texts suggests that Herringman's contains some errors that can be corrected from the Cowper MS (although the possibility that the latter contains scribal errors has also to be taken into account). For example, the structure of the opening section of the poem is much stronger in the Cowper text than in Herringman's, which omits 'and Witt' in the first line. Through this omission the parallel between the qualities of beauty, strength, and wit in l.1, and the verbs in l.4, 'fair,' 'large,' and 'high,' is lost, as is the link with the same sequence of qualities in ll.11-12:

> With Beauty generous Goodness he Combin'd,
> Courage to Strength, Iudgment to Wit he joyn'd.

Some of the other variants are evidently the result of deliberate revision, either authorial or editorial, the Cowper version being probably the earlier of the two. The final lines of the fourth stanza of the poem in the Cowper version,

> Which was the happiest Conqueror of the two
> One Conquerd England, the other Conquerd you,

are replaced in the Herringman text by: 'Which was the Happiest Conqueror of the Three' (l.70). This alteration may have been made by Cowley himself after the Restoration, with the purpose of adjusting the poem to the new political climate by eliminating (or, at least, making less explicit) a laudatory reference to Fairfax's victories over the King's forces during the Civil War.

'To the Duke of Buckingham' and *The Civil War* considered together provide striking evidence of the perils which faced the seventeenth-century political poet: while the one poem was too vehemently Royalist for publication after the defeat of the King's party, the other implied too sympathetic a view of the Parliamentary cause for publication after the Restoration. The fate that the two poems suffered amply demonstrates the truth of Cowley's comment: 'a warlike, various, and a tragical age is best to *write of*, but worst to *write in*.'[4]

4 Preface, *Poems* (1656), sig. (a)2^{v}

Index

This is a selective index, principally of proper names in the Introduction and Notes. Peers are normally listed under the names or titles by which they were known during the period of the poem, rather than under later titles.